THE JOHN DEERE STORY

The

JOHN DEERE

STORY

A Biography
of Plowmakers
John & Charles
Deere

Neil Dahlstrom and Jeremy Dahlstrom

Introduction by David Vaught

NORTHERN ILLINOIS UNIVERSITY PRESS

DeKalb

© 2005 by Northern Illinois University Press

Published by the Northern Illinois University Press, DeKalb, Illinois   60115

Manufactured in the United States using acid-free paper

Design by Julia Fauci

Library of Congress Cataloging-in-Publication Data

Dahlstrom, Neil, 1976–

The John Deere story: a biography of plowmakers John and Charles Deere /

Neil Dahlstrom and Jeremy Dahlstrom; introduction by David Vaught.— 1st ed.

p.   cm.

Includes bibliographical references and index.

ISBN 10: 0-87580-336-9 (hardcover : alk. paper)

ISBN 13: 978-0-87580-336-4 (hardcover : alk. paper)

1. Deere, John, 1804–1886. 2. Deere, Charles. 3. Industrialists—United States—

Biography. 4. Deere & Company—History. 5. Plows—Illinois—History. 6. Agricultural

machinery industry—Illinois—History. I. Dahlstrom, Jeremy. II. Title.

HD9486.U6D432 2005

338.7′6817631′0922—dc22

2004023584

To our parents, Craig and Brenda

Contents

Acknowledgments

The John Deere Story began as a biography of Charles Deere, the son of John Deere and the general manager and president of Deere & Company from 1858 to 1907. Charles Deere has clearly been an overlooked historical figure. Even with John Deere's two hundredth birthday occurring on February 7, 2004, we had at first decided to stay clear of his story. The legend seemed unapproachable, and we were certain that there was little new information to be discovered. It did not take us long, though, to realize that the story of one could not be told apart from that of the other and that, in fact, much of John Deere's story was yet to be told.

This book is a unique undertaking. Almost all books written about John Deere are about John Deere tractors. Not surprisingly, few people today know that the company was almost a century old before its first tractor was even conceived. Like many historical figures around whom have been built an impenetrable legend, the association of John Deere and the invention of the steel plow is basic American history. Yet John Deere never made the claim, nor did the need for such a claim ever occur to him—it was simply not important to his business. His son, though, disagreed. Charles understood the value of his father's reputation and later became the architect of the more idyllic version of the John Deere story: the invention of the steel plow and the conquering of the prairie. Charles Deere was a genius at mass marketing. His father's role in the development of the plow (stressing constant development), personal integrity, and dedication to quality were the unshakeable bases for all of the company's marketing activity during the nineteenth and into the twentieth century. Even after his father's death, in 1886, the portrait of Charles Deere in company catalogs followed a portrait of his father. Charles even identified himself first as the son of John Deere and second as the president of Deere & Company. It was a seamless combination of unwavering devotion and smart business.

This book in many ways is the context of a seemingly simple distinction made by Deere & Company's board of directors in 1913. After that date, the epitaph below portraits of John Deere in company catalogs and

literature was modified from "Inventor of the Steel Plow" to the more appropriate "He Gave to the World the Steel Plow." But American history
rarely pays attention to such revision, and still today John Deere the man
is known almost exclusively for an "invention" that never occurred.

It is a credit to many people at Deere & Company for seeing past the
inherent risks of allowing the publication of an objective biography that
shows how and why events actually occurred, not necessarily how we
want to think they occurred. Curt Linke and Betty Hagberg not only saw
the value of the project but also gave us the complement of unrestricted
access to Deere & Company's resources. Clair Peterson gave us much-
needed early words of encouragement.

Curt Roseman read the earliest manuscript and somehow saw
promise in an almost unintelligible narrative of seemingly unrelated
facts and dates. Mary Jane Brinton, Katherine Deere Glover Findlay, Liz
Marino, and Connie Ganz also read early drafts and provided invaluable
personal insights into the Deere and Tate families. To them, as well as
Gretchen Small at the Butterworth Trust, we owe great thanks.

Former Deere & Company corporate archivist Les Stegh read many
chapters, catching factual errors and providing advice on style and content. This book is very much the result of his work over more than
twenty-five years in the Deere & Company Archives. The staff of the
Deere & Company Archives, Ann Lee, Lisa Spurgeon, and Yu An Chang,
were champions from the start, and each contributed more than they
will ever know, whether pulling material, talking through unfinished
ideas, or listening to our frustrations. The Deere & Company Archives is
an extraordinary collection of materials in which much of our research
was conducted.

The early newspaper collections and city directories held by the Rock
Island County Historical Society proved invaluable. In addition, resources at the Illinois State Historical Library, R. G. Dun & Co. Collection in the Baker Library at Harvard Business School, and the Illinois Regional Archives Depository at Western Illinois University provided
insights into the financial resources of the Deere's early business and
John Deere personally.

Martin Johnson at Northern Illinois University Press saw the early
promise of the book and took on the substantial challenge of working
with two first-time authors. Melody Herr followed that challenge
through, giving us the guidance that allowed us to transform a rough
manuscript into a readable narrative and, in the process, teaching us

the importance of disciplined writing. For her support and guidance we are ever grateful.

Most especially, thanks go to Deere & Company corporate archivist Vicki Eller, whose constant encouragement, depth of knowledge, and uncanny ability to track the most obscure lead was of tremendous value to the project from start to finish.

Still, any errors in facts and interpretation remain the responsibility of the authors alone.

Introduction

DAVID VAUGHT

The period 1815–1860 has long been regarded as "the farmer's age," and with good reason. If there was ever a time when farmers took center stage in American history, this was it. As the American population spread westward at a rapid pace, farmers (particularly in the North) adopted labor-saving equipment, improved their techniques, produced surplus crops, and experienced a higher standard of living. Everything seemed to be expanding, from transportation networks, to markets, to people's very horizon of experience. By 1860, however, clear signs were emerging that the great age of the American farmer was drawing to a close. Indeed, the latter third of the nineteenth century might well be called the age of paradox in American agricultural history. Farm output, after doubling between 1840 and 1860, more than tripled from 1860 to 1900, yet for farmers themselves this was a time of deep and bitter discontent. John Deere came of age during the earlier period, his son Charles during the latter.[1]

Western migration had already begun in the late eighteenth century, when settlers eager to escape the increasingly crowded Northeast poured into upstate New York and the Old Northwest. Land was plentiful, but without adequate transportation to eastern cities, farmers produced primarily for themselves and local markets. Geography was their main obstacle. Most of the rivers in the eastern half of the United States run north-south, but east-west routes were needed to link the growing cities along the Atlantic seaboard to the growing hinterland. The region's few roads and bridges, moreover, were poorly constructed and maintained. The Erie Canal, which opened in 1825, changed everything. This engineering marvel transformed the lives of northern farm families and the American economy itself. The canal stretched 364 miles from Albany to Buffalo, but of even greater significance it connected, by extension, the Great Lakes and upper Ohio and Mississippi valleys to the Hudson River, New York City, and the trans-Atlantic world. Just like that, the isolation that made self-sufficiency a virtue out of necessity for western farmers was gone. The flood of farm products from America's interior soon made New York City the most important commercial center in the nation. It would have been hard to say who was more ecstatic—Western farmers or Eastern businessmen.

Western farmers and Eastern businessmen had more in common than meets the eye. For much of the nineteenth century, Americans held two competing conceptions of the West (the Midwest in today's parlance). According to the Jeffersonian intellectual tradition, each settler in America's new heartland was to be an island unto himself—producing for his own needs on a modest piece of land and practicing bucolic virtues, free of the corrupting influences of the marketplace and the rude intrusions of industrialization. The second idea, normally associated with Alexander Hamilton and Henry Clay, envisioned an aggressive, expanding commercialized agriculture, in which a farmer produced not only for himself but also for the nation and indeed the world. For farmers themselves, the two conceptions were not necessarily mutually exclusive. Many who streamed across the Appalachians to new settlements saw themselves as chosen people carving out an agrarian paradise in the wilderness. Despite what they may have thought, farmers very quickly found themselves locked into the advancing market economy. To this day, we tend to think that this country evolved naturally from frontier settlement to industrialization—that these were two distinct historical phases. In fact, each drove the other.

In the 1840s and 1850s, additional canals, new roads, and especially railroads continued to break down old geographical barriers and provide routes for an increasing flow of farm products to the East. They also opened the Midwestern prairies to settlement in a manner that can only be described as remarkable. The process of farm making on the level, rich land gathered tremendous speed and momentum. Farmers could bring their acres into cultivation without the old restrictive requirement of a lifetime devoted to clearing trees, though the lack of timber on the prairies for buildings, fences, and fuel would soon present a grave problem of its own. In the decade of the 1850s alone, an astounding 2.2 million people were added to the population of Illinois, Indiana, Iowa, and Missouri. This constituted 25 percent of the total population increase of the forty-one states and territories. The population of Illinois increased more than any other state, and Missouri's growth was exceeded only by that of New York and Pennsylvania. Not all the newcomers were farmers (a considerable portion was concentrated in urban centers such as Chicago and St. Louis), but the vast majority resided in rural areas.

Key to this explosive growth, though often forgotten, were black-smiths, who themselves bridged the frontier-industrial dichotomy that has too often limited our perception of nineteenth-century America. Many of the tools and implements that farmers used early in the century were self-designed and self-made, including wooden plows, harrows, cultivators, rakes, forks, shovels, and numerous household items. If, however, they needed a piece of iron for the moldboard or for the share of their plow, wanted to sharpen an iron shovel, or wished to insert iron spikes in their harrow, they went to the local blacksmith, who could forge and hammer out almost anything the farmer desired. When farmers began migrating to the Midwest, blacksmiths followed very quickly. This was an especially attractive option to those in the densely settled Northeast, where blacksmiths found it increasingly difficult to find steady work. John Deere, at the age of thirty-two, left Vermont for Grand Detour, Illinois, in 1836 precisely for that reason.

He and other blacksmiths found their services in much greater demand on the fertile prairies of the Midwest. The deeply penetrating, thick, and coarse root system of the prairie bluestem grass proved virtually impossible to break with the ordinary plows that settlers brought with them. The wooden moldboard and cast-iron plows that worked well enough in the lighter and sandier soils of the East could not cut through these grasslands, let alone turn a furrow. Farmers intent on cultivating corn, wheat, oats, and other crops had no choice but to turn to the prairie breaker, an immense, unwieldy wooden plow whose moldboard and wrought-iron share alone weighed at least 125 pounds. From three to seven yoke of oxen were needed to pull it, and even then it cut only two or three inches deep. Plowing with a prairie breaker was slow, hard work; a farmer considered himself fortunate to break eight acres during the plowing season. Moreover, few farmers could afford to buy one. Instead, they hired custom breaking teams at the rate of $2 to $5 per acre, not including the costs for weekly visits to the local blacksmith to sharpen the plowshares. Surely, thought John Deere soon after his arrival, there had to be a better way.

While on a repair job at a local mill, Deere noticed a broken steel saw blade and got an idea. He took it back to his shop, cut off the teeth, crafted it into the shape and size of a plowshare, attached it to a wrought-iron moldboard, and gave his new implement a high polish. To his delight, the moldboard cut easily though prairie sod and allowed the soil to peel away without dulling or clogging the share. The new plow was lighter and much more efficient than the prairie breaker, and it required half as many draft animals to pull it. Before long, farmers called it the "singing plow" for the slight whine in made as it cut through the soil. Its impact on their quality of life and its price—as little as seven dollars—may also have prompted them to break into song on occasion. Deere may not have made the first steel plow—that distinction probably went to John Lane of nearby Lockport, Illinois—but for the men and women who settled the Midwestern prairies, his invention was truly a godsend.

The excitement generated by the steel plow was by no means an isolated incident. It reflected the extraordinary faith among American farmers, especially in the Midwest, in new technology and their vigorous response to market opportunities—so extraordinary and so vigorous that historians often refer to this period (the 1840s and 1850s) as the "First Agricultural Revolution." Technological innovation—plows, cultivators, threshers, and especially reapers—broke down production and cultural barriers by midcentury. Cutting grain with a sickle or cradle and grass with a scythe were backbreaking jobs and expensive in terms of man-hours. The reapers introduced by Cyrus McCormick, Obed Hussey, and others harvested grain more thoroughly and seven times more rapidly than the cradle, with half the labor force. Put another way, a man could cut one-half to three-quarters of an acre of wheat a day with a sickle, two to three acres with a cradle, or ten to twelve acres with a reaper.

In practical terms, this meant that farmers no longer had to limit their fields to the amount their families (and hirelings, if they could afford them) could harvest, a development that proved downright seductive. The breaking of the production bottleneck dramatically altered farmers' perception of the marketplace even more, from a corrupting influence in the Jeffersonian tradition to a near state of nirvana. Supply, they now believed, created its own demand. Farmers, so they thought, could not overproduce and the more they produced the better off they would be. That fundamental assumption—an expression of extreme confidence and optimism—both motivated and haunted farmers for the rest of the century and beyond.

Federal policy during the Civil War strengthened farmers' commitment to unrestrained expansion. The economic measures passed after the Republican electoral victory of 1860 were designed, in no uncertain terms, to stimulate production. Midwestern (and now far western) farmers had virtually all of their major demands satisfied: a homestead act that gave 160 acres of free public land to settlers who would live and labor on it; a series of grants to railroad companies to provide still more transportation for moving crops and opening settlements; and a federal Department of Agriculture to offer a myriad of government services. Aid of this magnitude assured the continuing rapid exploitation of the country's farming resources, heightened the farmer's commercial identity, and strengthened the link between agricultural and industrial sectors.

By the 1870s, there were four clear signs that farmers had firmly embraced the market. The first was the increasing specialization of cash crops. The so-called belts of American agriculture—wheat, corn, dairy, and cotton—were well under way, if not already entrenched, perhaps the surest indication of all of how few farmers still raised crops primarily for home consumption. Second, farmers actually showed little passion for the land they cultivated, in that they were not averse to picking up and leaving whenever their acreage appreciated substantially—a common occurrence in frontier areas. Third, when feeling prosperous, farmers rushed into debt to buy more land and more farm equipment. And fourth, they clearly relished the innovations of the industrial age, including the riding plow, gang plow, steam plow, and a great many other implements manufactured by Deere & Company, which Charles took over from his father in 1858 and greatly expanded. Labor-saving farm machinery, in fact, cut production costs for the leading crops by half from 1850 to 1900.

Farmers, in short, now stood at the center of a vast and complex network of trade and industry. A highly sophisticated array of commodity exchanges, run by brokers wearing shirts and ties in Chicago and other big cities, determined prices and found buyers throughout the country and overseas. Great processing industries turned wheat into flour, livestock into packaged meat, and, a bit later, fruits and vegetables into canned goods. Entire rail systems, port facilities, and fleets of ships were devoted to moving the products of American farmers. Farming, in other words, had irrevocably become a business. Jefferson has been rolling over in his grave ever since.

Though not as offensive to old-line agrarians, the implement industry underwent a similar transformation. McCormick tested his first reaper in 1831 but did not place it on the market until 1840 or build his Chicago manufacturing operations until 1847. Even as demand skyrocketed, it took McCormick several more years to perfect his machine, advertise it, and build a factory that could churn out more than a few hundred units a year. John Deere was equally content to produce only a handful of plows in the early years of his small partnership and to market them at state and county fairs. When his business-savvy son took control of the business, however, he quickly turned it into a modern company with stockholders, branch houses, an expanded, nationally advertised product line, and greatly enlarged factories. Although John never pretended to be more than a good blacksmith at a time when farmers on the Midwestern prairies needed one, Charles sought nothing less than to control the American plow trade. Charles brought a substantial level of security to the family business and great personal fortune to himself, but he also had to contend with labor unions, angry farmers, patent disputes, and the question of trusts.

Farmers' integration into the industrial age proved even more difficult. For all that they produced, they received less and less for their efforts. The laws of supply and demand worked against farmers, as they did against virtually all producers in the latter third of the nineteenth century. Indeed, in this long, drawn-out period of deflation, commodity prices fell precipitously across the board. Unable to face the possibility that their fundamental assumption—that the West could not overproduce—might be fallacious, farmers tried to fight back and find someone to blame. Largely through the Grange, originally a social-educational organization, they denounced railroads for discriminatory freight rates, banks for inadequate credit, grain elevators for excessive charges, state and federal governments for insufficient regulatory legislation, and implement manufacturers such as Deere & Company for gouging them mercilessly. To western farmers, there was something basically wrong about a system that enabled giant corporations to flourish while the men who supplied them with basic goods could hardly make a living. They vented their frustrations even louder during the Populist revolt at the end of the century, but in the end with no more success.

So ended the American farmer's initiation into the modern economic world. The paradox of market-oriented agriculture would become even more pronounced in the twentieth century. Only on rare occasions, during the two world wars in particular, would farmers be able to produce to their hearts' content *and* expect to receive higher prices for their crops. Far more often, their identity as producers—their inner drive to expand their acreage, maximize yields, and improve their productivity with cutting-edge technology—brought with it great surpluses, low prices, and misery. From the 1930s to the present, they have had little choice but to rely on the federal government to maintain the health and vitality of their "industry." Charles Deere, in his last days in 1907, told his cousin and business associate of sixty years, "I'm sick forever. I ought to have quit business twelve years ago." Though he was referring to his health and the depressed economy of the previous decade, Deere's words also seemed to predict the tough times that lay ahead.

Note

1. See especially Paul W. Gates, *Economic History of the United States,* vol. 3, *The Farmer's Age: Agriculture, 1815–1860,* (New York: Holt, Rinehart, and Winston, 1960), vi, 420 (quotes). On the latter period, an equally valuable starting point is Gates's contemporary (and series successor), Fred Shannon, *Economic History of the United States,* vol. 5, *The Farmer's Last Frontier: Agriculture, 1860–1897,* (New York: Rinehart, 1945). This essay also draws from Martin Bruegel, *Farm, Shop, Landing: The Rise of a Market Society in the Hudson Valley, 1780–1860* (Durham, N.C.: Duke University Press, 2002); William Cronon, *Nature's Metropolis: Chicago and the Great West* (New York: W. W. Norton, 1991); James A. Henretta et al., *America's History,* 3rd ed. (New York: Worth Publishers, 1997), 519–49; R. Douglas Hurt, *American Farm Tools from Hand-Power to Steam-Power* (Manhattan, Kans.: Sunflower University Press, 1982); Hurt, *American Agriculture: A Brief History* (Ames: Iowa State University Press, 1994); Morton Rothstein, "The American West and Foreign Markets, 1850–1900," in *The Frontier in American Development: Essays in Honor of Paul Wallace Gates,* ed. David M. Ellis (Ithaca, N.Y.: Cornell University Press, 1969), 381–406; Rothstein, "The Big Farm: Abundance and Scale in American Agriculture," *Agricultural History* 49 (October 1975): 583–97; Charles Sellars, *The Market Revolution: Jacksonian America, 1815–1846* (New York: Oxford University Press, 1991); George Rogers Taylor, *Economic History of the United States,* vol. 4, *The Transportation Revolution, 1815–1860,* (New York: Rinehart, 1951).

THE JOHN DEERE STORY

MOLINE, ILL.

O N E

Young and Enterprising

Today John Deere is recognized as the world's leading manufacturer of agricultural implements. And more than a century after his death, the legend of the company's venerated founder and namesake is more widely recognized than ever. The most spectacular story—the story that John Deere invented the steel plow—is false, but the true trials and tribulations, failures and successes of the man hold far greater and more practical lessons than this embellished tale of one-time inspiration. John Deere's story is more pragmatic, the story of a man who suffered, prospered, and left a much deeper and enduring legacy. He is remembered as a great inventor and businessman, yet he refused to live in the past or to define the success of his life from that day in 1837 when he built his first plow. In his mind, his successes resulted from the accumulation of daily effort over the course of his entire life, although he also believed that a lifetime could be lost in a single moment of moral compromise. Men worked for him, loved him, and revered him because he had started where they were starting. Perseverance, dedication, faith, and morality had guided him, and, by following his example, they too hoped to attain the respect, wealth, and influence that he enjoyed.

John Deere was not an overnight success as the tale of the invention of the steel plow suggests. He was thirty-two years old when he arrived in Grand Detour, Illinois, and thirty-three years old when he built his first plow. Even then, he did not take immediately to the plow trade. Demand did not warrant the move. He was a blacksmith, and, until that point in time, not a prosperous one. But like thousands of men and women of his time, he was not a failure because he lacked energy or ability. By all accounts, he was highly skilled at the forge. As a young upstart, though, he faced a profession highly saturated with veteran blacksmiths in the East. He moved west to find a place where blacksmiths were in demand.

After losing their father as children, John Deere, his three younger brothers, and his sister were raised by their mother and their older brother. For four years, John worked as a blacksmith's apprentice. Then, at the age of twenty-one, he left to earn his own living. He stood six feet tall, with broad, muscular shoulders, and by some accounts, fiery red hair. According to his few biographers, he was the prototypical pioneer—rugged, intrepid, and headstrong.

Arriving in Illinois in late 1836, John Deere built a small timber house near the Rock River. Friends and neighbors had been to Illinois and returned to Vermont, so he knew firsthand of the bitter cold and winter hardships on the prairie. Nonetheless, he made the trip and went quickly to work in his lifelong profession. In many ways he was living his dream. He owned his own business and was doing the work he loved, but he could not yet afford to bring his family west. The construction of his first plow provided him with an unexpected opportunity, although when he went at last into the plow business wholeheartedly in 1840, he took great financial risk with no guarantee of success. His ultimate success in business was not the product of a single moment but of a lifetime of adaptability, determination, and a deep understanding of his own strengths and weaknesses.

Demanding creditors and uncommitted business partners continued to waylay him, that is, until his only surviving son graduated from a Chicago business school and joined the family business. The financial genius behind the company's rise and the architect of the John Deere legend, Charles Deere joined the business at the age of sixteen. Over the next fifty-four years, he would turn an average plow business into a family dynasty and, in the process, would become one of the most influential men in the United States.

A Young Man Finds His Way

In the winter of 1804, as Lewis and Clark were preparing for their epic journey across the Great Plains, over the Rocky Mountains, and down to the Pacific Ocean, John Deere was born. It was an era of expansion and exploration, financial depression, and limited social mobility. Four of every five American citizens made their living as farmers, and few people lived in towns with more than 1,500 residents. Large families lived in tight quarters, aspiring for nothing more than self-sustenance and a better lot for their children. At a young age, many boys were apprenticed to cabinetmakers, silversmiths, shoemakers, and blacksmiths to learn a respectable, skilled trade, but a fluctuating economy offered the youth little security.

John Deere was born into this world of change and uncertainty on February 7, 1804, in Rutland, Vermont. His father, William Rinold Deere, was a tailor; his mother, Sarah Yates Deere, a seamstress. In his early twenties, William had left England and had come to the United States via Canada in the early 1790s. Sarah's father, Captain James Yates, came from Portsmouth, England, to Portsmouth, New Hampshire, and served in the king's army during the American Revolution. After the war he remained on American soil and pledged both his allegiance and his family's future to the infant nation he had fought against. William Deere and Sarah Yates married in 1793. In 1806, they moved with their five children from the economically stagnant Rutland thirty miles to the north, to the forward-looking Middlebury, a village of cascading hills tucked into the heart of a valley along Otter Creek, where John would live most of his adolescent life. The town had been burned to the ground during the Revolution; most of its mills, taverns, stores, and homes were only a few decades old when the Deeres arrived. Yet Middlebury was home to 1,200 hardworking, God-fearing citizens; and its future was bright. During its early century boom, Middlebury's tiny frame houses and businesses, nestled among forests of hemlock and pine and split by the waters of Otter Creek, became a regular stop for the stages and wagons. In the heart of town, passersby could find purveyors of handcrafted furniture and leather and iron goods, as well as the wares of a new general store.

With the income from a prospering tailor shop, William and Sarah were able to support themselves and their now six children, but the young couple was always looking for more rewarding opportunities. When William received notice of a cousin's death and was summoned to collect the inheritance, he decided to return to England. Later learning that the story of his cousin's death was, in fact, false, he did not cancel his trip but in June 1808 set out on the dangerous voyage to England. From Boston Harbor, he penned a letter to his namesake and eldest son, William, who had just taken an apprenticeship with a local cabinetmaker.

My Dear Child as I am to be absent from you many months I wish you to attend to a few kinds of instruction from [one] who has your welfare at [heart]. Be faithful to your master and to his interests, be obedient to him & Mrs. Warren be friendly and kind to all the family. Let Truth & Honesty be your guide & on no pretense Deviate from it

[B]e Dutiful to your mother Kind to your Sister & Brothers, have the fear of God before you, implore his protection & you will obtain it and likewise the good will of all mankind.[1]

Faith, obedience, kindness, truth, and honesty were the virtues that young William was expected to cultivate in himself and to impart to his siblings: nine-year-old Francis, eight-year-old Jane, five-year-old Elizabeth, four-year old John, and two-year-old George.

Meanwhile, their mother carried on the tailoring business and took up other odd jobs to support her family during her husband's absence, which she assumed would be brief. But fate held other plans for the young family. William's letter was his last, and his family would never know his ultimate fate. Perhaps the passengers and crew were impressed by the English navy. Perhaps they met a gruesome fate at the hands of pirates. According to one account, the ship arrived safely in England with William's trunk aboard, though he was not to be found. When it became clear that William would not return, Sarah broke the news to her children. The brutal realities of an unknown future hit the family like a thunderclap.

Suddenly, Sarah Deere was responsible for five children under the age of sixteen. Her husband was gone; and her youngest daughter, Jane, had recently died. For spiritual comfort she joined the Congregational Church, and to make ends meet she offered her services as a seamstress in the house of a Mrs. S. Hopkins. At home she did odd jobs for neighbors and friends. For now the family was getting by, but that was all. Despite his father's wishes that he be obedient to his master, consequences forced William, Jr., to leave his apprenticeship and return home to help his mother.[2]

John may have attended classes at the local grammar school and may have even taken courses at Middlebury College for a short time. He survived the fever epidemics that took many of the town's elders in 1813 and 1814 and was too young to be included in the draft of Middlebury men who fought in the war of 1812. As a teenager, Deere took a job grinding bark for Epaphras Miller, the local tanner. His mother was pleasantly surprised one day to find her son dressed in a new pair of shoes and a suit of clothes that Miller had given him as payment. Every little bit helped.

After a short employment with Miller, Deere's intermittent schooling ended indefinitely when, at the age of seventeen, he left his mother's home for an apprenticeship with a local blacksmith, Benjamin Lawrence. Captain Lawrence had settled in Middlebury twenty-five years earlier when the primitive village boasted little more than a tavern, a few dozen homes, and a small jail. Now it claimed more than 2,500 citizens. Lawrence's residence was a typical single story timber and frame house hiding in the tree line on the knoll above the river at Frog Hollow. His shop lay a short distance up a narrow path, cut into the hillside nearby, dwarfed by a neighboring pail factory at least twice its size.

Deere spent the next four years working and living with Lawrence, his wife, and their daughter, who was close to his own age. In addition to clothes, room and board, and an initial annual salary of thirty dollars (which increased by five dollars each successive year), Deere received the type of personal and professional guidance he had missed since his father's disappearance thirteen years earlier. Lawrence was a talented blacksmith of notable reputation who had honed his skills through years of service to the people of Middlebury.

Lawrence had a thriving business, employing seven blacksmiths to handle the demand of townspeople and travelers for kitchen utensils, horseshoes, wagon wheels, hitches, hinges, and other ironware. They all worked together, but each man forged his own reputation. For Deere, Lawrence proved to be a strict master and a skilled teacher, both traits of a strong masculine figure the boy had been deprived of his entire life. Under his watchful eye, the young man discovered the brutal intricacies of the profession, such as striking the hot iron and finishing a job on the first heat. Most important, he learned that a blacksmith's workmanship was his signature.[3]

In 1825, Deere completed his four-year apprenticeship and hired himself out to David Wells and Ira Allen, neighboring blacksmiths on Court Street in Middlebury. The very next year Colonel Ozias Buel hired him exclusively to fit the sawmill and linseed oil mill at Colchester Falls in Burlington. Deere was still an upstart in an area that boasted a number of highly skilled blacksmiths, but for the time being he found journeyman work satisfying.

Early Struggles

Deere was a dedicated learner at the forge and at the anvil, but life in Middlebury and the surrounding communities was not entirely confined to the shop. During his apprenticeship he met Demarius Lamb, a skinny, round-eyed woman whose family had recently settled in nearby Hancock. Demarius was attending Emma Willard's School for Young Ladies in Middlebury and may have been living in the home of her brother Charles. Her education included reading and writing, as well as instruction in etiquette and the other important responsibilities of a nineteenth-century lady. The daughter of a prosperous farmer and the third of six sisters, Demarius so far had led a life much different than that of her future husband.

The young couple was married in January 1827, eleven months after the death of Deere's mother. The marriage brought a great responsibility and put a great deal of pressure on his future success. Perhaps Demarius's father was sufficiently impressed by Deere's ambitious plans for self-employment to consent to the union. The newlyweds moved to nearby Vergennes, just north of Middlebury, where Deere secured a job with John McVene. A year later, in May 1828, Demarius gave birth to their first son, Francis Albert. That same year Deere's partnership with McVene ended, and with work becoming harder to secure, the young family began to travel from town to town in search of opportunities.

If he could not find work, the independent Deere reasoned, he would create his own. In 1829 he borrowed money to purchase a small tract of land from Stephen Sparks and erected his first blacksmith shop at the "Four Corners" intersection of the stagecoach line that went to Middlebury, Leicester, Brandon, and further east to Boston and New Hampshire. The location, officially in the town of Leicester, was good and the profession was important, but the small surrounding towns were already saturated with blacksmith shops, so steady work remained difficult to secure. A limited income meant that efforts to break out on his own would have to wait, and a few months later Deere entered a short-lived partnership with Darius Holman. Soon Deere sold his property to Holman and became a tenant in the shop he himself had built.

More trouble followed. Deere's shop was twice devastated by fire, a common problem for a profession that worked smoldering fire under the shelter of timber-framed shops. Broke and unemployed, the young couple headed to Royalton, where Deere traded his wounded pride for a steady job with steady wages, repairing stagecoaches for Amos Bosworth, half-owner of the Cascadnac Hotel and the proprietor of a local stagecoach business. The job provided Deere with a sense of stability for the first time since his apprenticeship with Benjamin Lawrence, and now with three children—son Francis Albert and daughters Jeannette and Ellen—Deere desperately needed stability.

By 1832, the Deeres had seen much of central Vermont. Itinerant work and frequent unemployment had forced them to pull up stakes at least five times, and each move was more difficult than the last. But even though Deere enjoyed a steady income and job security working for Bosworth, the twenty-nine-year-old blacksmith was restless. Unwilling to spend the rest of his days working for someone else, he left Royalton for opportunities in Hancock in 1833, borrowed money to buy another small piece of land from a local doctor, and built another shop. Living near Demarius's family, who was perhaps providing some financial support, the Deeres got along on income from shoeing horses, patching wagons, and making pitchforks. It was honest work, and Deere was finally in business for himself. If he remained steadfast and diligent, he hoped, his perseverance would be rewarded. In those troubled times, however, he was still having difficulty staying ahead of his creditors.

The 1830s were difficult for many families. The national banking system was collapsing during what later became known as the "Panic of 1837." President Andrew Jackson had declared the National Bank corrupt and unconstitutional and then proceeded to remove all government deposits and disperse them among several independent state banks throughout the country. In addition, years of wild speculation in land, roads, canals, and other government property, as well as an increase in the importation of cheap foreign goods, prompted the proliferation of new banks up and down the East Coast.

To check such operations and limit further speculation, Jackson issued the controversial "specie circular," which, as of August 15, 1836, required payment for government lands in gold or silver. Its effect on the fragile American financial system proved disastrous. Banks immediately began calling in their loans, forcing citizens to sell their properties at greatly reduced prices and causing a collapse in the market for government land. Many defaulted on loan payments entirely, while others—small business owners and entrepreneurs mostly—began demanding payment on outstanding debts.

Deere, a small sole proprietor with little or no reserve cash to his name, faced the same demanding creditors. As a result of the panic, state governments went into debt, as did the federal government, and the financial crisis triggered an exodus. The West promised fortune or at least an escape from debt. Americans migrated by the thousands, lured by the prospect of starting a new life in Ohio, Indiana, or Illinois.

Stories of those who had already made the trip and returned for their families, along with the steady stream of rumors of cheap land and rich soil attracted Deere. According to the booster Augustus Mitchell, who captured the Western euphoria in what soon became a pioneer guidebook, patriots had a responsibility to spread the "intellectual, moral and religious condition of our national glory." Mitchell even lauded the "genial nature of [the Western] climate," although it seems doubtful that he ever experienced a limb-numbing winter in Illinois.[4]

Mitchell described the ideal pioneer as "young and enterprising" and "turning for eager competition of industry and talent." Deere certainly met these criteria. Amos Bosworth, Deere's former employer and caretaker, had already succumbed to the hysteria and left cozy Royalton to tame the prairie. Returning to Vermont to collect his family, he brought eyewitness tales of opportunity. He had settled in the young Illinois village of Grand Detour, founded by another Easterner with ties in Middlebury, Leonard Andrus. Bosworth may have motivated Deere to push west, but another incident precipitated Deere's decision.

In February 1835, Deere took a loan for $78.76. The terms called for the balance and interest to be repaid by October 1836, but when the time came Deere could not pay. In November, he received a summons from the justice of the peace of Leicester, one of his many former residences, and when the deputy sheriff appeared on November 7, Deere was arrested. He soon provided bail money and was released, only to find the judge had also placed a lien on his property. The proud blacksmith had a fateful decision to make: either follow the trail of other Vermonters who had already made the dangerous journey west or stay and face the possibility of a term in debtor's prison. Grand Detour was without a blacksmith, and if Deere was not personally invited to fill this void, he had offered his services. He sold his shop to his father-in-law for $200 and said goodbye to his four children and his pregnant wife. He would call for his family when he could.[5]

Go West

There is no record of Deere's trip west. He spoke only of traveling by "canal boats and lakes" (which likely took him through Chicago) and then only of a collection of temporary buildings with no indication of its later importance. He made the rest of the trip through the stark, untamed early winter desolation of the prairie by wagon. A contemporary English author likened the tedious journey across the unending prairie in any season to "putting out to Lake Michigan in a canoe."[6]

The trip from Vermont took several months, and Deere arrived in Grand Detour in early to mid-December 1836, just in time to bargain with the impending Illinois winter. There was not yet much to speak of in the village, though Grand Detour already had a long and rich history. The Winnebago, Potawatomi, Sauk, and Fox Indians had settled the area before the arrival of French fur traders in the eighteenth century. Indian mythology claimed that the Rock River was so taken with itself and the beauty of the surrounding landscape that it doubled back to take another look, forming the great horseshoe bend that cradled Grand Detour.

Upon his arrival, Deere quickly became acquainted (or perhaps reacquainted) with the town's founder, Leonard Andrus. A thin, serious-minded widower whose mind was as sharp as his beak-shaped nose, the thirty-one-year-old Andrus had at one time attended Middlebury College, so if Deere had studied there, the two may have been classmates for a time. After graduation, Andrus returned to his native New York and entered the dry goods business, but the attraction of the West drew him early on.

Andrus found his way to St. Louis, then set out on an expedition through Illinois towards the Galena lead mines in the northern part of the state. Along the way, he was intercepted by John Dixon, who gave his name to the Illinois town near the Rock River. Andrus laid his first claim to Grand Detour in 1833. The following year, he bought a river-bank cabin from a French trapper and built a hydraulic plant. Other enterprises soon followed—a sawmill, a flourmill, and a cluster of small shops dependent on his waterpower. Other businessmen and speculators had also been seduced by the allegedly uncharted territories along the Rock River. Upon their arrival, however, they found that Andrus had already cornered most of Grand Detour's markets. Newcomers had little choice but to go into business with him. In addition to the mills, he had an interest in the ferry and the stagecoach, and, after a trip to Washington, he soon owned rights to the post office as well.[7]

Fortunately for Deere, Andrus needed his assistance. He hired the blacksmith for an emergency repair to a pitman shaft in the hydraulic company's mill on Pine Creek, a job that Deere completed even before he started construction on his own shop. Deere's claim near the river was not large, but its location was critical because it offered immediate access to water and timber. He built a modest blacksmith shop from timber and rock and, within a few days, began accepting work. With the shop in operation, he set about building a small house for his family, a New England–style dwelling that may have resembled his own boyhood home. The small, one-and-a-half-story house of hewn timber was simple and traditional: two rooms on the lower floor with a narrow stairway to an upper sleeping room. In total, the house was not more than eighteen by twenty-four feet, but additions to shelter the growing family would come soon enough.

John Deere's Plow

Deere's business catered to the newly arrived settlers, most of whom came to farm. Their hopes and dreams, however, soon confronted a harsh reality. Unfamiliar with the prairie environment, Grand Detour's settlers set about farming as they had in New England. Instead of taking advantage of the vast, open grasslands, they cleared the heavily timbered areas. If the land could not support the trees, they believed, it could not support anything else.

Along with their traditional farming practices, the settlers also brought Eastern farming tools, including the plow, an implement almost as old as civilization itself that had changed little in its basic form and function. The plowman followed his horse or ox in the furrow, gripping the reigns between his thumbs and forefingers while he guided the plow with his hands to control depth and direction. Inventors strove to increase the plow's efficiency, specifically through an improvement of two critical parts, the moldboard and the plowshare. The sharpened share pierced the soil and cut deeply into the ground, uprooting trash and roots and pulverizing the soil. The moldboard was a rounded, larger piece of wood, or recently of iron, that rolled the soil into a row beside the new furrow.

Many, most notably Thomas Jefferson, had claimed to have perfected the plow, but the new soil of the frontier demanded new designs. Charles Newbold filed the first American patent for a plow that was made of cast iron in June 1797. In November 1808, Richard Chenoweth of Baltimore filed for a new wrought-iron share for deep plowing in Pennsylvania, Maryland, and Virginia. Three more patents were filed before Jethro Wood received a patent in September 1819 for a series of improvements, the most advanced of which was a system of interchangeable parts.[8]

As Americans moved westward, they struggled with new soils. Unlike the sandy New England soil, prairie soil stuck to both the share and the moldboard. Illinois soil was fertile for the initial breaking of the land, but following seasons revealed a stubborn, sticky loam that grew more resistant year after year. It made plowing a straight, deep furrow a backbreaking chore. The farmers resorted to carrying a wooden paddle and stopping every few yards to scrape the sticky soil from the moldboards, a frustrating and time-consuming task. Iron shares that would slice through Eastern soils as a warm knife slices through butter were quickly dulled by the impenetrable prairie soils and became pitted and coarse with use.[9] Some pioneers continued to use the cast-iron plow, with separate moldboards and shares bolted together, built on the concept of Jethro Wood's system of interchangeable parts. More traditional farmers, convinced that the iron plow poisoned the land, refused to adopt it.

With an obvious market for better plows, dozens of Western inventors were working on the problem by the early 1830s. Near Chicago, in 1833, John Lane nailed strips of steel to a wooden moldboard in what was probably the first attempt to include steel in moldboard design. The scarcity of raw materials and a tendency for the plow to bend during use, however, prevented its commercial success. Over the next few years, newly established plow makers in Pittsburgh began incorporating steel into plows specifically designed for the prairie soil, although these manufacturers typically used the steel in bolts and supporting pieces—not in the moldboards or shares. In 1836 two Pittsburgh companies produced a total of 34,000 plows (worth $174,000), most made of wood and cast iron, for the lower Mississippi region and the cotton and prairie lands of the West and the South. Meanwhile, despite a shortage of capital and materials, plow makers in Illinois continued to work to perfect the iron plow, but with few tangible results.[10]

While Deere shoed horses, patched wagon wheels, and manufactured essential ironware in Grand Detour, he heard the grumbling of farmers around town. Some of his neighbors considered returning to the friendly soil of Vermont; others believed that the prairie could be subdued. Deere pondered the farmers' problem. His moment of inspiration came in 1837, during a visit to the Grand Detour Hydraulic Mill, another Andrus company in Grand Detour. Noticing a broken steel saw blade sitting in the corner, he asked Andrus if he could take the blade to his shop.

Deere cut the teeth off the long blade with a hand chisel, striker, and sledge, then heated one small section at a time and molded it with a hammer and attached the steel blade to an iron moldboard. Next, he dug up a sapling and shaved two plow handles, which he connected to a carved beam. An upright standard, molded from the bar iron stock used to make ironware, connected the beam and moldboard. When the plow was finished, Deere set it on a dry goods box in front of his shop. It was several days before a farmer saw the plow and asked to give it try.

That first plow has been lost. Current reproductions are based on one surviving plow of the two Deere made the following year. His idea in Andrus's mill may have had roots in Vermont, where in 1828 he worked for blacksmith John McVene of Vergennes. According to an 1826 advertisement in a local paper, McVene offered horseshoes, axes, and other tools made "from the best Cast Steel and English Blister." In this light, Deere's idea was likely less inspiration and more a marriage of experience and opportunity.[11]

At the time, Deere did not see plows as a new business opportunity, even though the demand for his blacksmithing skills was dropping. He was working alone, one forge at a time. He would not become rich as a frontier blacksmith, he knew, but he continued to earn enough to care for his wife and children. Accompanied by her brother-in-law, William Peek, and his family, Demarius brought the five children to Grand Detour in 1838. Little Charles Deere and his cousin had shared the wagon's feed box as a cradle during the westward journey. Charles was already a year old by the time he first saw his father.

Grand Detour now boasted several frame houses, a tavern, a hotel, a sawmill, a gristmill, and a general store as well as several dozen log cabins. To those who called it home, Grand Detour offered a close, well-rounded community with great opportunity for all. For the Deere family it offered new beginnings and a frontier way of life. The oldest son—who went by his middle name, Albert—shot ducks from the front porch of their home. With their father, Albert and Charles trapped quail and other game. Fishing was also a necessary pastime, and Charles later remembered his sister Emma's incessant worrying that he would someday drown in the river. The Indians had been pushed out of Grand Detour, but the children made a game of protecting the family from attack. Music helped to pass endless days on the prairie, and all of the children became competent pianists. Here, along the shores of the Rock River, they hoped to finally make their permanent home.

A Speculative New Business

The modernization of America was in full swing by the late 1830s. Samuel Morse was developing his design for a telegraphing instrument and the code that would bear his name, Samuel Colt was marketing his new invention, the revolver, and Charles Goodyear was working on his vulcanization process for rubber. Meanwhile, a shortage of work was pushing John Deere into the plow business.

Although many of Deere's acquaintances, including some of his early partners, did not consider him a "man of general inventive ability," he was sincere and motivated. Those same partners also had enough faith in him to cast their lot with his. Indeed, Deere's commitment and ability to solve problems were regarded as his most prized attributes. He often labored from four in the morning until late into the night. Unable to afford to hire assistants, he only drove himself harder when he added plows to his line of goods. He was not specifically interested in plow design before he built his first plow, but, thanks to his experience repairing farming implements and a wide variety of other tools, he proved resourceful and creative. Necessity had made him an inventor.[12]

Deere built only ten plows in 1839, and the shortage of steel makes it likely most were made of iron. Deere had also learned that the shape of the moldboard was as important as the materials. Several failed ventures in Vermont had taught him about the risks of entering a speculative new business that required capital and manpower he simply did not possess. At the same time, the advantages of starting a plow-making business were hard to ignore. Instead of waiting for odd repair jobs, he could count on a steady flow of work. Plows would net more income than the miscellaneous ironware Deere was producing. The market for plows was also greater, with the promise of growth as more and more farmers came to settle Ohio, Indiana, and Illinois. In addition to local customers, Deere could sell to farmers on their way south or further west. Indeed, soon farmers would pass through Grand Detour for the sole purpose of buying a plow.[13]

There were, however, drawbacks. In central Illinois alone, dozens of shops produced plows and other farming implements. An increase in production and competition drove down prices, while the difficulty in distinguishing the plows made by one manufacturer from those of another prevented any one from developing customer loyalty. The outlook for Deere's success in the plow business was hardly guaranteed, but two decades of personal financial uncertainty drove him to make efforts—and take risks—that would daunt even the most hardened pioneer. He had a great deal to lose and could not endure another failure.

In 1840, for the first time the census listed Deere's occupation as an agricultural manufacturer.[14] That year he had built forty plows. The next year he built seventy-five, and the year after, one hundred. He constructed an eight-hundred-square-foot addition to his shop. It was not long before he added another interior room as well as a shed roof so that he could work outdoors yet remain under cover. Outside the shop, a horse-driven treadmill turned the grinding wheel for polishing shares and moldboards. Opposite the forge stood a large furnace for heating the steel and iron for bending.

With no capital and limited resources, it was impossible to enter a new business with an unknown product and expect immediate success. Deere was not yet an expert plow maker. By closely examining plows made by competitors based in Springfield, Princeton, Galesburg, and other Illinois towns, he began to understand the benefit of constant improvement. The United States patent system, still in its infancy and lacking enforcement, allowed entrepreneurs the freedom to borrow and adapt the ideas of others, and Deere took full advantage of the system's laxity. His inventiveness, as he would prove over and over again throughout his life, consisted of taking solid products, greatly improving them, and then marketing the new product more effectively and less expensively than his competitors.

Deere's persuasiveness as a salesman soon matched his reputation for mechanical skill. To increase his product line, he also began to offer on commission the Patent Cary Plow, made by Springfield manufacturers Jewett and Hitchcock. When Grand Detour's first newspaper, the *Rock River Register,* was introduced in 1843, he took advantage of the new advertising medium to inform "his friends and customers, the agricultural community, of this and the adjoining counties, and dealers in Ploughs, that he is now prepared to fill orders for the same on presentation." Deere's plows were made of wrought iron, "ground smooth, so that it scours perfectly bright in any soil, and will not choke in the foulest of ground." Unlike the typical iron plow, however, Deere's plow boasted a steel share, 5/16 of an inch thick, with a sharp edge. The advertisement highlighted the key selling points: a highly polished moldboard to prevent sticking, and a thick, durable steel share that did not easily clog. Recognizing that the country was still in the throes of the financial panic that had driven Deere himself to Illinois, he assured customers that "[t]he Price of Ploughs, in consequence of hard times, will be reduced from last year's prices."[15]

Collecting payment from customers continued to prove difficult. In February 1841, for example, Deere brought suit against Levi Dort for a two-year-old debt of $14.56. In 1842 Deere won a judgment against Peter Wertz, whose purchases included one plow at fifteen dollars, for an outstanding balance of $10.62. No stranger to debt or the courts, Deere would spend the next twenty years either trying to collect or facing the creditors who were trying to collect from him.[16]

Deere knew the pitfalls of debt better than anyone. Indeed, he needed to collect from his customers so that he could pay off the collectors pursuing him. Ghosts from Vermont finally found him in 1843, when the debt of $78.76 that had forced him from his native state showed up, along with other overdue loans, in the Ogle County circuit court. By this time, thanks to interest and fees, his debts amounted to $1,000. Records regarding the settlement are incomplete, but it seems that Deere settled by paying the original debt and court costs. The nagging debt that had driven him from home and family was finally settled, and he could only hope that his early business failures were at last behind him.[17]

L. Andrus & Company

The Deere family had grown comfortable in Grand Detour by 1843. To Easterners, it appeared a promising frontier town, if somewhat uncivilized. Settlers had to be satisfied with only most basic material goods, and their primitive dwellings more closely resembled the pilgrim settlement at Jamestown than the high society districts of New York. Even successful men such as Leonard Andrus had little use for mansions and household luxuries.

Deere seemed positioned for a major business triumph, but he foresaw that the market in the sparsely settled towns around Grand Detour would quickly reach saturation. Venturing further and further afield, he began to sell plows at a greater distance from his home base. Yet increased travel meant increased costs, and he still lacked the resources to push his business forward. Only one man in Grand Detour could solve that problem; so, in 1843, Deere entered a partnership with Leonard Andrus. In addition to start-up capital, Andrus offered the new business discounts from the mill and the other local operations he already owned. A year later, the partners increased their capital with a $1,000 contribution from Horace Paine, a squat, narrow-nosed local businessman, and enlarged their factory.[18]

Andrus had a great deal of business expertise, but his early contributions to the partnership were probably more financial than administrative. In addition to the partners, the newly formed L. Andrus & Company employed between eight and ten men on an average day in the factory, which by this time was powered almost exclusively by steam. Horsepower ran the foundry, the only one for hundreds of miles around. Instead of purchasing the horses, however, the company borrowed horses from neighbors to walk the treadmills that drove the belts and stoked the fire to melt the metal for castings.

Deere was often meeting with potential customers in the field, and through a combination of quality products and professional integrity, he began to forge his reputation. A personable character, he clearly understood the workings of his plow and always tested new models himself. If a farmer made a suggestion, Deere would correct the problem, and if improvements were suggested over the life of the plow, he would make the necessary adjustments on new models. Coupled with an unmatched ambition and drive, Deere's willingness to learn and adapt had become a priceless asset: customers knew they were buying the latest and most advanced model he could offer.[19]

Deere's resourcefulness and determination soon became as well known as his plow. Once, facing a shortage of iron, he decided that he could not afford to wait for the shipment of his next order. He hitched up a one-horse spring wagon and made the trip of nearly two hundred miles to Springfield in south-central Illinois to acquire the needed materials. The blacksmith's determination, always a topic of conversation in later years, pushed him to make efforts few others would. But his strong will could also be problematic, and it often drove away associates. After two years, for example, Horace Paine left the partnership. His replacement, Oramil Lathrop, stayed a mere eight months.

Deere's strong will brought him into conflict with the equally hard-headed Andrus, and they argued over the best course for the company's future. While Deere struggled to reach more distant customers, for example, Andrus tried to prevent a proposed railroad from passing through Grand Detour. Deere also became suspicious of his partner's accounting procedures. If his overwhelming desire to succeed too often overshadowed his practicality, Deere was nonetheless learning a hard lesson. Perhaps Andrus was taking advantage of him, but regardless of whether he truly was, Deere was learning that the man who financed the company was the man who reaped the rewards. His labor made the business successful, but he would always be at the mercy of Andrus's money. Their renewed agreement in June 1847 lasted less than a year.

To complement the part-time assistance of the bookkeeper John Gould, Deere relied on his nephew, Samuel Charters Peek, who had worked on and off for Deere since the early 1840s, and his son Albert, who was completing his formal education at the Rock River Seminary, a Methodist academy in nearby Mt. Morris. With a trusted core of financially minded men—Gould, Peek, and his son Albert—and with the intangible assets the family dynamic brought to the business, Deere again seemed poised to strike out on his own.

But a crushing tragedy intervened. Falling suddenly and violently ill in January 1848, Albert was rushed home from school to be with his family. A flu epidemic was claiming lives throughout Ogle County, and Albert became its latest victim. Deere was devastated: Albert was the third of his children to die since the family had arrived in Grand Detour ten years earlier. Albert's intelligence and bright future had been a shining star; his death left the family heartbroken.

Albert's death provided an occasion for Deere to take stock of his life. Almost thirty-years of scattered unemployment and financial distress had pushed the Deere family from their kin and their home in Vermont. On the prairie, they had found a new life, and, despite personal loss, Deere's ambitions for a better tomorrow were beginning to show the promise of the rewards he and Demarius had always dreamed about. Deere himself had emerged from the clutches of an unstable childhood, from years of business failure and missed opportunity, to become a man who seemed to hold his destiny in his own hands. At last, he had found ways to balance his own integrity and deep family loyalties with the sacrifices that were required to succeed on the prairie. Now, more than ever, Deere had the motivation to leave Andrus and Grand Detour behind.[20]

MOLINE, ILL.

T W O

John Deere, The Plow King

John Deere and his family led hard lives typical of the times, but in Grand Detour they started to enjoy more comforts. His perseverance, which probably exasperated faithful Demarius during move after move, finally seemed to be paying dividends. Although he still labored most of the day, he had also created opportunities and earned rewards that would have been impossible in the East. Now it was time to look to the future. Deere recognized that the only way that he could run a business on his own terms was if he provided both the initial seed money and the business model. He could bring in other partners but only under the true meaning of a partnership: each man contributing a particular skill and performing his duties accordingly. This concept may have seemed almost utopian in its simplicity. For Deere, it represented a just, moral partnership, and the quest for such a partnership consistently shaped his future business decisions. Deere and Andrus had parted because they failed to achieve such a symbiotic relationship: Deere had carried most of the workload but received little of the profit. So, too, the contrast between Andrus's more detached, cautious approach and Deere's hands-on experience, combined with a forward-looking practicality, caused the rupture.

Deere looked to the future. How could the company obtain the additional raw materials needed to expand the plow business, he wondered. The nearby Rock River had proven too shallow for heavily loaded barges, so coal and steel had to be transported by carriage from the town of LaSalle on the Illinois River some forty miles southeast of Grand Detour. By 1846, Deere and Andrus had manufactured 1,000 plows, shipping them by various water and overland routes to their destinations.

But, as production increased, so too did the need for a steady supply of quality steel, iron, and lumber. No longer could the company afford to wait out frozen rivers and impassable roads during icy Illinois winters. Andrus believed the partners would continue to prosper in Grand Detour. After all, they had outfitted the shop with a new steam engine and installed new presses, grindstones, polishing wheels, and even a power lathe. Deere, however, saw the remodeling of the shop as a short-term solution. When Andrus offered $1,200 for his interest in the business, Deere quickly accepted. He never looked back.

When Deere left Grand Detour, he took with him Robert Tate, the blacksmith, machinist, and engineer whose passion and good sense would become a treasured asset. Deere and Andrus had hired Tate to install their first steam engine, and the workman's intelligence and dedication had already made a good impression. Tate and Deere had led equally tragic frontier lives. Born in North Shields, England, Tate had apprenticed for five years with several blacksmiths, then moved to the United States at the age of twenty-six. The enterprising immigrant settled in Pontiac, Michigan, where he built his own blacksmith shop, only to sell it the following year and move to New York. Three years later, after the death of one of his young daughters, Mary, and the birth of another girl, Ellen, he moved the family west. Finally, in 1839, he settled in Dixon, Illinois, where he ran a farm, operated a general store, and performed general repair work for neighbors. Two years of tedium on the prairie sent Tate back to New York, but in a few years he returned to Illinois. Deere and Andrus hired him shortly after his return, and soon he became a regular in Grand Detour.

Tate likely brought little capital to the proposed business venture, but Deere was not yet concerned with finances. First, they had to find a suitable location for their business, a location with all of the geographical advantages that Grand Detour lacked: abundant waterpower, unlimited fuel supplies, and navigable waterways. Deere was also looking for a young town with a good moral fiber and an eye to the future. A merchant in Peru offered two lots as an incentive, but Tate urged Deere to look further west. Frank Gilmore, a dealer working for L. Andrus & Company, introduced the duo to an entrepreneur in Rock Island. Unable to reach an agreement for the price of waterpower, Deere and Tate headed for the local inn. During the night, their sleep was continuously interrupted by a crying child—or what Deere thought was a crying child. In the morning he discovered that the wailing infants were bear cubs belonging to one of the other boarders.

The next day, Deere and Tate were introduced to General John Buford, a West Point graduate with an interest in the waterpower in neighboring Moline. Buford offered more enticing incentives, and in short time they reached an agreement. The five-year-old village of Moline had little to boast about as of yet, but, like Deere, its founders had ambitious plans.

By 1848, the banks of the Mississippi had sprouted dozens of western outposts for American trade. The end of the Black Hawk Indian Wars just sixteen years earlier had paved the way for permanent settlement in the Upper Mississippi River valley. The area had seen steady growth since the establishment of the military post on the island called Rock Island, but its civilian population exploded when a milldam was erected on the southern channel of the Mississippi River in 1842.

Moline was founded in 1843, although it was not legally recognized until 1848 because a fire destroyed its founding documents. Geographically, it stood at a propitious spot where the Mississippi River turns west, sandwiched by a slough and the Mississippi River to the north and west, and by the Hampton, Carbon Cliff, and Coal Valley coal mines to the east and the south. The Rock River flowed into the Mississippi nearby, just below the neighboring village of Rock Island. That town was growing more quickly than Moline: by 1850 it would boast more than 1,700 inhabitants. Directly across the Mississippi River and accessible by ferryboat lay Davenport, a burgeoning river town in Iowa. All three towns, known collectively as "the Tri-Cities," looked to the ancient river to sustain and nourish the growth of their communities.

When Deere and Tate arrived in Moline, only a few buildings had been erected in the flat valley between the river and the bluff. Except for a few farmsteads, much of the seventy-eight acres of land originally platted for Moline was still covered by a dense forest of statuesque elms. One of the first settlers, David Sears, built a dam of brush and stone between the river's shore and the island of Rock Island, located across the slough. Over the course of a decade, several more mills were built, hence the name "Moline" (a derivation of the French word "moulin") the "City of Mills."[1]

After settling upon a location for his new business, Deere returned to Grand Detour and extended an offer to his former employee, John Gould, a bookkeeper from New Hampshire with a formal education. Deere told Gould that he and Tate could make and sell plows but that they needed someone to handle the accounting. Gould hesitated because he could not raise the money he needed to join the business as a partner. Furthermore, he was under contract with Dana & Troop's general store in Grand Detour, and the owners released him only with great reluctance. Because they had no cash to buy his interest in the store, they completed the transaction in a manner typical of a frontier business: they paid him with a small amount of cash and signed over their wagon and horses. Gould still needed capital to join the Deere-Tate enterprise, so Deere offered him a loan at 6 percent interest—half the going rate—and at last the partnership was sealed.[2]

In their early search for additional capital, and in Tate's absence, Deere and Gould approached Charles Atkinson, a thinly bearded town founder who had lost the use of one hand in a gunpowder explosion. Atkinson was Moline's equivalent of Leonard Andrus, and surely the partners approached him with caution. Atkinson, the owner of equipment capable of harnessing the power of the Mississippi River, joined the firm and in short time showed his business prowess. Tate had gone to New York and upon his return was shocked to find that the company was now calling itself Deere, Atkinson & Co. Deere and Gould did not protest because they felt they needed Atkinson's resources. Tate, always outspoken, found Atkinson on the street and "accosted him at this change and told him they might take my name from their books as soon as they pleased." Atkinson and Tate each went to Deere, who promised to straighten out the matter. Pleased with the outcome of Deere's intervention, Tate confided happily in his diary that Deere "got unreasonably cross with Mr. Atkinson, and he never let him rest until he got rid of him." The four worked out a deal to close the concern, a simple barter arrangement that utilized Atkinson's already vast resources but allowed him to withdraw officially from the firm on good terms.[3]

Things moved quickly that summer. On June 19, 1848, Deere, Tate, and Gould finally signed an official agreement. Deere brought Demarius to see Moline on the third of July. Three weeks later, on July 28, 1848, Deere, Tate, Gould, and six hired laborers, old man Hibbard, Pomeroy, Wallace, Jones, Philander, and a mason, according to Tate, "raised the rafters of the plough shop," a sixty-foot by twenty-four-foot factory. Deere left for Grand Detour the following day and returned to Moline on August 16, just in time to witness the most thrilling event to that point: "Started our big belt and our machinery moved for the first time!" On September 26, Tate gleefully recorded in his diary that the fledgling company had "finished the first ten plows!"[4]

Doing Business on the Frontier

The challenges of starting a new business on the edge of the frontier were monumental. There were no banks, paper money was scarce, and there were few transportation options, none of which were reliable year-round. Gould set up a system of double-entry bookkeeping, which "seemed to be a curiosity to the merchants and business men." Tate purchased heavy equipment in New York, and a great deal of capital was spent on initial shipments of iron, steel, and wood. The most difficult challenge was supplying basic necessities: provisions for employee room and board topped the list. Near the factory, the partners opened a company store and a boarding house, charging employees $1.75 per week, the equivalent of two or three days wages. Money, however, rarely changed hands. Instead of paying cash, the company arranged for credit with local merchants in the form of materials that were used to build their products. The company also boarded single men with local families and paid their room and board with vegetables, meat, and fuel from farmers, who received plows in exchange. The merchants were repaid when cash became available, which was rarely, because gold and silver were almost nonexistent in Illinois and the nearest banks were a day's journey away in Galena and, on the other side of the state boundary, in Burlington, Iowa. Much of the hard currency that was available was Mexican, French, and English coin.[5]

Deere, Tate & Gould had few customers at this point, and converting farmers from their current plow of choice to something new was as daunting as raising capital. With the intention of concentrating his own efforts on field sales, Deere hired one of Moline's two resident blacksmiths, Cyrus Kinsey, to work with Tate at the forge. Beginning in August, Kinsey made plows for the company out of his own shop, but within a few months he moved to the Deere, Tate & Gould shop along the river. In one conversation, he asked how Deere meant to succeed in the plow market, which was already saturated by a number of skilled manufacturers. Deere responded that "he did not care so much about a large profit, but by a smaller profit and by the number he would make, he would be enabled to drive out competition."[6]

Despite his apparent confidence, Deere was in fact concerned about competition. He struck a deal with his former partner Leonard Andrus, who kept the plow trade going from Grand Detour. Deere, Tate & Gould claimed the territories adjacent to the Illinois side of the Mississippi River and the largely unsettled territories to west, as well as Wisconsin to the north and Missouri to the south. Andrus's newly organized Grand Detour Plow Company could sell its products in eastern and central Illinois and in all the states to the east. On paper, the deal appeared a cordial split although, in the spirit of competition, each party immediately trespassed on the other's territory.[7]

Following the precedent Deere had instituted in Grand Detour as early as 1843, Deere, Tate & Gould advertised heavily in local papers. "We have just completed our new, large and much improved Manufactory at *Moline,* and by our skill and long experience in the business, are enabled to furnish Plows of all kinds in complete order, and warranted to scour [or polish] in any soil, and of easier draught than any other now in use." The secret: "We have on hand a large quantity of CAST-STEEL which was manufactured expressly for us, at the River Don Works, Sheffield, England, by Naylor & Co., and imported by us, which we are converting into Plows, at a trifling increase of cost over the common articles generally in use."[8]

Deere had first imported the high-quality, high-cost English steel several years earlier. Now, at great cost and effort, Deere, Tate & Gould continued to purchase it through a distributor in New York—the only plow company in the country doing so. American steel production was in its infancy, but Deere kept an eye on its progress. In 1846, he ordered the first slab of cast steel ever rolled in the United States from the Pittsburgh manufacturer Jones & Quigg.[9] In the meantime, imported steel raised unit costs, yet, according to the advertisements, it made the plows more efficient and extended their working life.

Deere's steel plow soon became noted for its self-scouring capabilities. Whereas most farmers still had to stop in the furrow to scrape away the soil clogging the plow, the Deere, Tate & Gould plow actually polished itself with use, reducing resistance and thereby reducing work stoppages. The company may have offered a plow with a moldboard of solid steel, although most of its models featured a steel-laminated, iron moldboard attached to a sharpened steel share. This combination moldboard presented advantages for manufacturers and customers alike. It was cheaper to produce and allowed the farmer to replace a worn share without simultaneously replacing the moldboard. At the same time, demand for replacement parts lead to a new product line for the company.

According to a visiting reporter in September 1849, Moline's future looked bright, and the Deere factory was one of the town's jewels. In half a day the reporter toured five factories and mills, including the Fergus & Buford foundry and machine shop, which supplied Deere, Tate &

Gould with waterpower. And the plow works certainly needed water-power to run its equipment: a drill, an upright saw, two grindstones, and two emery wheels. Nearby, an additional woodworking shop, thirty feet long and eight feet wide, rising to two and a half stories, was under construction. On an average day, twenty workmen kept the plow works' shops humming. Since October 1849, a period of less than a year, the company had already sold more than 2,300 plows and fully expected to make 4,000 the following year. As Deere, Tate & Gould's reputation grew, the future appeared limitless.[10]

Thanks to Gould, orders were being shipped up the Ohio and Missouri Rivers and sold on commission in every town along the Mississippi River as far south as St. Louis, Missouri, and as far north as St. Paul, Minnesota. Taking advantage of the slow winter months, he traveled through the arctic-like cold by horse and sleigh, making political and business contacts throughout Iowa, Wisconsin, Missouri, and Illinois. He first contacted state legislatures for a list of the able businessmen in particular towns and then called in person to talk business.[11]

By late 1851, Deere, Tate & Gould was manufacturing seventy plows a week and holding more than $30,000 in accounts receivable over a sales area that covered more than a thousand square miles. "Our business . . . is lucrative," Tate wrote to his brother, "our factory one of the largest if not quite the largest in the state. In short, our name is up, and I don't know why we should not do well."[12]

Tate was correct: business was booming. Nevertheless, although plows were selling at an unprecedented rate, the company remained in debt. Only one of their dealers bought plows with cash; the rest provided only IOUs for future payment. The paradox of thousands of dollars in notes payable but no cash on hand continued to torment the partners. "Many nights," Gould recorded, "I have gotten out of bed and walked the floor, knowing that I had some money to pay in a few days and did not know where I could get it. My brain felt as though I had a swarm of bees in it."[13]

Whereas Deere and his partners relied on barter and credit, the firm's creditors operated in cash, and one in particular was calling for payment on outstanding accounts. Lyon Shorb & Co., a steel supplier based in St. Louis, sent an agent to Moline in the winter of 1851 to review the company's books. Surprised by the income he saw on paper, he demanded immediate payment. Gould explained the difficulty of collecting on IOUs and finally negotiated an additional loan by offering mortgages and unpaid bank notes as collateral. But soon Gould discovered the man's true motive: Lyon Shorb & Co.'s agent held stock in the Grand Detour Plow Company and hoped to break up Deere, Tate & Gould and eliminate the competition.[14]

Only Deere, Tate, and Gould themselves knew that the business was even shakier than the finances showed. Deere's urge to manage every aspect of the business himself caused contention with every partner and employee who ever worked with him. His compulsive worries about money created further tensions that hung over the business from its earliest days. "Deere kicks up another rumpus about money—Money!!!" Tate wrote in his diary in March 1849. Deere was not a wealthy man, and his constant worry again threatened to sabotage a successful relationship with partners who shared his frustrations.[15]

Deere knew the difficulty of collecting outstanding debt from personal experience. He had tried to collect in Grand Detour on countless occasions and had also played the role of the debtor. At least one time he had run out on creditors, and so he could certainly sympathize with a delinquent farmer. While in Grand Detour, he had many times taken space in the *Rock River Register* requesting payment of debts. In one four-year period, from April 1841 through May 1844, Deere appeared as the plaintiff in almost two dozen cases trying to secure payment for past services. The early years in Moline were no different. Any funds he could not collect, he had to write off as losses.

By late 1851 tensions among Deere, Tate, and Gould had reached the point of no return. Deere offered Gould $2,600 for his shares, and Tate soon sold out as well. "I have seen enough of his one-sided moves," Tate wrote in his diary in early 1852, "so I put an end to it, and so left the control of it all to John Deere." According to Gould, though, the issue between Deere and Tate was not so much financial as it was ideological. The disagreement was the same one that had split Deere and Andrus: Deere looked to the company's future, and Tate did not. In this case, Deere continued to push for constant improvement in plow construction, while Tate insisted that they continue to sell their current products.

"Damn the odds," Tate argued. "They have got to take what we make." Deere disagreed. "They haven't got to take what we make and somebody else will beat us, and we will lose our trade." Deere knew that the company had to remain innovative to stay successful. "These little bickerings lasted quite a long time between them, both being honest and sincere in their convictions," Gould conceded years later. The partnership was finally dissolved, though the three men remained close

friends and business associates who collaborated on numerous endeavors in Moline in the decades to come. Gould considered starting a new
partnership either with Deere or with Tate the following year, but both
plans fell through. Gould began selling woodenwares on the island
across the slough. Meanwhile, Tate opened a wagon and blacksmith
shop on Lynde Street, only a few blocks away from the plow factory.[16]

Ironically, the very traits for which Deere was admired—perseverance,
ambition, and focus—were the traits that drove partners away. Four
years after making the move from Grand Detour, Deere was again in
business for himself. This time, he had a factory with equipment and
staff capable of producing 4,000 plows annually. Yet he had never succeeded at self-proprietorship. Entirely on his own, he now faced the
challenge of running a business that had taken three skilled profession-
als to manage.

Deere & Chapman

Deere's family—Demarius and their six children, Jeannette (eighteen),
Ellen (sixteen), Frances (fourteen), Charles (eleven), Emma (eight), and
Alice (four)—moved to Moline in November of 1848, four months after
the plow shop was built. They first lived with Robert Tate, his wife, and
their daughter in what Tate called the old Harris House. Charles remembered the "uncomfortable winter" and more specifically that his "share
of the discomfort was to occupy a bed made up on a trunk in the hall."
John Deere had lived there since June, but, just over a week after his
family's arrival, the Tates moved to a house owned by Charles Atkinson.
The living conditions were cramped even after the Tates left, and the
Deere family suffered from cabin fever from December through April.
The Illinois winters were most usually "Cold, cold, cold," Tate observed
wryly, and when spring finally arrived, it brought "[r]ain, rain, rain"
with weather that remained "cold and unsettled." At last, in August
1849, they could finally afford to move into a two-story brick home on
the corner of Main and Atkinson streets, four blocks away from the plow
factory.[17]

In April 1851, Jeannette married a local lawyer and banker named
James Chapman. Her father may have prompted the match since, as fellow businessmen, he and Chapman frequented the same social gatherings. Also, like his new father-in-law, Chapman was an active member of
the Whig Party. After the wedding, the couple headed to St. Louis in the
steamer *Highland Mary* for a short honeymoon. As a wedding gift, John

and Demarius bought the newlyweds carpet and furniture, including a tick and straw bed, a washstand, a rocking chair, and lanterns.[18]

In December, nineteen-year-old Ellen married Christopher Columbus Webber of Rock Island. Webber was a serious-looking, self-made businessman who had lived in nearby Geneseo, where he and his brother operated a general store for a time. In 1850 he organized the Union Foundry in Rock Island, which furnished castings for Deere.[19]

The week of the wedding wreaked havoc on the plow works. According to Tate's diary, it began to "snow and freeze hard" on Saturday, December 13. By the next day, the snow was two inches deep, and the plow factory was without waterpower. On Monday only one person came to work, and the temperature reached twenty degrees below zero. Young and amorous, Ellen Deere and C. C. Webber braved the temperatures and married on Wednesday the seventeenth. Ellen was soon pregnant with John and Demarius's first grandchild, Ada Louise, born in August 1852.[20]

Chapman and Webber would both play important roles in Deere's business over the coming years, as their father-in-law struggled with the intricacies of keeping his business afloat. In many ways, they filled the void left by Albert's death, in 1848. In late 1854, Deere and Chapman gave notice in the local paper that they "have this day entered into Partnership under the name, style, and firm of Deere & Chapman, for the purpose of Manufacturing Plows and other Agricultural Implements." Chapman resigned his position as Moline's police magistrate and announced that he would close out all of his pending legal business and his justice docket.[21]

In the factory, eight forges now operated continuously, with the muted ringing of workers' hammers shaping moldboards and shares on anvils scattered across the floor "to form the beautiful and accurately proportioned plows, so popular in the West." Beyond the factory, the business had advanced beyond the "old-fashioned mode"—to borrow Tate's turn of phrase—as Deere made use of new transportation opportunities. The company was selling plows in Illinois, Wisconsin, Iowa, Missouri, and the Minnesota territory and promising that the steel plow would "be a most valuable auxiliary in the settlement and civilization of Nebraska and Kansas." Local newspapers reaffirmed what Deere already knew: his company's ultimate success depended upon his ability to market the plow in the new territories opening further west. "Without being a prophet," Moline's recently established paper, the *Workman* asserted, "we may safely predict that wherever the hardy pioneer shall bring the wilderness and prairies of the west under cultivation, there will the beautiful and substantial products" for which "the Moline Plow Factory be known and appreciated."[22]

Deere & Chapman continued to grow steadily. The factory produced more than 8,000 plows in 1855, and more than 10,000 in 1857. On average, Deere employed fifty-six men who each earned between fifty-eight cents and $1.50 per day. A highly paid blacksmith earned $240 per year. Rising productivity and new extensions to the plow works testified to the company's prosperity, but ever-present competition and a fragile credit system demanded a steadfast and conservative approach to business. The Mercantile Agency, a credit agency that had given Deere, Tate, & Gould a glowing recommendation in 1850, was concerned about the new company's outstanding debts. "J. Deer [sic] goes on," its agent reported, "G[oo]d but hard up."[23]

City of Mills

Meanwhile, Moline was also growing, and its growth brought opportunities and problems that the town and the plow company were destined to face together. As western expansion continued, it was hoped that the flow of farmers into Minnesota, Kansas, and Nebraska would help to stabilize economic conditions in the city. The health and security of Deere's business depended upon it, as did the health and security of Moline.

"This is one of the busiest towns on the Mississippi," a visiting reporter told his readers, boasting of its "honest industry" and constant "din of water wheels, steam works, saws, planes and hammers." Equally important, the visitor found, "No loafing, no guzzling, no speculating, no gambling, nothing going on but the operations of honest industry." The Puritanical vision of former New Englanders had a firm grip on the town, and, despite the occasional crime, rascal elements were hard pressed to disrupt the pervasive moral temperament. Both socially and professionally, Moline's leading men were not the spoiled sons of wealthy families but the beneficiaries of their own efforts, which they hoped would soon pay large dividends. They built the town on their own terms, by their own sweat and at their own risk, and expected to run it as they saw fit. But how long those convictions would endure in the midst of Moline's industrialization was yet to be seen.[24]

Moline was also embracing the new technology that Grand Detour had stubbornly rejected. On February 22, 1854, the long-awaited railroad finally reached the neighboring city of Rock Island. Tate recorded the moment in his diary with mixed emotions: "The Cars. The Rail Road Car! The train reaches Rock Island. . . . One thousand passengers, poor accommodations. Many places illuminated. The strangers cram into every house to pass the night. Such a hubbub, yet they are all merry." Tate understood the significance of the event. Passengers could now ride from Rock Island to Chicago in six hours, to Toledo in fourteen hours, and to New York in forty-two hours. In the time it had taken to get to Chicago the previous week, travelers could now go to New York City.

More important, in Deere's view, the railroad could ship freight year round. The Mississippi River, in contrast, was navigable only four or five months of the year. From August through December, it was too low for barges; from December through April, it was frozen. Two years after reaching Rock Island, the railroad put a bridge across the Mississippi River, linking Rock Island with Davenport and offering Deere the advantage of transporting larger numbers of plows to the western settlements burgeoning along the railroad lines. At the same time, the newly built Illinois and Mississippi Telegraph Co., which installed telegraph lines beside the tracks connecting Chicago, Rock Island, Moline, and St. Louis, offered instant communication. With the foresight that first brought him to Moline, Deere envisioned fresh opportunities, and his innovative mind discovered new methods of putting both his name and his product into the hands of more people, in shorter time and at less cost. At last the world seemed to be moving in his favor.[25]

As he built his business reputation and established a loyal clientele, Deere became more involved in Moline's development. In contrast to rapacious Eastern entrepreneurs, Deere understood that the success of his business depended upon the prosperity of its hometown, and he put great effort into turning Moline into a vibrant place to live and do business. He understood the challenges of building a business on the frontier, and he applied the lessons he had learned to the building of his town. Just as, time and again, he had saved his business with quick thinking, fearlessness, and resourcefulness, he saved the new railroad bridge over the Mississippi River. One day in 1859, Deere and "a Mr. Thompson from Quincy . . . were passing over the bridge, coming to Rock Island" when they "discovered the bridge to be on fire." Amid swirling winds and spreading flames they gave the alarm, "and had it not been for two barrels of water standing on the platform, nothing would now be left of the great Rock Island bridge save a mass of smouldering [sic] ruins." Apparently, sparks from the engine of a passing train started the blaze. The *Daily Islander & Argus,* however, was not very grateful for

Deere's heroism. The paper declared the bridge a "serious obstruction to the navigation of the river and a detriment to the trails of this entire region." The only citizens who profited were the railroad's shareholders, it contended.

As Deere surely knew from the loss of two blacksmith shops, fire was a constant threat. In 1855, he led the effort to create a fire department. Like many such matters of public safety, the fire company was a community project: each able-bodied man was required to work three days per year on behalf of the village. Both James Chapman and Charles Deere served executive terms with the fire department during its first few years. On one occasion, in fact, Charles badly injured his leg while climbing a ladder.[26]

Public safety was always a great concern in Moline, with its New England settlers taking as much responsibility for the moral welfare of the town as they did for the virtue of their own families. Chief Blackhawk and the Indian tribes that once inhabited the region had been long displaced, but the dangers of frontier life—as well as theft, vagrancy, fraud, and other vices—were growing, despite community efforts. In July 1854, for example, the railroad delivered a group of sick and destitute Swedes to Moline. Immediately, the town held a meeting, and "hovels of pine lumber" were constructed to house the immigrants temporarily. A week later the townsfolk were building coffins and a makeshift hospital. By early August, however, many of the immigrants had moved on to Rock Island or other locales and left the shantytown deserted.

Deere and his neighbors also organized the Moline Property Protection Society to supplement the police force. River towns were especially good targets for con men, thieves, and the like, because the Mississippi and now the railroad offered would-be criminals easy escape routes. A local newspaper applauded the citizens' efforts and warned "horse thieves in particular and the light fingered gentry in general, that a warm reception awaits them."

Crime was a reality. In 1855, two or three robbers attacked the farmer Samuel Bell. His wife rang the bell in alarm, and when the neighbors arrived they found her sitting on the farmhouse stairs in shock. Shortly afterward, eighteen-year-old Charles Deere discovered her "in shallow water of the river pretending to drown herself" and went for help.[27]

Two months later, robbers hit the Deere home. "Several articles [were] taken, a silver watch belonging to Charley worth $100 and several dollars in change and quite a lot of choice cake," Tate learned from Alice Deere. "The father's [John Deere's] pants were overhauled, rifled and thrown back to his bedside again." There were also rumors that counterfeit money was found in his pockets. And quite possibly it was, because he often accepted foreign currency and other unfamiliar types of money for payment. The risk of being duped by a counterfeiter was yet another pitfall in the collection of debt.[28]

Deere's business had experienced sweeping changes in just a few years. By the mid-1850s, the business had grown from the Deere, Tate, & Gould partnership, turning out 1,000 plows a year, into the family-owned enterprise of Deere & Chapman with an annual production capacity of 10,000 plows. Deere's reputation as a plow maker, the innovator behind the company that sold quality products at an affordable price, was spreading well beyond Illinois and Iowa, into the opening western territories. Production and employment were at an all time high, the product line was expanding, and customer loyalty was growing. But by no means was Deere's business a stable one. Oncoming economic depressions, shifting business cycles and a changing family dynamic would offer new challenges. But for now, as the *Rock Islander* confirmed in January 1855, everyone was proud to be associated with "JOHN DEERE, THE PLOW KING."[29]

MOLINE, ILL.

---- T H R E E ----

C. H. Deere's "Celebrated Moline Plows"

The 1850s were a period of explosive growth in American agriculture. Advances in implement design, the reduction of prices as a result of fierce competition among manufacturers, and the growth of the railroad spurred the settlement of the West. Companies such as John Deere's were making large fortunes as farmers in Eastern and Western states alike cleared and cultivated more land. Between 1850 and 1860, the number of farms in the United States shot from one and a half to two million. In Illinois alone, the number doubled, reaching 143,000. By 1860, only Ohio, New York, and Pennsylvania had more farms than Illinois.

At the same time, 9,000 miles of railroad track was laid in Ohio, Indiana, Illinois, Michigan, and Wisconsin, providing cheap transportation and, consequently, larger profits for manufacturers. The cash value of crops in those five states rose past $1 billion in 1860, an increase of 40 percent from ten years earlier. Over the course of three decades of railroad construction, from the 1820s through the 1850s, the price of corn had increased by 50 percent and the price of hogs by 100 percent. There was money to be made at every stop, for the implement manufacturer and the farmer as well as the salesman and the railroad stockholder.[1]

In 1860 at least 2,100 plow makers were operating in the United States. During the agricultural boom of the 1850s, the value of implements and machinery on American farms increased 63 percent (more than $94 million), and the cash value of farms increased by more than 100 percent. Farmers were tilling more land, enjoying greater yields, and buying the latest labor-saving machinery. John Deere's company was fast climbing into an elite position among plow makers, and Moline was successfully stealing the title "Plow Capital of Illinois" from its rivals Springfield and Peoria. Deere's new status was not completely secure, however, and another national crisis exposed any doubts he had. Fortunately, his son Charles would soon join the family business and inaugurate a new managerial approach that would stabilize the company for the first time.[2]

As the Panic of 1857, another period of economic depression, engulfed the country, the company was strong, yet creditors' demands for cash and customers' inability to pay IOUs continued to squeeze the company's finances. In 1856, John Deere & Company (as it was called at this time) made a total of 13,400 plows. For all of the acclaim Deere would receive as the inventor of the steel plow, he had made cast-iron plows for a decade until he could at last produce steel plows in quantity. Now his factory offered seven different models, including a large breaker plow and a double shovel plow, each engineered for a particular type of soil. A visiting reporter in 1856 recommended that "two or three of his plows—the large breaker and the double shovel especially—would be a very valuable addition to the AGRICULTURAL MUSEUM of the New York State Ag. Society." To complement the plows, Deere made arrangement with other inventors to market a variety of grain drills, beginning in 1851 with the Seymour drill. Grain drills similar to the Seymour combined the process of digging and planting in one step with a single-wheeled mechanism. The drill reduced the need for manpower while it increased speed and efficiency; all the farmer had to do was walk behind and push.[3]

The company's fleet of traveling salesmen continued to scour the countryside, making personal contact with farmers and demonstrating and selling plows, cultivators, and drills. Deere himself annually attended the dozens of county and state fairs that offered implement makers their greatest opportunity for publicity. A good demonstration not only won awards but also, more important, garnered mention in local newspapers and endorsements that could be reprinted in future advertising campaigns. Fairs also provided Deere with the chance to investigate the competition.

In 1853, Deere won two dollars for the best center-draft plow at the First Annual Fair of the Rock Island County Society for the Promotion of Agriculture and the Mechanic Arts. A month later, his display at the Henry County fair was so impressive that one newspaper ventured, "At very few fairs in Yankeedom will a more beautiful, or better article be exhibited." In 1855, Deere took his plows to the Illinois State Agricultural

Society's third annual fair and won its highest honor, an award in the "plow for Old Ground Prairie" category. Locally, John Deere had attained celebrity status. "Mr. Deere not only deserves a premium for it from the State Fair," a Rock Island reporter exclaimed, "but some kind of suitable memorial from his fellow citizens of this vicinity. He is the best, the largest, the most liberal, and studiously honest manufacturer of plows in the whole North-west."[4]

At the 1858 Illinois State Fair, in Centralia, Deere witnessed the trial of Joseph Fawkes's Lancaster, a thirty-horsepower steam plow that, according to reporters "conquered the face of nature" and made Fawkes "immortal." Deere spotted a great opportunity. That year the Illinois Central Railroad had offered a $3,000 premium to the first person to introduce a reliable steam plow, so, in addition to potential future applications of the machine, Deere had a short-term incentive as well. "It will be a great day when Illinois can show a steam engine taking along a breaking plow, turning over a furrow ten or twelve feet in width as it goes. I think we shall be able to see it before June passes away," Deere predicted, adding that his best mechanic was on the job."[5]

Soon realizing he had misjudged the challenge and unwilling to invest the capital necessary for research and development, Deere decided to contact Fawkes. At the state fair the following year and again a few weeks later at the U.S. Agricultural Society contest in Chicago, a Fawkes steam engine pulled an eight-bottom Deere plow. The Fawkes/John Deere team won the verbose category of "machine which shall supersede the plow, as now used, and accomplished the most through disintegration of the soil, with the greatest economy of labor, power, time and money."[6]

For Deere the heavy, unwieldy design of the steam engine, as well as the demands of keeping it running, proved too great to make it a commercial success. Through the trials, though, he had not committed himself or his company. Instead, he had ridden on the Lancaster's early success without suffering from its ultimate failure. He would continue to use this practical advertising tool whenever the opportunity presented itself.

In the office, Deere continued to rely heavily on his sons-in-law, James Chapman and C. C. Webber, both of whom would participate actively in the business through the early 1860s. With well-learned lessons from previous financial panics, the three men worked hard to transfer and hide assets from creditors while, simultaneously, they strove to raise additional capital for expansion. Chapman's banking experience proved invaluable, as did Webber's talent for short-term investment.

In 1856 Deere borrowed $700 from his nephew, George Vinton, who soon came to work for the family business as a salesman. On July 1, 1857, Deere promoted three bookkeepers, Luke Hemenway, David H. Bugbee, and his own son, twenty-year-old Charles, to the status of partners. On paper, each paid an equal part of the capital stock and agreed to share equally in the profits or losses, although in reality Deere held claim to the whole business. In fact, this arrangement served as an escape hatch, allowing Deere to divest some of his personal liability in case of a crisis. It also represented the first in a series of steps to bring Charles more fully into the business.[7]

Deere deeded a quarter of the land on which the plow factory stood and two adjacent lots to his son, who in turn sold the property to the company. Moving cautiously, Chapman transferred property and monies out of business accounts and into the personal accounts of John and Charles Deere. Father and son also looked for refinancing options, which they found with John Gould, who had gone into the banking business since the breakup of his partnership with Deere and Tate. Gould was surprised that Deere sent his son, then only twenty-one years old, to negotiate the terms. He was even more surprised that the young man was requesting a loan: Deere's company was worth ten or twenty times more than Gould, Dimock & Co.[8]

The company kept this shuffling of assets behind closed doors, and, despite the factory's continued reliance for waterpower upon the unreliable river, production increased steadily. The annual statistics were staggering. Sixty-five workers manned the factory, while the woodshop turned 200,000 feet of oak plank into plow beams and handles, and the forges devoured fifty tons of cast steel, forty tons of German steel, one ton of Pittsburgh steel, seventy-five tons of castings, two hundred tons of wrought iron, and eight tons of malleable castings. The smiths' furnaces burned five hundred tons of Illinois bituminous coal, seventy-five tons of Lehigh coal, and one hundred tons of coke.[9]

The spectacular growth of Deere's company was unmatched in the industry. Nonetheless, competition was on the rise. In 1856 the Grand Detour Plow Company burned to the ground, and Andrus quickly rebuilt it. That same year a new competitor appeared in nearby Rock Island, when a transplanted Kentuckian named Charles Buford and his son opened a plow shop and hired Robert Tate to run it. Refusing to compete directly with Deere, at least in Illinois and the surrounding states, Tate decided instead to build plows almost exclusively for the expanding markets in the West.

Charles Deere Takes Control

In 1857 and 1858, John Deere, Charles Deere, Chapman, and Webber undertook great efforts to reorganize the company. Late in 1858, the reasons for the reorganization became clear: Deere was turning the family business over to his son. Charley, as his friends called him, had been cultivated for this moment since he was a child. Only an infant when his father built his first plow in Grand Detour, he had grown up with the business.

Charles was given two advantages his father never had—fatherly advice and the best formal education money could buy. He led a more or less typical childhood, with "a boys usual troubles with his father," including "tight arguments sometimes." Charles was educated in a number of private Moline schools, for a time at the residence of Mrs. Cass, and then at a school, taught by an Englishwoman named Mrs. Hasbrook, in Moline's old engine house. Charles was an energetic and intelligent child who found little value in education as an adolescent. His father, however, understood its importance, and the difference of opinion often resulted in disciplinary issues at school and at home. As an alternative to applying the hickory stick, when Charles could not find "mother's protecting wing," his father would send him to the shop to work off his punishment at a drill press or some other laborious task. "This penalty usually gave me an excellent lesson in application," Charles later wrote with disdain, "though otherwise it was not all to my taste." When he was not in school, he accompanied his father on business trips, following the plow through the freshly cut furrow during demonstrations. Much to his displeasure, "there was always an unpleasant side of those trips" as his father quizzed him on "the multiplication table, spelling and the like."

After grammar school, Charles attended Iowa College, just across the river in Davenport and then Knox College, a nondenominational college established by abolitionists, located about forty-five miles south of Moline in Galesburg, Illinois. Charles had matured into a more serious student over the course of his studies. In 1852, he began attending Bell's Commercial College in Chicago, the equivalent of a postgraduate business college with "superior advantages and facilities." Indeed it had those amenities, including a library with more than 1,000 volumes. There he studied such essential subjects as "Commercial Law" and the "art of detecting counterfeit Bank Notes."[10]

In 1851 Charles received his first practical business lesson at his father's side. After the agent from Lyon, Shorb & Co. visited John Gould that winter to collect on overdue accounts, Deere decided to take his son with him on a trip to St. Louis. It was Charles's first excursion on a steamboat, though the wonders of the fire-belching giant are not what most impressed him. Instead, the memory of the "going over" his father received from his creditors was one that would stay with him his entire life.

After graduating in late 1853 or early 1854, the sixteen-year-old began working for his father's head bookkeeper Reuben Wells. Upon his return to Moline, Charles temporarily fell into old habits with former schoolmates, "sometimes at the great expense of my business." Sometimes he brought those habits into the workplace as well. On one occasion, when a customer came to the factory to buy several breaking plows, Charles took him into the shop and told him to wait. After standing alone for some time, the customer finally found his way to the office where he discovered that the young prankster was sneaking out after trying to lock him in the shop for the night. Soon, though, the pressures of the business and, more directly, the heavy responsibilities placed on his young shoulders by a father with the highest expectations would tame Charley.[11]

By the mid 1850s, the United States was reaching the end of its "Golden Age," the period of prosperity brought about by marked advances in business and investment. Moline was growing from the tireless industry and puritanical traditions of a single generation—men who fled failure, conquered the prairie, harnessed the awesome power of the Mississippi River, and achieved wealth beyond their most extravagant dreams. With a proliferating network of railroad tracks, a steady flow of immigrants into the labor force, and the increased availability of raw materials such as iron ore, timber, and oil, the United States was being transformed from an agricultural to an industrial society. Yet, for the decades to come, farming would remain the pillar of the American economy.

Closer to home, between 1850 and 1860 the population of Illinois more than doubled. Proportionately, the region soon to become known as the Midwest began to take the national lead in the production of agricultural equipment, with John Deere's company taking its place among the leading manufacturers in the country. Business was never better—until 1857, that is, when the bottom dropped out of the American economy and the ensuing panic demonstrated that such unprecedented growth had consequences.

Reporters who toured the plow works gave glowing reports of the company's position from a manufacturing perspective, but much of the $140,000 in gross sales from the previous year remained uncollected. Prospects for collecting outstanding debt disappeared as a result of the Panic of 1857. Whenever the company had a hundred dollars cash in hand, John Deere would confer with his fellow managers to decide how best to use the money. Heightened political tensions blighted hopes for a speedy economic recovery, and anticipation of a sectional conflict—possibly even war—prompted further shuffling of assets.

In 1858, Deere was paying heavy interest on his own debts and closing out many bad accounts in an effort to reduce assets and focus on what collectible debt he possessed. The Mercantile Agency, an Eastern credit bureau, predicted that he would be debt-free within six months. In the meantime, Deere had amassed small personal fortune, estimated at $80,000 to $100,000, although most of it existed only on paper. The 1860 census, more realistically, valued his estate and personal worth at $22,000. No one would guess that Deere was sitting on a small fortune, largely because he never considered it secure from creditors, the next national financial crisis, or a poor business decision on his part.[12]

Another reorganization in March 1858 temporarily returned full control of the company to John Deere, but only so that he could institute yet another new business arrangement, necessitated by a near disaster. He had imported a large shipment of steel from England, but, when the plows were made, the steel proved too soft to scour. With wagonloads of returned plows, he could not pay for the steel. His capital depleted, he faced a total loss. At the suggestion of Webber, Deere sold out to his son, who bought the company in October 1858 for $15,000. Although Charles gave his father promissory notes payable over the next eleven years, he was nonetheless taking a huge risk as a twenty-one-year-old still cutting his teeth in the family business. Charles now assumed responsibility for the financial success—or failure—of his father's company.[13]

A few months later, after losing a huge investment in a brother's venture, Webber sold his share of the plow business. No longer a partner, he continued to work for the Deeres as a salaried executive well into the 1860s. The Mercantile Agency observed that Webber's decision to step down was probably a good thing for the company. Although had considerable property, Webber's reputation for business was "decidedly bad," because he was "not prompt to pay—but prompt to collect." If Deere considered Webber's tactics wise, in light of the economic climate, the Mercantile Agency proposed that Webber had "worked himself into the Plow Factory for the purpose of mkg money, even at the sacrifice not only of Deer's [sic] reputation but of Deer [sic] himself." At the same time, the agency approved of Charles's increasing involvement in the management of the company, despite his relative inexperience.[14]

In early 1860, the company's assets were worth a mere thirty-five to forty-five cents on the dollar, and the company was feeling the worst of the national depression. But by the end of the year, with the country on the brink of war, Charles had bailed the company out of much of its debt. Quickly recognizing him as a "good & reliable," honest, and industrious man, creditors were pleased to do business with him. Since his early days as an assistant bookkeeper, he had learned every aspect of the business—from making plows, to purchasing materials, to marketing, to pressing debtors for payment. Never the type to run a company from behind his desk, he had spent the latter part of 1859 visiting customers and dealers in the field.

The world was changing rapidly. The Pony Express had just completed its inaugural delivery of mail, 1,966 miles from St. Louis to Sacramento, in a mere eleven days. The railroad, which had arrived in Moline only six years earlier, had already shrunken the country, and more transportation and communication wonders lay ahead. Charles was determined to put these wonders to work for the company. The established sales territories agreed to by his father and Andrus had long since been abandoned, and now he traveled throughout Illinois and neighboring states, making personal contact with farmers, implement dealers, and hardware stores.

The job of the salesman was not a romantic one; Charles was often on the road for months at a time. Plows were shipped via the Mississippi River to Galena, Dubuque, and Keokuk to the north and to Burlington, Muscatine, and other towns further south. Salesmen picked up a wagonload of a few dozen plows and began scouring the countryside, moving from farm to farm and making individual sales. They also tried to convince hardware stores and implement dealers along the route to stock a supply of plows on commission. Advertising and word of mouth helped sales, but the best way to sell a plow was to demonstrate its merits to the customer, as Charles quickly learned. Within a few years after joining the company in 1853, he was promoted to head salesman, and he often set out alone on expeditions into new territories to introduce the latest line of plows. "I was not slow in suffering the usual agony of the salesman," he wrote, "that of making bad debts—and had to cut my eye teeth."[15]

From late 1859 into the early 1860s, Charles kept a travel and account journal with pages of notes on individual sales and more general comments on the business and its future scribbled in pencil. His travels in November 1859, for example, began with a trip to the steel supplier Lyon, Shorb & Co. in St. Louis. Over the next two weeks, he made his way to fifteen different towns in western and central Illinois, some of which he visited multiple times before returning to Moline. From St. Louis he traveled up the Mississippi River 130 miles to Quincy, then journeyed by wagon to Augusta, Plymouth, Macomb, and back to Augusta. In addition to reconciling accounts and taking new orders, Deere compiled a list of companies offering complementary products. Typically, his expenses on the road ran to two to three dollars per day for food and lodging.

During trips through western Illinois, he reminded himself to fill orders upon his return: "Be sure to do it thoroughly," he wrote in one of the earliest notations. On another occasion, he reminded himself to keep his options open and not bow to one-sided negotiations. "If you cannot make satisfactory arrangements with them look out for other parties who want the plows," he wrote of one overly demanding dealer. Other accounts were a complete loss. G. K. Hall was "not of much account," and agents Chandler & Co. reported that he was *"[t]ruly up the crick."*[16]

Deere read avidly to pass the time on the road, and he made notes to purchase books he considered required reading upon his return: *Analysis of English Words; Self Help* by Samuel Smiles, a collection of biographies extolling the virtues of the self-made man; *Gold Foil* by Timothy Titcomb; *Homes in the New World* by Frederika Bremer; and *The Habits of Good Society*. The long days also offered time for reflection and occasional moments of simple inspiration. In February 1860 Charles dedicated an entire page of his journal to a thought years in the making: "I will never from this seventh day of February, eighteen hundred sixty A.D. put my name to a paper that I do not expect to pay—so help me God." Simple and straightforward, this resolution was the result of years of experience. As the fear of debt had driven his father, this resolution would now drive Charles.[17]

As a reward for his son's hard work, Deere reorganized the company yet again on November 5, 1860, to give Charles full leadership of the enterprise, which he renamed the Moline Plow Manufactory. "The Shop is now in full operation," a company circular announced optimistically, "and upon the opening of Spring will have the largest and best finished lot of Plows ever turned out here." The agreement was a pivotal experiment: for the first time in almost two decades, John

Deere's name was not attached to the company. Instead, Charles and the budding town of Moline came to the fore.[18]

During these formative years, Charles learned as much what *not* to do by watching his father as he learned what *to* do. But his father's experience could not prepare him for what lay ahead. The greatest crisis in American history, far more disastrous than any of the financial storms the company had thus weathered, was fast approaching. The ups and downs of past few years notwithstanding, Deere's business had reached its most prosperous period ever, and under the leadership of Charles it stood to dominate the plow trade for decades to come. Yet the future held unpredictable challenges, personal tragedies, and moral struggles that the nation seemed unprepared to face.

New and Improved

The Moline Plow Manufactory General Catalogue for 1862 tempted the farmer with several varieties of plows, not only the cast-steel clipper plow in a number of sizes but also corn plows, deep tillage plows, subsoil plows, Michigan double sod breakers, and plows custom made to the buyer's specifications. Product descriptions included information on weight, cut depth, and price per unit, as well as prices for spare parts. "Plows are manufactured from the best of English and American Cast Steel," the company boasted. Charles Deere still imported some steel, although he could now rely on Pittsburgh suppliers. Unfortunately, so could his competitors.[19]

To preserve his plow's reputation as the best in America, John Deere worked continually to improve manufacturing processes and implement designs. Competitors (and some former partners) swore that he lacked the knowledge and ability to make a decent plow himself. His new patents proved otherwise. In January 1864, almost thirty years after crafting his first plow, he secured the company's first patent for a "new and useful Improvement in Molds for Casting Steel Plows and other Articles." Whereas the standard process left air spaces in the castings of "moldboards, landsides and other articles in steel," Deere's patented method produced perfect steel castings more easily and at no greater cost than the traditional method for casting iron in sand molds. Following Deere's process, a smith first formed a mold with dry sand, then coated its inner surface with plumbago and an adhesive made of fired clay into which the melted steel was poured, and finally baked it to remove all moisture and form a perfect casting.

Later patents followed. Deere further improved upon his process and amended his original patent in April 1864. Over the next three years, he filed two more claims, thus putting his signature on a state-of-the-art process for making steel plows. Ironically, Deere never claimed to have invented the steel plow or even to have been the first to advance it. His contribution to the company and to its customers, as he understood it, was constant improvement, quality craftsmanship, and superior sales efforts.[20]

Along with the plows, the catalog for 1862 included cultivators, harrows, a corn sheller, and other new products promising a bright future for both the company and the farmer.[21] One key new addition to the Deere product line was the company's first riding implement, the Hawkeye riding cultivator. Webber had made arrangements with the inventor W. Furnas for the company to sell the Hawkeye. Unlike the Fawkes steam engine, riding equipment had a practical, realistic future in American farming. The Hawkeye was one of many early riding cultivators developed in this period. The return of handicapped soldiers from the battlefields of Gettysburg, Antietam, and Vicksburg partially accounted for the greater need for mechanical farming after the Civil War.[22] Charles Deere had accurately predicted market demand: in 1864 the company sold almost 500 machines.[23]

The catalog also served as the company's primary advertising vehicle. The 1862 edition, for example, offered over a dozen pages of testimonials and lists of awards won at fairs across the country. The company also placed advertisements in local newspapers for "C. H. Deere's Celebrated Moline Plows." In years past, the plow had been known as the "Grand de Tour Plow" and the "John Deere plow." The company had also recently used the name "Moline Plow." Adopting a town's name for a plow was common practice: Elgin Plows, Rock Island Plows, Lockport Plows, and Moline Plows were sold across Illinois.

Under Charles, business was running more smoothly and with more success than it ever had. His name now graced all advertising literature. It seemed as though John had been pushed into early retirement, but he could still be found daily in the shops and remained active within the community. Whereas his father had always struggled with partners who lacked his vision and endless financial difficulties, Charles brought a comfortable level of security to the business by surrounding himself with intelligent, forward-thinking men and—most important—family. No wonder he was optimistic, despite flooding in 1862 that forced the company to rebuild its workshops. He truly expected a boom after the war when the Southern market opened again.

Thanks in part to the implementation of a cash-only system, Charles had managed to alleviate burdensome financial worries. Hard currency remained scarce as the Civil War dragged on, yet manufacturers and importers of steel and iron refused to extend credit to their customers. Consequently, Charles was also forced to demand cash from his customers. As an incentive to buyers, he offered a 25 percent discount on catalog prices for full payment at the time of sale.[24] The tactics worked, making the company's finances more stable than ever. A credit report from R. G. Dun & Company (formerly the Mercantile Agency) in January 1863 observed that Charles had accrued good credit and a large amount of property.[25]

It was true, as the credit agency observed, that the property had been transferred to Charles by his father. Asset shuffling from the previous decade had left John Deere officially a nonentity; so father and son decided to reorganize the company once again. On July 1, 1864, John and Charles each contributed $70,000 in stock, buildings, machinery, and outstanding debt to create a new partnership under the name of Deere & Co.[26] The day-to-day life of the company changed little, but John could better reap the financial benefits of his lifelong investments. To complement the Moline farm secured a few years before by George Vinton in a barter agreement for an unpaid debt, the elder Deere bought a second farm outside the eastern edge of Moline, high atop the bluffs overlooking the Mississippi River. He called it Alderney Hill, after a popular breed of cattle. It was one of several farms Deere would eventually own in and outside of Moline.[27]

For Deere & Co., the early 1860s brought a change in leadership and a period of steady, if minor, growth. For John Deere and the citizens of Moline, those same years brought the hardships and personal tragedies of the Civil War. For the Deere family, those tragedies were interrupted by Charles's marriage and an optimistic outlook for the future. Charles had developed into the savvy businessman his father had been waiting for him to become. Together, they were now prepared to solidify their grip on the American plow trade.

MOLINE, ILL.

F O U R

Raging Abolitionist

With his son taking charge of the plow company, John Deere turned more attention to local politics, which reflected on a small scale the problems facing the entire nation. With the expansion of business, the emergence of powerful political newspapers, and the development of a new Western character on the frontier, the American economy and society were undergoing profound changes. Meanwhile, the antagonism between the industrial North and the agrarian South continued to escalate. No less horrific for its seeming inevitability, the Civil War threatened the very soul of the young nation.

Moline was spared neither the carnage nor the despair of the Civil War, and not even the town's most prosperous and influential men were sheltered from its impact. As communities across the country readied for a war that would become more intense than anyone predicted, politics in Moline followed the nationwide debate over states' rights and slavery. Bitter political rivalries became as destructive to the town as the floodwaters of the Mississippi River. Political parties rose and fell in step with the national dialogue, and families and friends were torn apart by moral and ideological transgressions in the Tri-Cities.

Like another rising Illinois politician, Abraham Lincoln, John Deere and James Chapman were both Whigs, members of the party formed in 1836 in reaction to the policies of President Andrew Jackson. Whigs collectively urged a program of national tariff protection, a continuation of the national bank, and a policy of conservative public land sales. Theirs was a platform that held strong appeal for American merchants and manufacturers yet also protected agricultural prices and other concerns of the agrarian population. Those concerns lay close to the heart of John Deere, who in 1854 served as chairman of the Whig county convention. That same year, he added his name to a list of the citizens of Rock Island County who opposed slavery and regarded party distinctions as secondary to their moral cause.[1]

Delusions of disappearing party lines were, however, short-lived. Whigs and Know-Nothings, a new nativist party opposed to immigration and foreigners in general, slowly dissolved while the Democratic Party became more militant in its defense of slavery. Most of Moline's citizens, primarily settlers from New England, were strongly against slavery, in a sharp contrast to their neighbors in Rock Island, most of whom were the descendants of Southern landowners and planters. When the Republican Party rose from the ashes of the Whig and the Know-Nothing parties and began to organize in Rock Island County in late 1854, Deere was not an immediate convert, though in due time he transferred his loyalties as new partisan lines were drawn solely around slavery. The final catalyst for Deere was the heated controversy over the Kansas and Nebraska territories, the roots of which were already four decades old. When the citizens of Missouri applied for statehood in 1818, the long-standing balance between free states and slave states was threatened by a congressional bill to ratify Missouri's inclusion in the Union, complete with an amendment prohibiting the entry of slaves into the state and providing for the gradual emancipation of those already living there. The bill was defeated, but the debate raged on. When Maine applied for statehood the following year, Henry Clay, a Whig and the Speaker of the House, warned that, unless Northern congressmen changed their position toward Missouri, their Southern counterparts would reject Maine's petition. In the spirit of compromise, the congressmen agreed to a provision forever prohibiting slavery in any of the territories encompassed by the Louisiana Purchase north of the Mason-Dixon Line. Missouri and Maine entered the union together in February 1820, thus ensuring that free states and slave states would have equal representation in the Senate. This arrangement set the precedent for adding new states to the nation until the passage of the Kansas-Nebraska Act on May 30, 1854. The new act, sponsored by Senator Stephen A. Douglas, allowed people in the territories of Kansas and Nebraska to decide for themselves whether to allow slavery within their state borders. Although the silver-tongued Democrat from Illinois declared the triumph of "popular sovereignty," the amendment to the Kansas-Nebraska Act specifically repealing the Missouri Compromise sparked a chain of events that led to the dissolution of the Whig Party and ultimately to the Civil War.[2]

In February 1856, Deere's name appeared first on a petition from Moline citizens who favored repealing slavery in the state of Kansas. Deere's often fiery and passionate rhetoric stirred controversy, and, not surprisingly, he swiftly gained a reputation as a firebrand. His fellow citizens should not have expected anything less, because his political intensity mirrored his work ethic. Indeed, he was passionately intense about his work; as his nephew remembered, no lazy man dared to ask him for a job.[3] When a meeting of the local Democrats was rudely disrupted in 1858, Deere took the blame. The *Daily Islander and Argus*, a fork-tongued Democratic paper founded in Rock Island in 1852 by men who, as they themselves professed, were "not among the number who believes that 'all is fair in politics,'" gave a slanted report of the "mean, dirty and disgraceful affair." Supposedly under Deere's leadership, a group of Whigs had marched in "yelling, hooting and bellowing, in a manner that would disgrace the lowest brothel in existence."[4]

During his political rise, Deere also began to clash with his son-in-law, James Chapman. Chapman had served as an officer on the Whig county committee, but in June 1856 he joined the Democratic Party. Balancing political and business pursuits, the two men put aside their differences with great effort. When the Civil War broke out, both rallied behind the Union, but still backed different parties. The relationship, however, soon became hostile.[5]

In the years preceding the war, Chapman became good friends with the editor of the *Rock Island Argus*, J. B. Danforth, a curly-haired journalist who spent his entire career moving from one high-paying government patronage job to another. As their friendship flourished, Danforth printed without reserve anything Chapman wrote. Denying the charges of his detractors, Chapman claimed that he was neither a politician nor a political aspirant, but that he much preferred the quiet of home to the excitement and turmoil of political controversy. Living in Moline, as former friends and colleagues divided over the slavery question, however, Chapman found himself on the wrong side. One contributor to the *Moline Workman* took offence at one of Chapman's published letters that mingled religion and politics. The contributor suggested, with a hint of suspicion, that Chapman had joined the Democratic Party not because of necessity, but because of some other selfish, hidden motive.[6]

Seven days later, Chapman answered his enemies in the columns of the *Workman* with an attack on the paper itself for professing neutrality but holding "covertly Republican" loyalties. His remarks, Chapman claimed, typical of the two-sided approach of Republicans, targeted

"those so ignorantly bigoted, they would fain believe all like themselves," to the point of "speculating as to the low muttered curses of the
democracy, because of the course you are now pursuing." American
democracy would not be threatened by the "ignorant or willfully bigoted" and would not be destroyed by a political party seeking power.
The *Workman* followed with a nonpartisan rebuttal. Its editors acknowledged Chapman's friendly spirit and open-mindedness, as evidenced by
the contributions he and other Democrats had made to the growth of
Moline. But in the present crisis, the editors continued, Chapman and
his colleagues must be treated as friends once loved but now departed.[7]

While Chapman fought the newspapers' attacks, his extreme views
threatened his relationship with his father-in-law and, consequently, the
relationship between John Deere and his oldest daughter Jeannette.[8] Yet
the *Workman's* position aptly described Deere's own handling of a tense
situation. Eager to avoid personal conflict whenever possible, he decided
to treat members of the Democratic Party as individuals, regardless of
their political ideas.

Chapman was, after all, setting an example for community service
and civic leadership. In 1856, he served as secretary of the new fire company. Along with Robert Tate, he was also one of the leading figures in
the formation of the Moline Lyceum, an organization founded upon the
belief that "prosperity and wealth have a favorable influence on the
morals and manners of a people." This creed may not have sounded particularly democratic, but it was noble.[9] All the while coyly denying his
own political aspirations, Chapman helped to organize the Moline
Democratic Club and the spin-off Buchanan Club to elect James
Buchanan of Pennsylvania to the presidency.[10]

Moline and the Politics of War

While Charles scoured the countryside making sales and settling accounts in late 1859 and early 1860, the Union was devouring itself. The
presidential election took place in November 1860, with heavy sectional
voting decisively splitting the country in half. Republican Abraham Lincoln carried almost all of the northern states, and, although he received
a minority of the popular votes, he was elected the sixteenth President
of the United States. Lincoln was, of course, a local favorite in Moline.
Most residents of Rock Island County first learned about the lanky rail-
splitter during his much-publicized senatorial debates with Democratic
congressman Stephan A. Douglas in places such as Quincy, Freeport, and

Galesburg. Lincoln himself became familiar with Rock Island County during his days as the captain of a volunteer unit during the Black Hawk War, and later, in 1856, his law practice had taken him to the town of Rock Island for a controversial court case involving the railroad.

When the railroad built a bridge over the main channel of the Mississippi River at Rock Island, numerous steamboat owners felt threatened. Just weeks after the first locomotive crossed the bridge, a tragedy focused public attention on their concerns. Shortly after departing Rock Island en route to St. Paul, Minnesota, the steamer *Effie Afton* collided with a ferryboat. The initial clash caused only minor damage, and the *Effie Afton* continued under the drawn bridge. But once it had cleared the passage and the bridge was lowered, the boat's side paddle stopped turning and the swift Mississippi current threw the steamer back against the bridge, igniting first the boat then the wooden bridge. Steamboats along the shore blew their whistles in triumph, joyous to see the bridge in flames. When James Hurd, owner of the *Effie Afton,* filed a lawsuit against the Rock Island Railroad for damages, Lincoln was hired to argue the case. The trial eventually ended in a hung jury, although similar cases continued to pepper the dockets of federal courts until 1862, when Congress passed a law declaring such bridges legal structures and dismissing all pending suits.[11]

With Lincoln now on his way to Washington, the new decade brought clear signs of a different kind of political friction. In Moline, Democrats and Republicans argued vehemently over Lincoln's election and, of course, over the fate of slavery. Danforth, a vociferous Democrat, rallied his minions against the "black republican disunion" party.

The Civil War finally broke out in the middle of 1861, and, though the first battles seemed distant, the rippling effects of the war soon reached Moline. After Lincoln's initial call for 75,000 troops to put down the rebellion in April 1861, Rock Island citizens held a mass meeting at the county courthouse to air their views on the conflict. By the end of the week, they had organized an entire company of infantry, which the governor swiftly endorsed. Illinois men flocked to volunteer. By the summer of 1862, the state had gathered 130,000 men for the war effort. Before war's end, Illinois would send more than 250,000 men to defend the Union and house within its boundaries several prisoner-of-war camps, including the notorious prisons in Chicago, Alton, and Rock Island.[12]

The war years would be the greatest test so far of the Deere family's resolve and adaptability. Since 1857, under Charles Deere's guiding hand, the company had undergone a complete changing of the guard. A new wave of managerial appointments began to transform the company into a professionally run organization, and, as more educated men joined the firm, business and politics overlapped. These improvements notwithstanding, the plow business stagnated during the war and would not show much progress until peace returned

Charles Deere's political leanings, which he had formerly kept private, finally became apparent as he too became swept up in the war. The *Argus* provided up-to-date news on April 10, 1861. "NO FIGHT YET—For several days sensation makers have been busy with rumors of expected hostilities in the South, but . . . we believe the administration will endeavor to preserve peace." The editor could not have been more wrong: just five days later he rescinded faith in the Lincoln administration. "The terrible reality of civil war, a war between our own country—men, our own kindred, has been precipitated upon us." The war inevitably "must result in the subjugation of the southern states, through a long and bloody war, or perhaps an annihilation of our own government."[13]

On April 25, Mayor Bailey Davenport led Rock Island's first company of volunteers through town. After Rock Island successfully recruited the first company of soldiers—120 men in all—Moline followed suit. Deere's three-man selling force, George Vinton, Alvah Mansur, and Charles Deere, were "all for the war," and Mansur helped raise a company that was soon attached to the 19th Illinois Infantry regiment. In the excitement, the townspeople offered command not to Mansur, but to Peachy A. Garriott. Forty years later, Charles remembered him as "a good democrat whom we were all afraid had copperhead instincts," and he still felt that Garriott's command had been "greatly to the detriment of the company."[14]

Charles did not go to war, though it is likely that he attempted to join the army on several occasions. That a healthy young man was not accepted into service would seem puzzling, except for two considerations: his overly protective father had a great deal of influence and, as the manager of one of the country's largest agricultural implement manufacturers, the young man made an important contribution to the war effort. Soldiers relied upon farmers to raise food, and farmers relied upon the Moline Plow Manufactory, as Charles Deere renamed the company, to supply their equipment. Nevertheless, Charles admired the courage of those who did serve in the military. Little did he suspect that he would soon witness the suffering of the war up close.[15]

Wartime Business

John Deere, at that time an amateur politician with strong local influence, was equally swept up in the fevered excitement of war, which the people of Moline could not ignore. By February 1862, Rock Island County had contributed men to at least eighteen companies of infantry, cavalry, and artillery. Reports of Union defeats filled the papers, and it often seemed that there was little hope. John's close friend Robert Tate, still working at the Buford plow shop in Rock Island, paid close attention to the progress of the war, and as reports of the fighting made their way to the banks of the Mississippi, he became less and less optimistic about the possibility of a Union victory. "Secesh [sic] has driven us back to Manassas again," he wrote in his diary in August 1862. "The 29th, 30th and 31st, the second Bull Run fought, Friday, Saturday and Sunday. Whipped again sorrowfully." Despair filled his heart. "Cecesh [sic] is too much for us."[16]

Sales routes through the Confederate states had been completely obstructed; rail and water shipments could not get past the southern tip of Illinois at Cairo. But the Lincoln administration was looking out for Midwestern businessmen and farmers. On May 15, 1862, after a two-year campaign run by the Republican Party, the president signed a bill creating the Department of Agriculture. The new department would assist with price and tariff regulation, endorse incentive packages for farmers and implement manufacturers, and generally promote the welfare of the country's largest economic enterprise. That same year Republicans joined with Free-Soil Democrats in Congress to pass the Homestead Act, making 160 acres of public land available on the Western frontier to every American citizen over the age of twenty-one. In July Congress passed the Morrill Land-Grant College Act, providing 30,000 acres to each state for each representative and senator it had in Congress, to be used for the creation of an agricultural college. Such acts would contribute immensely to the growth and mechanization of the American farm. In the past, the typical Midwestern farmer had worked a farm of forty or sixty acres, but the agricultural and geographic records for the 1860 census showed that the average-sized farm had grown to 146 acres. Compounding this increase, the Homestead Act resulted in enormous agricultural growth west of the Mississippi during the war. And naturally, with the increase in acreage under cultivation, came an increased need for farming equipment.[17]

Although the farming legislation would have far-reaching consequences in the decades to come, other presidential acts had more immediate impact. In September 1862, Lincoln issued a proclamation to free all slaves in states currently in rebellion, effective January 1, 1863. The citizens of Rock Island and Moline reacted predictably; Deere was no exception. They held a public meeting at the Rock Island County Courthouse on the day the proclamation went into effect, in order, the *Argus* explained, to discuss "the most effectual mode of preventing the immigration of Negroes and mulattoes to this state." Danforth, who had hoisted Rock Island's Democratic flag up the Republican flagpole in a display of nonpartisan unity in 1860, now headed a committee to study the issue. The committee passed several resolutions, the most disturbing of which called upon the governor of the state to prevent all people of color from settling in Illinois.[18]

Thanks to personal experience, the citizens of the Tri-Cities had intense feelings on the subject of slavery and the moral questions it posed. Davenport had at one time been home to the slave Dred Scott, who sued for his freedom after his master had taken him through a number of northern states. When his case reached the United States Supreme Court in 1857, the justices ruled that black men had no rights as citizens and, therefore, Scott could not sue for his freedom. Danforth agreed wholeheartedly with the court's decision, although he was aware of the close attention his readers had paid to the case and their strong feelings about its outcome. Danforth printed the Emancipation Proclamation in full on January 2, along with the president's remarks making the act effective. For some Moline residents, the act represented a moral triumph, the cleansing of a great stain upon the country's soul.

A Growing Family

While other Deere company employees were fighting in Southern states, Charles Deere was well sheltered from army life, left to focus on his business and social activities. The twenty-five-year-old was all business all the time, or so it seemed to the casual observer. That quickly changed when he met Mary Little Dickinson, a petite, attractive, and well-educated twenty-one-year-old Chicago socialite. Though both Charles and Mary had been born in Vermont and raised in the Midwest, they were from very different social spheres—Charles, the son of a typical frontier family, and Mary, a child of wealth and influence. Mary's mother, Judith Atkinson Dickinson, was a cousin of Charles Atkinson, one of John Deere's early partners in Moline, who remained a close friend and business associate. Mary's father, Gideon Dickinson, had lived in Vermont, Massachusetts, and California before he settled in Chicago in 1854. There he made a fortune in real estate and served on Chicago's powerful board of trade.

What the young couple had in common was education and ambition. Mary was a member of the first graduating class of Chicago's Dearborn Seminary, located on Wabash Avenue near Washington Street, in 1855, just two years after Charles graduated from Bell's Commercial College. The union would prove a powerful combination in the upcoming years; Mary's headstrong, independent personality balanced her husband's outwardly shy and passive demeanor. More at ease in social circles, Mary worked hard to elevate her husband's reputation through those channels. The couple also shared ideals, both professionally and socially.

On September 9, 1862, Charles and Mary were married in Chicago, the same day that Mary's younger sister, Anna, wed army officer William D. Hawley. After the weddings, Charles and Mary returned to Moline.

A few weeks earlier, Stephen Velie and his wife, Emma Deere, had returned to Moline from Princeton, Illinois, where they had lived for two years, so Velie could join the family business. Charles would find in Velie an intelligent, motivated business associate and, over time, his most trusted personal confidant. Unlike his father, Charles was a visionary who thought in terms of results instead of processes, so his success depended upon men capable of overseeing the day-to-day details of the business.[19]

Strengthened family relationships were gaining significance at a time when business took back a back seat to political turmoil. James Chapman spearheaded the recruitment of a local company from Rock Island County and managed to be elected a first lieutenant. In September 1862, he joined the 129th Illinois Volunteers in Louisville, Kentucky, and was then transferred under the command of Brigadier General R. S. Granger's Tenth Division. While in the field, Chapman provided Danforth with short letters for publication in the *Argus*. Chapman reported in January 1863 that his company had lost only two soldiers to death, while only three others were currently in the hospital.[20]

Compared to other units, the 129th Illinois had seen little action. On the other hand, Captain P. A. Garriott's 19th Illinois, the group that, as Charles Deere said, "stole Moline's flower," took part in some of the heaviest fighting in Tennessee. A rumor reached Moline by telegraph in the first week of January that Garriott had been killed at Murfreesboro. A few weeks later, however, more accurate reports confirmed that he had merely been shot in the leg.[21]

Chapman proved less heroic. In October 1863, just before the 129th was transferred to guard a critical railroad line between Bowling Green, Kentucky, and Gallatin, Tennesee, he and a number of other officers were deactivated, allegedly for "disloyalty." Danforth informed his readers that the "crime of Lieut. Chapman consisted in not wishing to serve with Negro soldiers, and for saying so, in a letter published in the *Argus*."

Despite their disagreements, John Deere stood by his son-in-law. He did not approve of Chapman's support for the Democratic Party, but he was family, after all, and was serving the Union Army. Seizing the opportunity to throw mud once again, Danforth asserted that Deere, whom everyone knew was an ardent abolitionist, had journeyed east to visit General William Rosecrans of the Union Army. Danforth claimed that at that meeting, Deere had "whined, and sniveled, and cried," pleading that Chapman had fallen under Danforth's bad influence. "It was all Danforth's work, . . . Danforth led him into it." If anyone was disloyal, Deere supposedly insisted, it was Danforth. He was the "copperhead, [the] rebel sympathizer."

After launching his own impressive barrage of slanderous name-calling against Deere, Danforth spoke for Chapman. "Lieut. Chapman, we suppose, is a democrat—and 'that's what's the matter.' We don't think he wants anybody to cry or be for him. We suppose he will endeavor to survive the calamity of being dismissed on account of his politics, when so many other Democrats are served in the same way." Danforth went on to advocate solidarity, listing several other Democrats who had met the same fate. "We could extend the list indefinitely," Danforth concluded. But "Lieut. Chapman is in good company, and he don't ask any favors of abolitionists."[22]

At home, John and Charles had further problems to deal with. In July 1863, their shop superintendent, a Swedish immigrant named Andrew Friberg, punched a man named Fred Calkins after a political disagreement in a local store. Danforth, always ready to cast Moline in the role of Rock Island's ugly, corrupt stepsister, painted a picture of an unprovoked assault. According to the newspaper account, Calkins, a small, weak man, was attacked by the big "Moline bully" Friberg without warning. The case was taken before a Moline judge, but, because the man was known to be an abolitionist, Calkins asked that the case be moved to Rock Island. The next day the Rock Island judge fined Friberg three dollars plus court costs and put an end to matter.[23]

Early the next year Danforth had more favorable news from an old friend: Chapman wrote that his resignation as first lieutenant of the

129th Illinois Volunteers had been accepted. In Chapman's defense, and perhaps in direct opposition to John Deere, Danforth claimed Chapman had dealt with a great deal of harassment and numerous false accusations during his military service. His return to Moline was not a joyous one. The Union Army did not want him, and his family did not celebrate his homecoming. In fact, evidence of any relationship with his wife, Jeannette, and the rest of the Deere family all but disappears from the surviving records. Neither his personality nor his politics ever met his in-laws' approval, and when the company no longer had need of his financial expertise, his usefulness to the family he had rebelled against waned.[24]

"Real, Live Rebels"

As the war dragged into its fourth year, many patriotic and able-bodied men marched off to distant battlefields. Many never returned, leaving a host of Moline and Rock Island wives, children, and elderly parents to brave the realities of life and an uncertain future on their own. Even in an industrial town like Moline, where a natural social division between the laborer and the businessman had developed, death came indiscriminately.

Nestled in the middle of the Mississippi River, directly across the slough from John Deere's plow works, was an island, three miles long and half a mile wide, owned by the federal government. Sauk myth claimed that the island was inhabited by a great white swan living in a cave within its bowels. In 1816, Fort Armstrong had been built at the foot of the Rock Island rapids; and in July 1862, after much campaigning by several local citizens, the United States government appropriated funds for the establishment of a government arsenal on the island. A year later, as construction continued, the island's location and natural topography suggested another use for the island, one that brought the realities of the Civil War to Moline's doorstep: a Union Army prison camp.

The camp went up quickly on the north side of the island, "exposed to the bleak northwest winds," according to Danforth, who continued to attack the United States government and any project sponsored by the Republican Party. The prison was built on the Iowa side of the island only to "please Davenport shoddy contractors," he insisted. Despite Danforth's protests, work over the next five months saw the construction of eighty-four prison barracks and a twelve-foot prison wall surrounding them.[25]

"It was on a dark, raw, gloomy day, December 3, 1863, when the first Confederate prisoners came," a woman visiting relatives in Rock Island wrote. "I promise you, it was a day fraught with intense excitement, never to be forgotten. . . . Real, live Rebels were coming!" Almost five hundred ragged and hungry prisoners captured during the recent Union victory at Lookout Mountain in Tennessee stepped from the train into below-zero weather. "And, ridiculous as it may seem, it is a fact that many [citizens] were frightened, actually afraid of a disarmed foe. Still, they had curiosity to see how he looked, blankly disappointed, no doubt, to find him minus the horns and cloven hoofs."[26]

The prison camp brought the war to the area in a most personal way. By February, with more than 7,600 Confederates confined at the facility, Rock Island Prison had already exceeded its maximum occupancy. Townspeople on both sides of the river collected blankets, tobacco, and newspapers to help ease the prisoners' suffering and rededicated themselves to the Union war effort as a daily reminder of the haunting price of failure now lay within their midst.

Contractors in Moline, Rock Island, and Davenport were doing well by the prison, though. Chamberlain, Reynolds & Co. of Rock Island split the lumber contract with a Davenport firm. Dimock & Gould, makers of woodenwares formerly located on the island but now in Moline, provided buckets and other wood products, and a number of smaller merchants made considerable income from the hastily constructed prison barracks. Danforth, who protested incessantly that too much of the work was going to Davenport, estimated that $10,000 to $20,000 were to be made every month simply by supplying the island with dry goods, liquor, cigars, newspapers, and other sundries. The editor was disgruntled because prison advertising was denied him on account of his affiliation with the Democratic Party.[27]

For local residents, the prison camp was a constant reminder of the war, which, with a string of Union victories in the South, was slowly drawing to the close after the reelection of Lincoln in 1864. More than 600,000 Americans were dead by the time of General Robert E. Lee's surrender in April 1865, and, despite smoldering hatred and grief, conciliatory efforts began. Rock Island soon began releasing prisoners, and the surrounding communities looked forward to times of peace. With such promise, the Deere family was no doubt devastated, along with many of their fellow citizens, at the news brought by the April 15 edition of the *Argus:*

DEATH OF THE PRESIDENT AND THE SECRETARY OF STATE.

President Lincoln was shot through the head last night at Fords Theatre and died this morning. The assassin is supposed to be J. Wilkes Booth, the actor. About the same time a desperado called at Sec'y Seward's pretending to be a messenger from his physician but being refused admittance he attacked Fred'k Seward, son of the Secretary, knocking him down, then passing to the secretary's room, where, after cutting down two (2) male attendants, he cut Mr. Seward's throat.[28]

The initial report was only half correct: Seward's wound was not fatal. But Lincoln was indeed dead. The country mourned him as a great martyr. Rock Island designated Wednesday a day of prayer and vigil, while newspapers offered daily reports on the pursuit of Lincoln's assassin until John Wilkes Booth was shot in a Maryland barn on April 26, 1865. While the nation mourned, John Deere returned to Vermont with his daughter Jeannette, leaving Charles in Moline to organize a business strategy to take advantage of peacetime conditions.

Mourning and Recovery

Throughout the war and the year immediately after its conclusion, the Deere family suffered a number of devastating personal tragedies. Ellen Webber's eighteen-month-old son, Frank Alvin, died in January 1863. Demarius, John's wife of almost forty years, suffered a series of illnesses, which in the years to come would seem an inherent family curse. When she had taken seriously ill several times in the late 1850s, friends were surprised at her survival. But now the birth of ten children and the physical demands of raising this large family really took their toll.[29]

In the summer of 1864 there were two new additions to the Deere family. Ellen Webber gave birth to her sixth child, Mary Ellen. In August, Charles and Mary were blessed with their first child, Anna Caroline. The name took on greater sentimental importance that December when her namesake, Mary's sister Anna Caroline Hawley, died at the age of twenty-four from a disease she contracted while serving as an army nurse.

That winter seemed to carry all of the misery of the past four years into 1865. It was one of the coldest winters on record, and the continued near-zero temperatures provided no respite. In February 1865, temperatures still hovered around zero. The river remained frozen and people crossed it on foot.[30]

On February 17, Demarius died at age sixty. Three days later, she was buried near her children. She died as quietly as she lived, for almost nothing is known of her life. Two weeks after the death of her mother, Ellen was at the bedside of her husband, C. C. Webber, who was then serving as an alderman in Rock Island. The forty-nine-year-old was "dangerously sick with erysipelas," an often-fatal skin disease, and despite early signs of recovery, Webber succumbed. The opinions of creditors notwithstanding, he had bailed John Deere out of financial trouble on several occasions. In addition, he had made great contributions to his in-laws' family business, and his influence upon both products and personnel would shape the company's future. Although he himself had left the business prior to the outbreak of the Civil War, he had brought into the company Gilpin Moore, an inventive man with a knack for mechanics who stayed with Deere after Webber's departure. Webber had also introduced his former clerk and boarder, Stephen Velie, to Emma Deere. Velie and Moore would help pilot the company successfully for the next forty years.[31]

More than a year after the death of his wife, in the spring of 1866, John Deere returned to Vermont with much of the family. His native state had seen many changes in his absence, although his name was more familiar now to his former neighbors than when he had gone west in 1836. On May 20, 1866, Deere married Demarius's sister Lusena Lamb. He was sixty-one years old; Lusena was fifty-six. Physically, she was a fair reminder of her sister, a petite, fragile-looking woman with round eyes and long black hair. A great source of comfort for both the bride and the groom, the marriage further strengthened the bond between the two families and their homes—the Vermont of Deere's youth and the Illinois of his present and future. His visit to Vermont reminded him of his humble roots and a bygone era. Eight days after the wedding, Deere took his bride home to Moline.

The years leading to the Civil War and especially the war itself were tumultuous times for the nation and for the Deere family. The plow business had been put in the capable hands of young Charles Deere, a modest intellectual with a deep appreciation for his father's vision and his customers' needs. The family saw weddings, births, and funerals, but at last, with years of war behind them, a sense of normalcy and, for the business, explosive growth, was imminent.

MOLINE, ILL.

---— F I V E ——---

The Case of "The Moline Plow"

John Deere's former shop foreman Andrew Friberg returned to Moline in 1866 after spending several years in the West to receive treatment for his respiratory ailments. Ever wary of Friberg, when C. C. Webber first took charge of the blacksmith shop, he had brought in Gilpin Moore to keep an eye on the untrusted Swede. Now, upon his return to Moline, Friberg found that he had been replaced. Unhappy in his new position working under Moore, he offered to run Robert Tate's Rock Island factory for a wage of five dollars per day. To avoid a confrontation, he made the offer the same day that John Deere left for Vermont. Clearly, Friberg preferred being the head man for the competition to being an underling for Deere. He was, after all, a skilled mechanic and competent foreman. Convinced that he was alone responsible for the superiority of Deere's products, he reasoned that success would follow him.[1]

Tate accepted Friberg's proposal, maybe because of his qualifications, but more likely because he thought Friberg and his partners, the Bufords of Rock Island, deserved each other. Shortly after Friberg was hired, Tate sold out.

Robert Tate's departure, combined with the employee swapping of recent years, added a tumultuous dynamic to the otherwise friendly competition between the Rock Island and Moline plow companies. Now, new players in the local manufacturing scene were enacting plans that would create a further conflict that would take Deere & Co. by storm.

During John Deere's trip to Vermont in the spring of 1866, a new Moline plow maker, Candee, Swan & Co., founded by local businessmen Henry Candee and Robert K. Swan, published its first catalog offering plows and other farm equipment. The agricultural implement business showed great growth potential after the Civil War, and the new firm wanted a piece of the profits. Adding to the continued competition of the Rock Island factory was now a competitor literally in Deere's backyard.

Candee had come west from Connecticut in 1838. After shifting about between Peoria and the Tri-Cities, he settled in Moline and went into partnership with a manufacturer of fanning mills. In 1854, Candee joined Swan as a manufacturer of chain pumps, horse rakes, and other miscellaneous iron goods in a factory along the Mississippi River. This business ran successfully throughout the Civil War. Afterward, jealously eyeing Deere & Co., the partners decided to offer some friendly competition. Candee and Swan provided the start-up capital for the new endeavor. The firm's expertise, however, was provided by a heretofore silent partner, Andrew Friberg.[2]

Moline, now a village of 2,000 residents, was so small that its leading men of business and industry frequented the same clubs and dance halls and enjoyed leisure outings and other amusements together. So, too, in business affairs, partners who had separated over irreconcilable differences in the past still collaborated on future projects to the benefit of both themselves and the city. In 1863, for example, John Deere joined with other local businessmen, including Robert K. Swan and his own former partners Charles Atkinson and John Gould, to organize the First National Bank of Moline.

Deere's relationship with Swan, though, would take a much different direction than the continuing friendships he shared with Tate and Gould. When the Candee, Swan & Co. catalog appeared in 1866, it looked overly familiar. In fact, it was nearly identical to Deere's catalog in almost every respect, down to the typeface, layout, and product engravings. It was even run off the same printing press by the same Peoria printer Charles Deere had hired just months earlier.[3]

Furthermore, Candee, Swan & Co.'s line of agricultural implements bore close resemblance to the line sold by Deere & Co. Deere's circular of 1866 offered ten woodcut images of Deere plows, each with the company's trademark, "John Deere, Moline, ILL." prominently stenciled onto the beam. Candee, Swan, & Co. printed almost identical woodcuts in its catalog. The company not only employed nearly identical advertising and hallmarks, but with Friberg running the shop, Candee, Swan & Co. adopted the same numbering system, a combination of letters and numbers to denote specific parts, making construction and replacement of worn parts more efficient.

Almost immediately, Deere & Co. responded defensively in its advertising. "The high reputation attained for them, has led other manufacturers to attempt imitations, and, for the purpose of making sales, claim that they make the Moline Plow," the ads boasted. "We would say to parties who might otherwise be misled by such representations, that the only genuine Moline Plows are made by us, and are branded: John Deere, Moline, ILL."

Charles Deere was livid. Although he accepted all fair competition, he would not stand for the outright theft of what his father had spent so much time and effort to establish. What, he wondered, would possess honorable businessmen to organize an identical plow operation right under his nose, copy his designs and organization, and then deny that they had poached on his territory? It seemed almost ridiculous, but here it was happening right before him. And nothing, apparently, could be done to prevent it from recurring. Patent litigation was still in its infancy, and it was a time-consuming and expensive process. Charles Deere attempted to resolve all lawsuits himself unless the situation required costly outside council. For the time being, he merely continued to observe Candee, Swan, & Co. through the fall and winter of 1866 and to take note of any suspicious sales or advertising tactics. He also met frequently with his lawyers, John B. Hawley and George Pleasant.[4]

At the factory, Charles grew ever more suspicious of spies. On February 26 a man named William Miller managed to sneak into the workshop and examine the Southern Plow. The next day Deere discovered that Miller worked for Burnam Bros. in St. Louis and that he had come to town to meet with the proprietors of a number of Illinois plow companies in an effort to hire skilled workers. Deere pursued the scoundrel to Rock Island, only to learn that his Rock Island competitors had uncovered the spy's plot. By the time Charles arrived, Miller had already skipped town.[5]

Charles had seen enough. That day he and his lawyers met Judge Ira Wilkinson in his chambers at the Rock Island County courthouse with an application to restrain Candee, Swan & Co. from using certain trademarks upon plows they were manufacturing. A local newspaper candidly summarized the charge. Candee, Swan, & Co. had been manufacturing plows with the size, shape, marks, numbers, style of finish, coloring, and lettering in exact imitation of the well-known Moline Plow manufactured by Deere & Co. for the purpose of misleading customers and capitalizing upon the name and tradition of its established competitor.

Long gone were the days of John Deere's Grand Detour, when plow makers openly adopted the designs of colleagues and competitors solely for the purpose of improving the farmer's armory. By the mid 1860s, the industry had grown much too lucrative. Long-established manufacturers now guarded their own designs. Consequently, plow makers were sending an unprecedented number of applications to the patent office.

In this case, Wilkinson had to decide two key questions. First, did Deere & Co. have an exclusive right to the name "Moline Plow" and any assumptions of quality that came with it? Second, if Candee, Swan, & Co. did not intend to take advantage of the popularity of Deere's plow and trick customers into thinking that both companies were one and the same, then why did the company attempt to imitate Deere's plow, call it by a similar name, and advertise it as "the old and well established Moline Plow"?[6]

In Deere's view, competing was one thing, but purposely misrepresenting a product to mislead potential customers was quite another matter. Since entering his father's employ in 1853, Charles had made his work a personal tribute to his father's hard-earned success. Any assault on the business was a direct assault on his father and his family. He warned all of his salesmen to beware of Deere look-alikes. One of his St. Louis agents rushed a circular to its customers. "You are doubtless aware that a firm in this city are advertising for sale, and have quoted in their price lists, the 'Moline Plow.' We wish to acquaint the public to this fraud, which they are attempting to perpetrate by offering an inferior article."

"We have just been advised by Messrs. Deere & Co. that they are about instituting suit against all engaged in this piracy upon their trade marks, both manufacturers and those selling," the St. Louis circular announced. "Messrs. Deere & Co. are fully alive upon the subject of exposing this fraud, and will prosecute one and all implicated, to the extent of the law, which affords them abundant protection."[7]

Deere was true to his word. On March 19, 1867, he filed an injunction against Candee, Swan, & Co. with the purpose of preventing them from manufacturing their imitation "Moline Plow." Deere's injunction requested that his competitors be completely restrained from using the name in advertising and, particularly, from painting on their products in imitation of Deere's distinctive stencil. But there was one problem: Wilkinson recognized that Deere's plows were not patented. Consequently, Candee, Swan & Co. had every right to make similar plows if it chose. But that issue was not in dispute. The dispute was over the words, letters, and figures, especially their combination, which Deere & Co. considered its unique brand.[8]

Deere maintained that the combination of words, letters, and figures stenciled into the plow had become a trademark, regardless of whether this was the original intention. Deere's mark included the words "John Deere" in capital letters and black paint, in a semicircular pattern, with the words "Moline, Ill." in a straight horizontal line underneath, in smaller capitals in like black paint, with a dash between them. Candee, Swan & Co had copied it right down to the details. The company's name appeared in smaller capital letters, in a semicircular pattern at least two inches longer than that of "John Deere," along with the address "Moline, Ill."

By virtue of the constant use of the term "Moline Plow" in advertising literature, could Deere & Co. claim that this was, in fact, its trademark? Not only advertisements but also the farming community referred to the company's chief product as the "Moline Plow." Similarly, the company marked each model of plow and its parts with certain letters and figures—such as "A, No. 1," "AX No. 1," "No. 1," "X. No. 1," "B, No. 1,"—to designate particular qualities, sizes, and patterns.

Candee, Swan & Co., as Wilkinson observed in a ruling handed down in April 1867, duplicated the markings almost exactly and merely replaced "John Deere" with its own name. The final decision rested on a simple point of law. According to Wilkinson, the words "Moline, ILL." were not originally intended to distinguish Deere & Co. and therefore could not be claimed as a trade name. Moreover, since "Moline, ILL." merely designated the place of business, neither company owned the exclusive right to use of the town's name."[9]

The defense sighed in relief. Candee, Swan, & Co. informed customers in a July circular that anyone assuming that the company would be discontinuing the manufacture of plows was incorrect.

With his injunction denied, Deere and his attorneys looked at the case again. They had not proven misrepresentation in any form, nor had they shown that Candee, Swan, and Friberg were maliciously profiting from John Deere's name. It was time to change tactics. Almost immediately Deere filed charges again, and the case was placed on the Rock Island Circuit Court's docket for May 1867.

Before the court hearing commenced, neutral friends and colleagues tried to reconcile the two firms. Charles Atkinson, who for a short time after his arrival in Moline had been Deere's partner, urged John Deere to talk to Swan and, simultaneously, pressed Swan to approach both John and Charles with the hope that the two parties could resolve their differences. Atkinson told the elder Deere that Swan was willing to stop using "Moline, Ill." on his plows and to reform his numbering system if Deere would drop the suit. At the same time, Atkinson told Swan that Deere would agree to such terms, although neither businessman had actually consented. The alleged compromise was Atkinson's invention, and by this point a great personal distrust and animosity had evolved. Neither side would let the matter drop as company circulars and editorials in agricultural journals and newspapers blasted charges of counterfeit plows and blatant misrepresentation.

"We have the exclusive sale of the celebrated Moline Plows in the section, and sell no others," a Deere advertisement in the *Chicago Republican* insisted.

> [N]early every farmer knows that if he gets a Plow branded "John Deere, Moline, Ill." that he has got a reliable Plow, and no chance for a failure. We can say from experience that there is no tool that the farmer uses which, if good, is so pleasing, and if poor, so aggravating as the plow, and we really believe that no man can live an exemplary Christian life and use a poor plow. We therefore think that every farmer should spare no pains to get what he knows to be reliable and not allow himself to be deceived by flaming advertisements, claims of scientific principles, red stripes, etc., which are nearly always used to cover up bungling, awkward, inferior and useless implements.[10]

In the normal cycles of business, Deere & Co. suffered from temporary lapses, but never because of inferior products or lack of customers. Instead, it was the imitators, not the legitimate competitors, that depleted the company's financial resources. More important, by attempting to steal the Deere & Co. identity, those imitators pirated the Deere reputation. Despite the financial drain of legal fees and court costs for both Deere and Candee, Swan & Co., the pending suit demonstrated the worth of the Deere name and the Deere tradition. The company had created its most effective sales strategy yet: emphasizing that Deere's history was older and more celebrated than any of its competitors, especially Candee, Swan & Co. Placing John Deere himself at the head of the concern, whether actively or figuratively, emerged as one of the company's most powerful advertising tools.

Although Friberg had acted as foreman of Deere's shop for more than a decade, he still could not claim seniority. John Deere had been selling plows long enough to capitalize on "the liberal patronage extended to us through a course of business of many years duration." Claims to tradition filled Deere & Co.'s 1867 general catalog, which was now being printed in Chicago. "The business has been carried on as long as the life-time of a generation," it boasted, "the senior partner having commenced it over thirty years ago. The varied knowledge of the wants of agriculture, and the experience and numerous facilities for manufacturing accumulated during this extended period, enables us to offer to the public a Plow constructed on the most scientific principles, of the most suitable material, in a thorough and finished style, and at a price affording simply a fair remuneration for the capital and labor employed."[11]

Candee, Swan & Co. responded in kind. Friberg was the oldest *practical* plow maker in the Northwest, the 1866 catalog alleged. "Our Mr. Friberg for twelve years had charge of the Iron Department of Mr. Deere's shop, and to his skill as a Mechanic they in great measure owe their justly merited popularity," the company asserted.[12]

And although the rivals publicly debated the merits of their respective businesses, privately the lawsuit was well under way. Between August 1867 and January 1869, thirty-one witnesses testified. On Monday morning, March 23, 1868, Robert Tate appeared in the office of John Hawley, the Deere company lawyer. Tate would prove a key figure in the case because of his long relationship with John Deere and his experience in the manufacturing of agricultural equipment. Called by Candee, Swan & Co.'s attorneys, Tate spoke directly and truthfully in his numerous appearances; but his early recollections, taken in fragments, inadvertently painted Deere as a petty thief filching ideas from others. When questioned about inventors of the different plows made by John Deere, Tate offered a brief history lesson. The earliest he could recall was an implement named the Diamond Plow manufactured in Princeton, Illinois, by a man named Hitchcock. He also recalled that, soon afterward, a man named Henry May from Galesburg, Illinois, had begun making a similar plow; it was the first plow with a steel moldboard that Tate could remember.

Plow makers had incorporated small amounts of steel into their products since the early nineteenth century, though they used this steel only in a supporting capacity, in the form of a bolt or plate. In 1830 Samson Felton of Huntingdon, Pennsylvania, received a patent for a plow with a pointed steel share. Three years later, Charles B. Taylor invented a layered plow with two shares, the lower one made entirely of steel. Either because the majority of farmers were plowing in the soft, amenable soils of the East or because of limited production, steel plows retained their primitive, early nineteenth-century form until, as Tate acknowledged, May made improvements around 1843. Soon thereafter, Deere and Andrus began producing similar plows in Grand Detour. They were not alone. Someone in their own town named Denney and someone named Doane in Palestine, Illinois, manufactured plows much like May's. Tate himself had helped to produce steel plows in a similar manner, first as a partner of Deere, Tate, & Gould, in Moline, and later as a partner of Buford & Tate.

When pressed to point out what was original about the John Deere plow, Tate could not identify a single original part. The beam and handle were essentially the beam and handle used by Pittsburgh manufacturers Ruggles, Mourse & Mason. The cast block, intended to give form to the moldboard, was copied from the Evans plow of Galena, Illinois. The clevis was purchased from Warner, who manufactured this same piece for Ruggles, Mourse & Mason, and other plow makers. Tate explained how he and Deere then introduced what they called the muley share, copied from the Occidental, another plow brought to Moline in 1850. But such copying was standard in the industry, Tate offered in his friend's defense. The plows Tate himself had until recently manufactured adhered to the same basic form of the plows that he manufactured while with John Deere.

When the questioning turned to Deere's personal attributes, Tate did not give Deere credit for an inventive creativity as much as for an ability as a "good judge of a plow." Tate further suggested that Deere was ignorant about the fundamental structure of the plow. In light of the fact that Deere had four patents to his name, Tate's claim seems surprising.

When the defense returned to the particular plow designs that Deere had supposedly copied in the early years of his business, Tate did come to his old friend's defense, clarifying his assessment of Deere's inventive capabilities. In Grand Detour, Deere had been responsible for the entire manufacturing process. During the early days in Moline, however, Deere had directed his energies toward marketing and sales, so he did not have much opportunity to prove his smithing skills. Tate recalled that the only time he ever saw John Deere take part in production at the Moline shop was when one of the blacksmiths asked him to inspect a job or to answer a question.

How then, Tate's interrogators wanted to know, could Deere & Co., a firm built on the work of others, sue a competitor for copying a plow that John Deere himself had copied? Was not Deere only a middleman?

The plow handles were a case in point. Were the handles on Deere & Company plows not the same as the ones first used by John Deere? Asked whether Deere was contesting ownership of earlier handle designs borrowed from competitors, Tate replied that, in fact, the handles were not manufactured in the same way. In the current process, he explained, plow handles were steamed and bent to their desired form before the plow was finished, then bolted to the beam at a later stage. So too, the beam, the clevis, the share, the landside, and the moldboard had been improved not only by using more durable iron and steel, but also by discovering better ways of attaching the individual pieces. Finally, Tate conceded, his own products were also based directly on the designs of others. Manufacturers across the country all built plows according to more or less similar designs. Imitation was the standard and, apparently, the greatest form of flattery.[13]

The Moline Plow Company versus the Moline Plow Works

Despite more deliberate attempts at belittling John Deere's accomplishments behind closed doors, his reputation remained fully intact in Moline and beyond during the trial. The company's position, the *Chicago Republican* noted after a visit in May 1868, "is the result of twenty years untiring labor. . . . John Deere may be called a pioneer, if not *the* pioneer, plow manufacturer in Illinois. No man has done more, and few, if any, have done as much to establish for Illinois plows a reputation that has never yet been eclipsed anywhere." Not only in Moline, "all plow makers respect and honor him for his skill and success, and concede the service he has rendered Western agriculture by his efforts."[14]

Meanwhile, the case was providing a boom to Candee, Swan & Co. In July the company offered a circular explaining why it had been unable to fill orders as quickly as expected. The circular also explained that the company had to decline unsolicited orders at present but was increasing production capacity with extensive additions to the manufacturing facilities. The neighbors watched as the company doubled the size of the wood shop, built a new foundry, and constructed 117-foot-long by 50-foot-wide addition to the grinding and polishing shops. Of course, the new expanded facilities required additional waterpower as well.[15]

But as old buildings grew and new ones rose from the ground, behind the scenes a financial crisis was ravaging Candee, Swan & Co. The costs of the yearlong lawsuit, combined with the overwhelming need for capital and extended credit—a plight John and Charles Deere knew too well—was threatening to destroy the young company. The new construction drew heavily on finances and forced the parters to seek financial assistance. Stillman Wheelock, a thickly bearded New Yorker, had come to Chicago in 1839, two years after John Deere passed through the young town. In 1851 he arrived in Moline and, with a partner, first bought N. B. Buford's old foundry, then built the Moline Paper Mill. Joining Candee, Swan & Co. in 1871, he infused the business with $75,000, and the company was again armed to fight its Moline rivals.[16]

Wheelock also gave the company a new name: the Moline Plow Company. The name change caused even greater confusion between the two rival companies as a Chicago clerk, J. E. Winzer, testified. Winzer worked for J. N. Bradstreet & Son, a company whose primary business was reporting the commercial standing and credit of business firms for the protection of trade. The name "Moline Plow Company" had caused great problems, he explained, because it so closely resembled the name of Charles Deere's company, the "Moline Plow Works."

J. N. Bradstreet & Son had received an inquiry from the Moline Plow Company but mistakenly responded to the Moline Plow Works, unaware that the two businesses were not the same. Unofficially, the Deere factory had always gone by the Moline Plow Works and even printed that name on its letterhead. Charles Deere, who personally sorted the company's mail every morning, detected the error and requested a copy of the original letter. As he suspected, it was a request from his Moline competitors.

Unaware that there was now a second plow company in Moline with a similar name, Winzer assumed that the Moline Plow Company and the Moline Plow Works were one and the same, which was exactly the point Deere was trying to make. True, he could not claim the word "Moline" as a trademark, but Deere considered a trademark implied because "Moline" had been used in advertising and it was the name by which his plows were called. Whether the judge would consider such an argument convincing remained to be seen.[17]

The Birth of Deere & Company

While his son fought for his company's name in the winter of 1868, John Deere had adventures of his own. In January 1868 the *Rock Island Union* reported that one of his horses broke from a hitching post in town and pulled his wagon wildly through the streets. He was shaken but unharmed. Two months later, he concluded arrangements for the purchase of some property in California with the intention of spending his winters there. As much as he enjoyed the time he spent at his Moline farms raising Jersey cattle and Cotswold and Leicestershire sheep, slow, dry West Coast afternoons held great appeal for a man of sixty-two.[18] That year Deere also erected a monument for Demarius, which Tate referred to as "John Deere's Warrior column." The light gray, granite obelisk struck Tate "as the work of a people, not a parent or a husband. . . . One would suppose it had been erected in memory of some hero by the rank and file." He estimated the cost at $1,000, "which amount [Deere] could well afford."[19]

On August 15, 1868, John and Charles took steps to solidify their hold on the agricultural market, following a trend of incorporation in response to expanding national markets. After thirty-one years of differing business configurations since the first partnership of John Deere and Leonard Andrus back in Grand Detour, Deere & Co. completed incorporation procedures in the state of Illinois and formally adopted the name Deere & Company. It would be the company's final name change.

Four shareholders were named in the enterprise: John Deere, Charles Deere, Stephen Velie (Charles's brother-in-law), and George Vinton (Charles's cousin). Capital stock of $150,000 was divided among the four partners, with John and Charles assuming the majority. John Deere was no longer deeply involved in the daily operations of the business, although as the company's president, he presided over all board meetings. He continued to work in the shop on occasion, make demonstrations at county and state fairs, and, most important, serve as the company's most recognizable figurehead. Thirty-one-year-old Charles Deere, by now a well-established, veteran leader, was named vice-president and continued to wield all of the executive privilege necessary to run the business. Velie, a serious-looking, cool-headed, and fiscally responsible businessman, was named secretary. In this role, he would continue to drive all corporate advertising and promotion. Vinton, a salesman with fourteen years of service, would continue to manage the company's ever-expanding sales territory.[20]

A year after Deere & Company's incorporation, in the summer of 1869, the company added two minor stockholders. Gilpin Moore continued as the superintendent of the iron works and he now received a minority interest for his service. John Deere's nephew C. O. Nason, who had arrived from New Hampshire in 1857 and worked for his uncle in the wood department ever since, also received an interest in the company. The new agreement redivided the stock among six men: Charles Deere claimed 40 percent; John Deere, 25 percent; Velie, 14 percent; Vinton, 10 percent; Moore, 6 percent; and C. O. Nason, 5 percent. Only

Moore was not related to the Deere family by blood or marriage, and Friberg's recent betrayal had given the company all the more reason to prefer the men of the family.

In view of its origins in Grand Detour in 1837, when John Deere manufactured only one plow, the company's progress was impressive. The company's property was valued at $105,100, and its machinery and equipment at $45,265. In 1869, Deere & Company would sell 41,133 plows, harrows, and cultivators for a gross income of almost $650,000, netting profits of almost $200,000. John Deere's credit problems seemed a distant memory, and, as of yet, the nagging court case had caused no visible problems.[21]

Apparently none of the court proceedings greatly concerned John Deere. He and Lusena felt free to spend the summer in Vermont. But during his father's absence, Charles was busy devising an experiment that time would show to be as critical to the company's expansion as any arrangement to date. As the company expanded, putting greater pressure on Vinton to reach the overwhelming number of salesmen and independent dealers he was responsible for, it became increasingly clear that some attempt would have to be made to create more permanent, company-controlled sales affiliates throughout the country. In addition, an uncontrollable independence had grown among company salesmen who were raising and lowering prices in the field for their own personal gain and taking advantage of both the company and the customers.

As Deere prepared to take action, he procured the services of Alvah Mansur, a small, stern-looking man who had first joined the company in 1859. He had served in the Union Army, and, after his discharge, he went to the Colorado Territory, where he engaged in several mining operations and served two terms in the Colorado legislature. In 1868, he returned to Moline to embark on Charles Deere's innovative and potentially disastrous new business venture. For many years, Deere had trusted jobbing firms in places such as St. Louis to sell his products on commission. Yet he did not have the desired managerial control over these firms, and establishing branch houses seemed to be a natural solution. Finding a competent manager was the first step, and Deere fully believed that Mansur was the man for the job. Among his qualities, creditors reported that Mansur was a married man (marriage in those days was thought to be a sign of stability) with good habits, character, and capability, as well as attentiveness and honesty.[22]

Deere announced the opening of the first branch house in September 1869: "We take pleasure in announcing that we are establishing, at KANSAS CITY, MO., a General Depot for the distribution and sale of the

John Deere Genuine Moline Plow, Deere's Walking and Hawkeye Cultivators, &c." The depot would keep "at all times, a full assortment and supply of our Implements, thereby enabling dealers to obtain any Plow, or part thereof, at short notice." And besides the ready supply of stock, this location, "accessible to every Railroad," offered a "material reduction in our list of prices." The company, "under the supervision of Mr. Alvah Mansur, the resident partner, a practical Implement man, and the style of the firm, DEERE, MANSUR & CO.," would carry not only Deere's standard product line, but also "other leading farm Implements of the latest Improved patterns."[23]

Deere & Company's first branch house was a unique concept in the agricultural market and the first sign of Charles Deere's visionary approach to expanding sales territories as the country continued to grow further west. Ironically, it was the antithesis of the centralization strategy that spurred Deere & Company's incorporation in the first place, though the creation of a partnership reduced the parent company's risk. The partnership made sense to Charles Deere, himself a player in the volatile agricultural marketplace. Careful study and a conservative yet decisive approach were the keys to his success.

Deere, Mansur & Co. was launched with $20,000 capital, half from Deere & Company and half from Mansur, who would be responsible for on-site management and the ultimate success of the business. The partners drew up a five-year agreement and the great experiment began. If it succeeded, the new arrangement would greatly reduce the stress in Moline, especially for Vinton, whose control over expanding sales territories was diminishing year by year. In its most basic form, the branch house would stock a full line of Deere plows and eliminate the delay in shipping implements and parts from Moline.

Ever an idealist, Charles Deere was a lifelong proponent of the benefits of competition, and the branch house structure was the clearest evidence of this belief. In addition to Deere plows, the Kansas City house would stock complementary equipment from other manufacturers. The move was a stroke of genius. Deere now received a cut of his competitor's profits as commission, and at the same time he could offer his own agents the opportunity to sell a complete line of products and realize some of that added profit themselves. Furthermore, farmers could buy all of their products from one salesman. On the surface, Deere was promoting competition—which he truly believed in—but he could do so because he also believed that he had a better product and a greater talent for salesmanship than his competition.

The earliest known image of John Deere's Grand Detour home comes from the *Ogle County Atlas,* which was published twenty-four years after John Deere moved to Moline. Courtesy Deere & Company Archives

Demarius Deere. John Deere married Demarius Lamb in 1827, nine years before he came to Illinois. Courtesy Deere & Company Archives

Leonard Andrus was John Deere's first partner in the plow-making business in Grand Detour. Courtesy Deere & Company Archives

John Gould, 1860. Courtesy Deere & Company Archives

John Deere. This earliest known image comes from an advertising poster printed in 1856. Courtesy Deere & Company Archives

1838 Plow. The oldest surviving John Deere plow was built in 1838 and is now at the National Museum of American History. Deere's first steel plow likely resembled this design. This plow is missing its handles. Courtesy Smithsonian Institution

Advertisement in the *Country Gentleman* for the John Deere Improved Clipper Plow with rolling coulter, 1857. Courtesy Deere & Company Archives

Polishing Shop, 1856. Water power from the Mississippi River ran the grinding and polishing wheels in the Plow Works. This artwork is from an 1856 advertising poster. Courtesy Deere & Company Archives

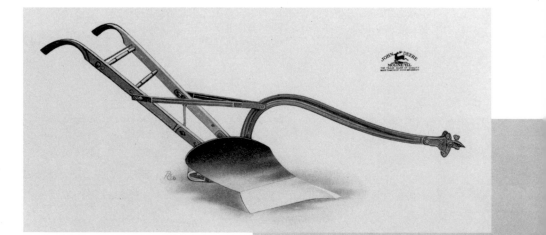

(above) The steel-beam walking plow was introduced by John Deere in 1867. It would remain in the product line until the 1940s. Courtesy Deere & Company Archives

(right) This lithograph from the late 1800s shows John Deere watching a Gilpin Sulky plow at work. Below them is the John Deere Plow Works along the Mississippi River. Deere is shown in his typical dress: a long black coat and fedora hat. Courtesy Deere & Company Archives

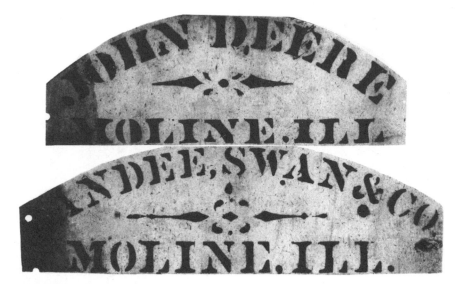

Exhibits G and H from the *Candee, Swan & Co. vs. John Deere* trademark case. Although the trademarks were similar, the ultimate ruling favored Candee, Swan & Co., which by that time had changed its name to the Moline Plow Company, further confusing it with Deere & Company's Moline Plow Works. Courtesy Deere & Company Archives

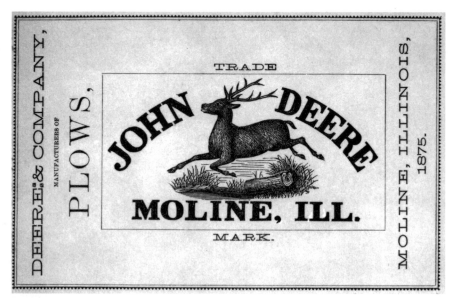

Deere & Company's first leaping deer trademark, designed by family friend M. A. Gould, appeared in 1873, two years after the *Candee, Swan & Co. vs. John Deere* case had been decided. Courtesy Deere & Company Archives

Twenty-one-year-old Charles Deere *(middle)* in 1858, the year he became general manager of his father's business. Courtesy Butterworth Trust

(left) Charles and Mary Deere's "Swiss villa" mansion, Overlook, as it appeared in the 1870s. Courtesy Deere & Company Archives

(below) Charles and Mary Deere had two children, Anna *(bottom)* and Katherine *(top)*, 1880. Courtesy Deere & Company Archives

(right) John Deere. An undated photo of John Deere, possibly taken during his term as mayor of Moline from 1873–1875. Courtesy Deere & Company Archives

(below) This view from the Mississippi River looking south shows Moline as it appeared two years after John Deere was mayor. Courtesy Deere & Company Archives

(above) Red Cliff. John built Red
Cliff just down the street from
Overlook on the bluff overlook-
ing Moline. Moline's 11th Avenue
became known by two names:
Deere Row and Millionaires Row.
Courtesy Deere & Company
Archives

(right) Lusena Deere. After
Demarius's death, John Deere
returned to Vermont and married
her sister, Lusena. Courtesy Deere
& Company Archives

Interior of the John Deere Plow Works forge shop, circa 1910. Deere & Company was the first factory in the Tri-City area to introduce electricity, in February 1881, replacing some of the torches and kerosene lamps with 13 electric lights, each with power equivalent to 2,000 candles. Further efforts to increase production and provide safer working conditions included the installation of an extensive air-filtering system in 1885.

By 1910, the belt pulleys were powered by both steam and electric power. Courtesy Deere & Company Archives

At the time of Charles Deere's death, the Plow Works alone had 1,400 employees and made more steel plows than its eight largest competitors combined. *Above:* Plow Works employees, 1872. *Below:* The 1894 office force. The front row from left to right, includes C. O. Nason, Stephen Velie, Charles Deere, and Gilpin Moore. Courtesy Deere & Company Archives

Skill and Integrity

While Deere & Company and Candee, Swan & Co. underwent major restructuring, the lawsuit between them continued. On August 22, 1868, John Gould, John Deere's former associate, testified that he believed himself to be the first to refer to Deere's plow as the "Moline Plow" when he was still a partner with Deere and Tate at the time they first moved to Moline in 1848. When questioned further, he explained that the partners thought they had made improvements over other plows and so they chose this name to distinguish their plow from those manufactured elsewhere. Deere & Company was establishing the case that it was, in fact, the only manufacturer of *the* Moline Plow and that by association it alone held claim to the name "Moline." This point would have ramifications throughout the country, because companies traditionally adopted the name of their town. The Rock Island Plow Company, the Grand Detour Plow Company, the Peru Plow Company, and others dotted the Illinois landscape, yet, strangely enough, Moline was the first town to spawn two similar, competing companies.[24]

On December 4, Deere & Company lawyers called Joseph Jaeger, a thirty-year-old hardware dealer from Missouri who had been selling the Moline Plow for twelve years. His testimony provided the much-needed evidence of misrepresentation when he reported an uneasy confrontation in December 1866 in his store in Macon with Robert Swan.

> After I had given an order to Mr. Swan for horse rakes, he told me that he would like me to take the agency for a Moline Plow. I told him I would not take it just now. He then had quite a talk with me, and tried his very best to have me buy a few. I came pretty near giving him an order, but before I did, I asked him what Moline Plow he was selling; if it was John Deere's Plow he was selling? He said not, it was not John Deere's plow, but a plow just as good as John Deere's, made in the same place, and the same brand on, 'Moline, Ills.' He also told me that they had Mr. Deere's foreman employed, and that the plow was just exactly like Mr. Deere's, and he said that it would sell just as good on account of having 'Moline, Ills.,' on.[25]

Jaeger's loyalty spoke volumes. "I then told him if I should buy any Moline plows, I would buy none but Mr. John Deere's, because that plow has a large reputation in the country."

Then Swan's tactics crossed the line. According to Jaeger, Swan asserted that it did not matter who the manufacturer was as long as the plow had the words "Moline, Ils." on it, because farmers could not tell the difference. Swan was right. Jaegar repeated conversations with local farmers who had purchased plows that had "Moline, Ill." painted on the beam, assuming they had bought a Deere plow. The reason for the confusion was that they did not identify the manufacturer of either plow and simply purchased the one marked "Moline, Ill.," as they had done for years, only to find that now there were two firms selling under such a name.[26]

It was damaging testimony indeed. Could the lawyers prove that Candee and Swan were intentionally misrepresenting themselves as purveyors of John Deere Plows? Another nine months of testimony delayed any answers.

Spring 1869 brought the much-anticipated testimony of forty-year-old Andrew Friberg, one of the many Swedes who joined the Deere factory upon their first arrival in Moline. So many Swedes worked for Deere that finding English-speaking employees in the plow shops was not always easy, and a prerequisite for a foreman's position was the ability to speak two languages. Hjamer Kohler, arriving in Moline from Grebbestad, Sweden, in 1868, took part-time work translating letters for Deere & Company. "I could not use the most elegant English, but my translations were true," he wrote, "and from time to time I was called upon to translate letters from Sweden and articles in Swedish newspapers pertaining to their plows."[27]

No employee caused more trouble for Deere & Company than the able, intelligent Friberg. He testified that on several occasions Deere had unscrupulously copied the designs of other manufacturers: the two-horse Galena plow and the Diamond Plow mentioned in Tate's testimony were only two of many. Whereas Tate defended his former partner by rationalizing the rampant borrowing of designs among all plow makers, Friberg attacked John Deere's lack of skill and credibility. Hearing about the Diamond Plow made in or around Galesburg, which farmers seemed to like, Deere "went and got one for a pattern; then he went and bought stock for fifty of them," Friberg alleged. "Then he made out a bill of sale of that stock to one of his workmen; so he went to work to help in making the plows, and they sold them. He done that so that the patentee could not come at Mr. Deere for the use of his patent."[28]

On another occasion, Deere copied the Double Michigan Plow. He suspected there was a patent on the cast-steel plow, the casting method, and, as Friberg explained, the general "manner of making it." Deere claimed it was his own patent, when in fact it belonged to "a Mr. Smith of Connecticut." Friberg remembered when Smith came to visit the

Deere factories, and "Mr. Deere told me the day before Mr. Smith came out here, to remove all suspicious things in regard to the cast iron mould and the hardening, and be careful what I said to him when he came to the shop."[29]

In his testimony, Friberg compared Deere & Company's plow with the Moline Plow Company's plow. He was walking delicate ground in trying to prove that Deere copied other companies' plows, while claiming that he himself was an innovator. The designs were not alike, he insisted, and he listed several distinctive features of his own plow, including a lower land side and the positioning of the handle. Furthermore, he continued, "When we commenced making plows we made a long point on them. Mr. Deere, at that time, was making a short point to his plows. When Deere & Co. saw our plows, they commenced making their plows with a longer point, so as to correspond with ours." Deere, Friberg claimed, had stolen *his* designs.[30]

The rest of the defense's line of questioning continued to target Deere's claim as an innovative plow maker. "What is there original about the plows made by you while in the establishment of Mr. John Deere, that was invented or originated by the said John Deere?"

"There is not anything that I know of, or that I can remember," Friberg replied. But even he conceded John Deere's real innovation when asked how the plows manufactured by Deere had been perfected. "In constant improving and experimenting," he stated, "and also having other plows to see and copy parts from."

His comments may have appeared damaging, but the suit was not about copying and improving plow parts. It was, instead, about markings, and neither Friberg nor any other witness to that point had been able to deny the similarities between the two insignias and who had used the markings first. During the cross-examination, John Hawley bombarded Friberg with questions about his own processes and his indebtedness to John Deere.

Deere had taken the Swedish immigrant, who knew almost no English and had never made a plow, into his employ in 1851. Five years later he asked him to oversee the entire shop, but Friberg "did not like to take the responsibility and . . . asked to have another man do that." A year later Deere offered him the job again. After much prodding, Friberg accepted. When he went west during the latter half of the Civil War for health reasons, then returned to Moline to find he had been replaced by Moore, he felt jilted and went to work for Buford & Tate in Rock Island before joining Candee, Swan & Co. When Friberg started there, as Hawley confirmed through a series of questions, to a large extent the business was modeled on Deere & Company. Candee, Swan & Co. had price lists from other companies but fixed their prices primarily according to Deere's. As for the patterns, Friberg skirted the issue, claiming to have "bought some, made some, and one or more (don't remember how many) took out of old plows."

Hawley continued the pursuit. "Where did you buy the blocks you speak of, and from whom?"

"I bought them from Mr. Deere, the biggest part of them; I sent different parties down there to buy them."

"From what old plows, and whose manufacture," Hawley pressed, "did you copy or prepare the block patterns, as spoken of by you?"

"They were Deeres," Friberg finally relented. He had made some of his own patterns and made variations on a few others, but the bulk of the plows from which he had copied were Deere plows.

Tearing yet more holes in Friberg's testimony, Hawley next came to the subject of markings. Friberg had testified that Deere took the idea of marking his plow parts with letters and numbers from other manufacturers, with the implication that he acted deceitfully. "Do you mean by that," Hawley demanded, "that he copied the same letters and numbers, or combinations, or do you simply mean that thereafter he used letters numbers and combinations?"

Again Friberg stumbled. "I don't mean just the same letters and numbers; I meant he got the idea of combining letters and numbers, that is all." By the time he was finished, Friberg had answered 223 questions from Deere's attorney, many of them attacks on his memory, which became hazier as the grilling continued. On one occasion the court broke for lunch, and when the session resumed Friberg tried to amend a previous statement. Coaching was obvious, and distrust between opposing attorneys was growing as quickly as it had between the two companies. But since the case was being tried behind closed doors, the press was banned and the public heard no news about the important case. In the meantime, the two firms continued to work next door to each other in Moline's industrial district.[31]

The Court Decides

As Charles Deere worked tirelessly to iron out the details of the new branch house, visits to his attorneys punctuated the workweek, although these visits became more pleasant as the suit against Candee,

Swan, & Co. progressed. The parade of witnesses called on his company's behalf testified to John Deere's integrity and the value of his products and, in particular, emphasized the company's already long-standing tradition as the maker of the Moline Plow. Evidence showed that Deere & Company had used the name in advertising in the early 1860s, well before the Moline Plow Company was established.

On November 5, 1869, after the case had dragged on for nearly two years, Judge William Heaton, temporarily serving on the Sixth Judicial District Court in the courthouse at Rock Island, made his decision. While Charles Deere focused on the claim to the word "Moline" and what he called the "pirating" of employees, products, and manufacturing processes, the defense had turned the case into a personal attack against John Deere, challenging his integrity at every turn. Heaton took the issue of misrepresentation into serious consideration in his summation. He forbid the Moline Plow Company or any form of the company and its agents to use the current company name and ordered the company to cease advertising, selling, or marking its plows as the "Moline Plow."

Turning to the contested number system, Heaton declared that the Moline Plow Company was "forever restrained and enjoined from" imitating Deere's letters, numbers, and combinations of the two in marking individual parts of implements. Also, the Moline Plow Company name—past, present, or future—could in no way be stenciled on the plow beam in a circular form "in imitation of the complainants' brand."[32]

The ruling was a victory for Deere & Company, but it was not a conclusive victory. Judge Heaton transferred all depositions, printed evidence, and case files to the Illinois State Supreme Court in Ottawa. The defense had thirty days to appeal. Candee, Swan & Co. wasted no time.

Ongoing construction of the new Deere & Company buildings near Main Street was a constant reminder to the stockholders of the company's success. Compared to large, spreading cities like New York or Philadelphia, Moline's borders remained compact. The town's factories still depended on the Mississippi River for their most basic power and transport needs. Competitors, as the case of Deere and the Moline Plow Company showed, were still neighbors both in business and at home. Robert Swan, Henry Candee, and John and Charles Deere all lived within a few blocks of each other. Familiar faces of friends and of enemies alike were seen daily in the windows of Moline's storefronts.

Despite the appeal by Candee and Swan, the decision against the Moline Plow Company must have at least given some temporary satisfaction to Charles Deere. Generally a man of few words, he had publicly defended his father's name and reputation in the face of dishonesty. John Deere's reputation rested on quality and integrity, and the majority of his customers were returning buyers who had formed a personal relationship with the company's network of salesman throughout the Midwest. Charles was fighting hard to strengthen that relationship in his father's name, and so far he had succeeded.

Plows dominated the Deere & Company product line in 1870, as they always had and would for the rest of the century, although variations and specialization in the company's essential product became increasingly important as Deere's plows spread to farms across the country. Deere's general product catalogs now dedicated their first pages to a history of the plow, which dated back to a time when a stick sharpened to a point was the only farming implement available. Deere & Company's 1871 catalog boasted on its cover Deere's "Celebrated Moline Plow," the "Improved Hawkeye Cultivator," and Deere's "Walking Cultivator." The Hawkeye corn cultivator had been introduced in 1864 as the company's first riding machine and had since become a farm favorite. Catalogs bragged that the cultivator was manufactured to the point of perfection: for the past three years the company had received no complaints or suggestions for improvement. Quality and integrity continued to drive the company's mechanics, salesmen, and office force, but the looming appeal by the Moline Plow Company threatened the company's reputation and dominance of the market.

The appeal process made any celebration of Heaton's verdict both uneasy and premature; so the battle between the two firms continued unabated in catalogs and circulars. Deere & Company went to great lengths to differentiate its own plows from "confessedly inferior imitations" and to vaunt its own improvements for which the "uniform reliability, strength, finish and working qualities of The Genuine Moline Plow is universally acknowledged," as the 1871 catalog declared, with the emphasis on the *Genuine* Moline Plow. "The high reputation which our Plows have achieved and enjoyed for nearly a quarter of a century, under the name of Moline Plow, is well illustrated in the fact that other manufacturers have sought to and are fraudulently appropriating *the name*. . . . Any others purporting to be the Moline Plow, are fraudulent imitations gotten up to deceive the farmer."[33]

The Moline Plow Company tenaciously held to its claim as the oldest practical plow maker while Illinois Supreme Court continued to review the appeal. Finally, as spring knocked on Moline's door in early 1871, the case was put to rest. On March 11, 1871, the *Daily Davenport*

Democrat, which had provided the most complete and up-to-date news on the ongoing trademark battle in Moline, reported the court's decision. The verdict was far different than what Charles Deere had hoped it would be.

Illinois Supreme Court Associate Justice Sidney Breese, recognizing that the case was one of very great importance, announced the court's conclusions. There were several points at issue. It was true that, when John Deere moved from Grand Detour to Moline, he formed several partnerships. Yet Deere had been the lead partner in each of them, and his work and perseverance were the primary forces behind his company's rise from a one-man operation to one of the largest manufacturers of farm equipment in the United States. Enjoying a monopoly over the trade for more than twenty years, his company had prospered, and the field plow had been greatly improved upon through his careful study of the successes of others and his ability to reconcile those ideas with his own. Breese recognized Deere's ability to identify and incorporate improvement, conceding that "his great recognition and praise is, that he had the sagacity to discern to what profitable use the inventions of others could be applied, and by a well directed judgment he has constructed a plow not inferior to any in use in our wide-spread agricultural community, all which entitles him to as much credit as if an original inventor."[34]

Having thus trudged through the question of John Deere's claim to the invention of the steel plow—a claim Deere had never made in the first place—the court moved to the pressing question of trademark. After citing a number of definitions from legal texts and treatises, the judge examined Deere and Company's contention that it held the exclusive right to the markings. According to the evidence, a Deere & Co. circular dated 1859 showed neither a trademark nor any mention of the words "Moline, Ill," or "Moline Plow." Instead, the circular used the name "John Deere." The Supreme Court considered this evidence "an abandonment of any claim to the words 'Moline, Ill.' or 'Moline Plow,' as their trade mark, and the mark being a trade mark by being placed on the beam, is a virtual disclaimer of all rights to any other, claimed in circulars and price lists." While noting the obvious similarities between the two company's semicircular logos, Breese pointed out that the names of the respective manufacturers were not at all similar. He noted that the name of "Candee, Swan, & Co." was so much longer than "John Deere" and that the letters of the former were so much larger that, even at a glance, the differences would be noticeable.[35]

Furthermore, Breese found no evidence of intentional misrepresentation. Even though both companies were selling Moline Plows, the Moline Plow Company did not claim to be selling on behalf of John Deere, and, because Deere had no registered trademark, the Moline Plow Company was acting within the law. In addition, because Deere & Company had no patents on the shape of the plows, anyone could legally copy them, down to the smallest detail.

The entire case led to a larger question for the Supreme Court. The exclusive use of a town's name by one manufacturer was a move toward monopoly, Breese declared. In keeping with the public sentiment of the day, he castigated "odious" monopolies and proclaimed that nothing could be more abhorrent than a monopoly on the manufacturing of plows. In his final remarks, he harshly reprimanded John and Charles Deere. The only fault of the Moline Plow Company was "their audacity, in so interfering" with the "monopoly appellees had created." The court further denied "any discussion of the questions presented by the supplemental bill, deeming it unnecessary; satisfied, as we are, that appellees have no standing in a court of equity."[36] Thus ended the case. The Moline Plow Company could manufacture Deere look-alikes free from challenge.

In October, after a vacation in Hot Springs, Arkansas, with Mary and his daughters, Charles Deere was in Ottawa, Illinois, fighting for another hearing, but the court proved immovable. The judge had decided, once and for all, that both companies had the right to continue to manufacture plows of the highest quality as they deemed best. Robert Tate, weary of the entire case, wanted to move on. "The injunction served on the Moline Plow Company has been removed, and I hope there will be no more of it," he confided to his diary.[37]

Charles had lost the case, but he learned valuable lessons in the process. First, Deere & Company's claim to its heritage, its integrity, and the quality of its products were all essential to the company's reputation. In future attempts to corner the plow market, he would remember Breese's unsubtle warning against his company's domination of the industry. He had also taken a valuable lesson in protecting his investments. But above all else, he now knew who his friends were.

Although Moline appeared the center of the agricultural universe, the court's overturning of what became a landmark case in the trademark world was far from the most dramatic events unfolding in the agricultural market. During the unending summer of 1871, the United States was suffering from severe drought, and, as a result, business was also drying up; however, while others suffered, Deere & Company showed no sign of slowing down. Profits continued to rise, and the Kansas City branch house experiment gave all indications of success.

Long past the mischievous days of his youth, Charles had grown into one of the state's most widely recognized business magnates. His company had not experienced the overwhelming financial boom enjoyed by the railroads, but a steady course had resulted in great stability and controlled growth. Taking advantage of technological innovations, particularly the railroad, Deere & Company adapted to the times but continued to hold on to the hard-earned traditions of its past. Charles continued his soft-spoken ways, but his reputation for shrewd, decisive action was fast growing. The personal habits and contrasting management styles of father and son were also becoming more evident as John stepped further away from the company's operations. It was a foreseeable shift. Much more in tune with the rapidly changing world, Charles continued to push the company toward new frontiers. His father, meanwhile, dedicated his energies to Moline's future.

For Charles, strict warnings against monopoly came as an unexpected rebuke, because he and his father had clearly earned every bit of their success. But now, it became clear, his success and role as standard-bearer had made him a target for less-capable speculators. A new era of vulnerability, the uneasy period of transition between the company's hard-earned successes, and impending public fears of industry domination was unavoidably upon them.

MOLINE, ILL.

Supply and Demand

By the early 1870s, John and Charles Deere were going separate ways, professionally speaking. John retained a local focus, as the era of big business with all of its intricacies had grown well beyond his adaptive capacity. Charles, on the other hand, rose to the challenge, and his efforts increasingly pushed him into the national spotlight. Although John still took an active interest in the business, presiding over board meetings and finding time to work in the shop on occasion, he spent his winters in California and had all but retired from the plow business to devote himself to his Moline farm.

Charles Deere was in many ways an anomaly: a soft-spoken entrepreneur who shied away from personal praise and criticism, preferring to run his operations from behind closed doors. While his father's political interests led him to the mayor's office in Moline, where he focused on infrastructure development, Charles strove to maintain the expansion of his company amid growing resistance from a new organization of farmers—the Grange. In the coming years, Charles would struggle with this underground movement and its attempts to undermine the fabric of his business.

Moline's town limits had crept closer to Rock Island during the 1860s, until many thought that the two towns would soon become one. This merger never occurred, despite the new churches, homes, and businesses springing up on the southern edge of Moline, pressing its limits to the foot of the bluffs that sandwiched the town between the mighty Mississippi River and the lush hills to the south.

Morally and politically, the City of Mills traded the atrocities of the Civil War for the social crusades of its aftermath, particularly the temperance movement and the rebalancing of the middle and working classes. The industrialization of America brought waves of immigrants to the United States, and by the 1870s organizations working on behalf of the laboring class were beginning to create new issues for corporate managers who had never before needed to negotiate wages and shop conditions with their employees. Moline, which the *Daily Davenport Democrat* in July 1869 called "a first class Puritan town," was accustomed to a way of life that conflicted with the cultures of hundreds of German, Irish, and, most recently, Swedish immigrants who had found work in the factories along its riverfront. The influx of immigrants, combined with the repeal of many prohibition laws at the conclusion of the Civil War, created a tense social environment in cities around the country. As he had done in local abolition campaigns before the Civil War, John Deere again threw himself into the heat of the battle. He understood the opposing sides of the temperance issue as well as anyone and sought the middle ground. A New Englander by birth, like many of Moline's original settlers, Deere held tight to his moral temperament, though it often caused conflict with the immigrant population that flocked to Moline to work in his factory.[1]

Mayor Deere

John Deere's name was synonymous with Moline. He frequently attended meetings of Moline's early settlers, cofounded the First National Bank, and financially supported local schools and churches for twenty-five years. He was a trustee and deacon of the First Congregational Church, and when a new building for its growing congregation was completed in 1870 and the cost had overrun capital, Deere started the fund-raising with a $1,000 pledge.[2]

Religion had always been a guiding force of his life, and, although a devout Congregationalist like his mother, he gave to churches regardless of their denomination or location. In 1871, for example, he gave $112 to the Thomas Jewitt Sunday School. In February 1873 a donation earned him the title of Life Director of the Chicago-based American Home Missionary Society. Over the next several years, he gave to Moline's Swedish Lutheran Church, the Chicago Theological Seminary, Rock Island's Augustana College, and his son's alma mater, Knox College in Galesburg. He would later become a trustee of Knox College as well.[3]

Deere was not Moline's only benefactor. The manufacturing facilities and mills along the river had made many men rich, men who believed that with prosperity came a moral obligation to Moline's less fortunate citizens. Controlling every aspect of an employee's life, manufacturers ran the saloons where their employees drank, owned the homes in which they lived, and sold them the food they ate. They were fulfilling their civic obligations, and, of course, they stood to gain.

In 1872, many of those businessmen, all amateur politicians by virtue of their moral and religious responsibilities, looked to Moline's future. On April 10, Moline was incorporated as a city; in August the townspeople held their first election. The election provided Deere an opportunity to become the designated moral and financial leader of a city split by the temperance controversy that was deciding many elections nationwide. In the absence of official statistics from Moline for the period prior to the town's first mayoral election, comparisons can be made with Davenport, its neighbor across the river. Between April 1, 1871, and April 1, 1872, Davenport recorded 312 violations for intoxication. The next most frequent crime was disturbing the peace, with 128 violations, followed by vagrancy at seventy-two violations, and "keeping house of ill-fame" at sixteen. Davenport elected strong, Democratic candidates in favor of temperance in April 1872, and Moline also appeared to be leaning in that direction.[4]

The earliest liquor regulation in Moline was an ordinance passed in 1853, which permitted the sale of liquor only in quantities of more than one quart and only for mechanical and medicinal purposes. Moline's city charter of 1855 included the stronger Neal Dow Law of Maine, passed in June 1851, which prohibited liquor sales *in any amount* except for mechanical and medicinal purposes. The charter also gave Moline's board of trustees power to regulate or prohibit liquor in town, a power they put to use from 1858 to 1861 and again from 1864 to 1867.[5]

By the time of Moline's first mayoral election, crusaders fighting "America's besetting evil" were at their strongest. Moline was a devotedly Republican town, and its first election pitted John Deere against temperance advocate Daniel Wheelock. The families knew each other well, because Charles Deere continued to compete with Daniel's entrepreneurial brother, Stillman Wheelock, who only the year before had saved the Moline Plow Company from bankruptcy during the bitter trademark case. Daniel Wheelock was also familiar to voters. Only a week before the town's incorporation, he had been elected as one of Moline's four trustees, a position that incorporation now made obsolete.

Moline's citizens were not the only ones considering temperance; nearby Chicagoans were facing the same debate. In 1872 Chicago's mayor ordered the closing of all bars and saloons on the Sabbath. The *Chicago Tribune* came to the defense of the targeted population—immigrants. "Beer is the national beverage of the German," the paper declared. "He has drank [*sic*] it daily from youth up. It is the bread and meat of the peasant, and as indispensable to him as water to the American laborer."[6]

On election day, the citizens of Moline voted 368 to 192 in favor of Wheelock, although a short election cycle granted the new mayor only a short, seven-month term in which there was little time to accomplish anything. In the meantime, in November, Moliners helped to reelect Republican president Ulysses Grant, who had openly denounced temperance during the campaign. Only months after the presidential election, Moline again went to the polls. On April 16, 1873, John Deere won the city's second election by a landslide.

At its last meeting before Deere took office, the outgoing city council voted to revoke the licenses of saloons in Moline. The new council, however, was deadlocked on the issue and brought it back for a vote. Mayor Deere was to cast the deciding vote, but he instead suggested that the question go before the people. Theoretically the move was a democratic gesture, although Deere felt certain that the small number of temperance crusaders, no matter how influential they were, would be soundly defeated. The result was chaos.

Moline's twenty-eight saloons fought adamantly for an extension of their licenses against the opposition of local churches, the newly created Reform Club, and other social crusaders. Main Street now became the stage for protest. Opponents of prohibition drove a loaded beer wagon from Rock Island into the heart of Moline, providing drink for a large street party that soon drew a large crowd of temperance advocates who tried to disrupt the festivities. Mayor Deere ordered city police marshal Follett to disperse the crowd, but, unable to control it with a force of five policemen and "receiving some very unpleasant remarks from a high official in authority" (likely Deere himself), Follet resigned on the spot. "It was a disgraceful affair," declared one paper.[7]

Deere practiced temperance himself, but with Deere & Company's German, Belgian, and Swedish employees at the center of the debate, he had to consider the consequences for his business. The issue also had larger fiscal implications for the city. Income from saloon licenses was Moline's largest source of revenue, amounting to $4,300 in the year ending in April 1875, and, if city violations reached anywhere near Davenport's numbers, fines generated a sizable income. Having witnessed enough protest, Deere used the city council's split to his advantage to push a liquor license ordinance that gave the mayor the sole power to grant or refuse all liquor licenses. Because the people could not come to a sensible agreement, he took the matter into his own hands. He was running Moline as he had run his business, although in this case there was more room for compromise.[8]

Deere's ordinance allowed the sale of liquor but severely regulated saloons, causing "hard conditions," or so the *Argus* asserted. Saloons could operate only on the ground floor, and the bar had to be in clear view of the street so police could patrol without entering. No liquor could be sold between ten at night and five in the morning, or between ten o'-clock Saturday night and five in the morning on Monday. Cards, dice, and billiards were also illegal during the weekend hours. "Such a law in Germany would result in a revolution in less than 24 hours after its passage," wrote the *Argus* editor in disgust, "and yet we boast of personal rights and personal liberty."[9]

Meanwhile, reformers lamented that the saloons could operate at all. The recently established *Moline Review* cried in despair, "Oh, Moline! What has become of thy moral atmosphere?"[10] By offering a compromise, Deere had lost the approval of both camps.

Fortunately for Deere, the temperance battle would not be his only legacy as mayor. He deserves credit for dramatic infrastructure improvements and the elimination of corruption. In the midst of complaints of impropriety, Deere replaced Riverside Cemetery's board of trustees with a board of directors appointed by the city. Also at his direction, the city paid $15,000 for eighty-three acres of farmland owned by William Mill and Jackson Bell for the creation of a city park. Other beautification and infrastructure efforts during his term included the long-overdue construction and repair of sidewalks and streets as well as the installation of street lighting throughout the city. "We like the generous way in which Mayor Deere and Street Commissioner Head are giving their attention to the streets," the *Moline Review* wrote less than three months after Deere took office. "Men and teams are consistently at work, and what is better, there is evidence that something is accomplished." But there was still plenty to do. The street commissioner was asked to provide lanterns for sections where workers were removing entire sections of sidewalks without notice, causing nasty falls in the dark. A year later, Deere appropriated $10,000 for additional work on the streets and alleys.[11]

In a time when no homes had indoor plumbing, outhouses were the norm, and the contamination of public water was a constant threat to citizens of a growing city unprepared for the collection of waste. Deere spearheaded a series of public health initiatives. The cholera epidemic of 1873 had claimed at least forty lives in Moline. Now, under Deere's direction, the city began to replace a haphazard network of open drains with separate sewer pipes to prevent contamination.

Equally pressing, especially in the manufacturing district, was the need for an adequate system of fire prevention. The devastation of the Great Chicago Fire in October 1871 was an all-too-eerie reminder of Moline's own great fire in May 1855, which destroyed the stores of Benson Bros, S. P. Hodges, John Burt, and Chamberlain & Dean, resulting in estimated losses of $20,000. Moline's riverfront factories were built close together, connected by a maze of train tracks and streets. The Moline Plow Company, Wheelock's Paper Manufactory, and the Deere & Company factories stood adjacent to one another, sandwiched between the Mississippi River and Main Street, along with furniture factories, flourmills, and other businesses. The spread of the fire of 1855 demonstrated that one small blaze had the potential to destroy the entire district.[12]

Though far from home, the Great Chicago Fire was nonetheless devastating to the Deere family. Since John Deere passed through in 1836, Chicago had grown into the most important city west of the Appalachian Mountains. With a population of 300,000, by 1871 the city had become an industrial Mecca, with 21 mainline railroad tracks, 12 bridges, and 530 miles of street. From the elegance of Michigan Avenue's Terrace Row to a room in the recently completed Palmer House on the corner of State Street and Monroe, Chicago's charm could not be equaled anywhere in the Midwest. On Sunday evening, October 8, 1871, just after nine o'clock, that charm turned to horror as a fire broke out in the barn behind the home of Patrick and Catherine O'Leary at 13 DeKoven Street. The city had already witnessed more than two dozen fires during the preceding week. That night it was entirely engulfed in flames.

Upon hearing of the fire, Charles boarded the first train to Chicago, arriving to find only the smoldering ashes of the city that had become his second home. The two limestone wings of the courthouse, only recently finished, stood gutted and charred; between them, the wooden main structure lay in ashes. The fire's devastation was "more widespread, soul-sickening desolation than mortal eye ever beheld since the destruction of Jerusalem," wrote the *Chicago Tribune*. "Everything had disappeared." The tragedy struck the Deere family on a very intimate level. Mary Deere's parents, Gideon and Judith Dickenson, lost their home and soon moved to Moline.[13]

Back in Moline, the Chicago fire provided Mayor John Deere with the impetus to sign a thirty-year contract with the owners of the newly formed Moline Water Power Company, Charles Atkinson, Charles Deere, and John Gould. The water company agreed to lay 5,000 feet of pipe before July 1, 1875, with another 5,000 feet in 1876 and another in 1877. Extensions were planned whenever the spread of the city required. The city committed itself to building hydrants at 400-foot intervals. In the first year, the city installed thirteen street hydrants; twelve more went up in each of the next two years. In addition, Moline agreed to pay for the use of the water at an annual rate of eighty dollars for each hydrant for ten years and then a reduced rate of sixty dollars per year per hydrant.[14]

The improved waterworks laid the groundwork for the establishment of a regular fire department in December 1873, replacing the volunteer fire company that had protected Moline for the past two decades. Eighteen months later, the fire department proved its worth. On a dry Tuesday afternoon, the straw room of Stillman Wheelock's paper mill went up in flames, and, of the hundreds who rushed to the scene, the *Argus* commented, "there were those in that anxious group who fancied they saw only the smouldering [*sic*] embers of two of Moline's best and most enterprising establishments, and imagined their livelihood gone." Wheelock learned his lesson. Five days after the fire, he replaced his wooden straw room with one of brick. In time Deere & Company, the Moline Plow Company, and other downtown businesses organized their own fire brigades to complement the city's fire department.[15]

Deere spent two years in office, but the onset of chest pains and chronic dysentery that at one point forced him to take an extensive leave of absence, forced him to retire and not seek reelection in 1875. He was probably grateful not to be the scapegoat a few years later when a mule pulling a wagon of beer was found drunk outside of a Moline saloon![16]

"The Farmer's War"

Upon completion of his mayoral term, John Deere, who had temporarily resigned from Deere & Company's board of directors, was reelected its chairman. He was often absent, spending his winters in California and making frequent trips to visit family and friends in Vermont. Meanwhile, Charles was beginning to appear more and more often in the Chicago papers and agricultural journals—and not always for enviable reasons. With the country on the verge of another depression and farmers suffering from a national drought, the financial divide between

Deere & Company executives and the farmers buying their products seemed to be growing. The company's competition was facing the same criticism, but Charles Deere's personal attachment to his employees and his customers led him to speak publicly about his operations for the first time.

Aware that conspicuous evidence of his personal fortune would, in the public eye, indicate the prosperity of his company, Charles began construction of Moline's most impressive mansion. After purchasing land high atop the bluff overlooking the sprawling Deere & Company factories, Charles hired a progressive, white-haired architect from Chicago named William LeBaron Jenney to build his home. Noted for his engineering brilliance during the Civil War, Jenney had designed Union fortifications at Corinth, Shiloh, and Vicksburg. His architecture would help transform Chicago after the Great Fire. His Home Insurance Building, built in 1884–85, for example, was the first steel-framed skyscraper. In 1891, he designed the second Leiter Building on South State Street.[17]

When complete, Deere's modern Victorian-style house was indeed magnificent. Boasting nearly 5,000 square feet of floor space, with rising turrets and spires of the "Swiss Villa"–style roof, it sat majestically upon the bluff. Visitors would arrive at the lavish mansion via a driveway that wrapped around the hill and delivered them to a covered carriageway on the home's west side. Inside, the house displayed three floors copiously furnished with the most modern amenities, all of which were continuously updated with the latest designs from New York and Europe.

Instead of playing near the manufacturing facilities near their home on the northwest corner of Ann and Atkinson streets, young Anna, age nine, and Katherine, age seven, roamed the expansive halls, unending rooms, and rolling gardens of the mansion. Overlook, as Charles and Mary named the mansion, even included running water. At the time, the Moline Water Power Company was moving toward an agreement with the city for a contract to build a municipal water works. "Private enterprise is always ahead of the public," claimed the *Moline Review*. "Charles Deere proposes to enjoy the luxury of water works in advance of the city.[18]

Overlook represented a fundamental difference between Charles and his father, who continued to live a modest lifestyle. John traveled extensively, but not lavishly, and remained in the Main Street house he had occupied for more than twenty years. Charles, on the other hand, felt no guilt about spending the money he had labored so hard to earn. He had not inherited a fortune, and he was in many ways as much a self-made man as his father, yet some chose to see him as a spoiled boy who had ridden his father's coattails. He made no apologies for his growing wealth and influence and merely continued with business as usual.

Construction at Overlook was only a minor distraction for Charles. What demanded most of his energy at this time was the rise of a new labor organization pitted against the nation's largest implement producers. Discontented citizens pointed to the widening gap between Moline's working class and the opulence of its growing upper crust, which Overlook symbolized only too vividly. The gap was brought to the attention of the American public in 1873 in a biased book entitled *The History of the Grange Movement or the Farmer's War against Monopolies*. Citing the "great Railroad Monopolies that have sprung up in our midst" and the inauguration of "a series of abuses which have gradually and effectually undermined the solid finances" of the farmer, the book's author, Edward Winslow Martin, sought support for an agricultural movement that had been gaining momentum since the early days of the Civil War. Martin placed the blame for the farmer's woes primarily on railroads, the "coal ring," and the federal government, but he condemned implement makers as well.[19]

The Order of the Patrons of Husbandry, better known as the Grange, was officially founded on December 4, 1867, in Washington, D.C., by a group of clerks and other government officials at the impetus of Oliver Hudson Kelley, a former reporter and self-taught farmer working in the newly formed U.S. Department of Agriculture. During a tour of several Southern states at the request of President Andrew Johnson, Kelley was struck by the farmers' low standard of living, which he attributed to excessive prices for land and equipment, on the one hand, and low market prices for crops, on the other. After more than a year of discussions with members of the Department of Agriculture, the Department of the Treasury, and key Washington insiders, Kelley created a secret society of farmers to put pressure on the corporate businessmen responsible for the bloated cost of farm implements.

At first farmers hesitated to join a secret society, but the Grange soon spread across the country as Kelley organized new branches in Washington, and then in Harrisburg, Pennsylvania, and Fredonia, New York. The hierarchical structure included local, or "subordinate," granges and county and state granges, with the National Grange, located in Washington, D.C., at the top.

The Grange's mission was general and straightforward: increase the wealth, happiness, and prosperity of farmers. Its underlying tenant was that the basis of all wealth comes from the soil, and therefore farmers had more of a claim to the rewards of national prosperity than anyone else. The Grange vowed to educate farmers and—more important—to organize "intimate social relations and acquaintance . . . for the advancement and elevation of their pursuits *with an appreciation and protection of their true interests.*"[20]

To this end, the Grange created social and intellectual opportunities never before offered to the country's most prevalent profession. Still, its intent was more specific. Kelley, himself a failure in most of his farming endeavors, founded the order as an organized attack on big business. Earning revenues of more than $1 million for the first time in 1875, Deere & Company was one of the largest equipment manufacturers in the country.

The Grange itself took on all the machinations of a secret society. Earned titles included the Gate Keeper, Master, Overseer, Lecturer, Steward, and Chaplain, and biblically laced meetings began with an invocation and ended with a benediction. Women also played an influential role in the movement, because they were accepted on equal merit and allowed to take the ceremonial titles of ancient Greek and Roman goddesses such as Ceres, goddess of grain. The organization was, however, far from ceremonial. The Grange fought on a number of fronts: railroads, banks, land speculators, and above all, the implement-peddling middleman. In January 1873, the national Grange office adopted a constitution, and by October the number of subordinate Granges reached 6,914. The first Grange in Illinois started in the offices of the Chicago-based magazine *Prairie Farmer* in April 1868, but through 1872 only seven more had been established in the state. Those numbers were about to change.

The Grange "has grown by the process of nature, out of the pressing wants of the time; and it has spread and waxed strong steadily and rapidly ever since it came into existence," reported the *New York Tribune.* "Within a few weeks it has menaced the political equilibrium of the most steadfast States." Granges had begun to develop an internal network of manufacturing facilities and dealers in an attempt to bypass implement companies altogether and prevent "combinations of any kind." Not only would such moves cut the profits of the manufacturers but, if successful, would eliminate the detested middleman who was the first to profit from increased prices. The Grange's program created a dilemma for Charles Deere, because in most respects Deere & Company was working toward the same goals as the Grange: less reliance on credit, wider distribution of information through printed material, education of farmers, and lower manufacturing costs. The only difference was that Deere also aimed to make a handsome profit, and for that reason the Grange saw Deere and his fellow manufacturers as the enemy.[21]

Deere & Company was itself working in conjunction with a larger group of Midwest implement manufacturers that had first met in Chicago in 1864 to discuss the rising costs of steel and other materials as well as the early rumblings of loosely organized farmers. George Vinton represented Deere & Company at the initial meeting. The group met again in June to formalize what would soon be called the Northwestern Plow Makers Association (N.P.M.A.), with Colonel John Dement of Dixon, Illinois, as president and Charles Deere as secretary.[22]

Steel prices continued to rise through 1864, posing a serious threat to Deere and his colleagues. According to the *Prairie Farmer,* the country's premier agricultural journal, it cost one dollar more to make a plow in October 1863 than it had in October 1862. Between 1861 and 1864, the prices of lumber, coal, and pig iron almost tripled, and years of war had further crippled the demand for skilled labor. In reaction to the rise in prices, members of the N.P.M.A. agreed to increase the base price of plows and similar products, then prepared for the customers' reaction. Some of the manufacturers pressed for a drastic price increase and a greater profit margin while others, led by Deere, advocated a "medium advance" in price. The group had first come together in the interest of controlling such costs, and, although Deere would be publicly accused of using the group to raise prices over the coming years, in reality the price of plows was kept within reasonable bounds thanks largely to his efforts.[23]

In the manufacturers' view, the N.P.M.A. was working toward a mutually beneficial relationship between themselves and their customers. Farmers, however, suspected collusion and conspiracy on the part of some of the country's largest agricultural implement manufacturers. In the decade since the group's founding in 1864, N.P.M.A. members had strengthened their position. As he always did, Deere took accusations of corruption personally. Refusing to be intimidated, the N.P.M.A. continued to meet throughout the summer of 1873 and into the winter to discuss the growing influence of the Grange, which, according to the *New York Tribune,* "was not the origin of the Farmer's movement" but so far its "only outgrowth."[24]

In November, the N.P.M.A. again met at the Matteson House in Chicago. Member companies agreed to sell their plows only at retail prices and to offer no discounts to Granges or similar farmer clubs. Exceptions, of course, would be made for large orders paid in cash. This exception was permitted because cash sales reduced administrative and bank fees, which accounted for some of the retail markup. Most of all, it eliminated risk. Charles Deere arduously defended the cash system. The lessons of several financial panics had convinced him that a cash system was the only way to secure payment on goods and keep his business in good standing. "While we want to do a large business and intend to do all we can to make ours so," he wrote to his cousin and one of his traveling salesman, A. F. Vinton, in 1872, "we cannot do it by loose manner of trading or a long credit system. . . . You know well the necessity of selling to good houses, and while we do not want to miss any of them where it is desirable for us to sell, we cannot give them the old line of credit and continue in the business."[25]

Just as his father had faced divided interests on the question of temperance, Charles was now caught in the middle of a problem with no clear solution. On one side, steel barons continued to raise prices, which in turn raised Deere & Company's production costs. On the other side, farmers were pushing for reduced equipment prices, which, if Deere capitulated, would eliminate any profit margin. Such a chain of events would prevent investment in high product development costs, and in no time Deere & Company would be unable to compete. As it was, Deere continued to struggle to collect payment on previous credit purchases.

Another severe financial panic gripped the nation and pushed Deere further toward the cash system. Failing banks and hard-pressed railroad companies only added to the plight of the implement giants with escalating interest rates and transportation costs. "I am considerably waked up about collections and propose to make that my business this winter and sales shall be a secondary consideration," Deere declared again to Vinton a month after his previous letter. "It is costing so much money to run our business since these high prices of iron and steel that we have *got to have our pay,* and we don't propose to send any party goods unless he has paid up."[26]

Chicago was the country's railroad hub, and its powerful board of trade controlled the price of grain and other commodities. Hence, the city became the central focus of the Grange's activity. The farmers' chief target was the manufacturer Cyrus McCormick, who was most famous for the development of the mechanical reaper. Since his first patent in 1834, McCormick had done for the harvesting of grain what John Deere had done for the plow, though much more ruthlessly. McCormick frequently undercut the competition, paid his dealers less, and required them personally to pay freight charges for the machines they shipped.

Whenever the market allowed, he raised prices. So far he had gotten away with his tactics because, even at an outrageous initial price, his thresher was a sound farm investment. Well protected by a number of patents, it dramatically reduced labor costs and increased crop yields. By 1864, the McCormick reaper had already "yielded its inventor a princely income."[27]

By virtue of his reputation and proximity, McCormick bore the first wave of the farmers' attack. Yet, ignoring both the Grange and the N.P.M.A., he continued with business as usual. His company thought that the Grange posed no cause for alarm. Besides, there was "no law to prevent people making fools of themselves," as one office clerk wrote. Apparently, McCormick planned to wait for the Grange simply to go away and, in the meantime, to use it to his advantage. In 1873, he agreed to bypass the middleman and began selling directly to Grangers at factory prices for cash. Grangers were buying at reduced costs, and, to the displeasure of the N.P.M.A. and other competitors, McCormick had again undercut them and simultaneously retained his profit margin.[28]

In March 1873, two Granges organized in Rock Island County, and over the succeeding months newspapers reported railroad strikes and farmers lobbying in Springfield and Washington. In December, the N.P.M.A. met again and agreed on standardized price lists. Just two months earlier, Deere had drastically reduced prices. The price of an eight-inch steel plow, for example, dropped from $10.50 to $8.00. In 1875, Deere agents were selling eight-inch plows at a target price of $9.50, splitting the difference in the extreme prices of the previous two seasons. Nevertheless, the Grangers showed no signs of compromise with what they called the "Plow Ring." After its own meeting that same month, the Grange opted for a boycott.[29]

Normally reclusive and reluctant to comment publicly on the Grange, Charles Deere now spoke up. In January 1874, as his father fought temperance crusaders in Moline, Charles sat down with a reporter from the *Chicago Tribune*. To the reporter's surprise, Deere was very free in his discussion. Even more surprisingly, although Deere openly disagreed with the Grangers' tactics, his comments showed a desire to work with, not against, them to control prices. "Rightly directed, much good will grow out of it [the Grange]," he asserted, and he urged the Grange not to overlook the cash system as a promising solution. Indeed, he felt that the cause of the current price inflation was the continued use and abuse of the credit system, specifically the high cost of credit to farmers and their inability to remove themselves from the crushing constraints of debt.

Deere cited the prosperity of farmers over the last several decades, which was stimulated by "legitimate demand." Strenuous competition had lowered prices, providing farmers with otherwise unavailable financing options "by which the farmer has been involved in debt for much that he could more profitably have got along without." The farmer also could help himself by maintaining his equipment. Deere estimated that careless treatment cost farmers "millions yearly."[30]

Deere noted the dangerous expansion of agricultural implement companies and their extended networks of dealers and agents, which only "overload the purchasers, involving an unhealthy and unsafe credit system." But, he stressed, "this is not an evil of monopoly, but of competition." The *Tribune*'s reporter, whose questions hinted at a dislike for the implement giants, suggested a "fair division of territory" and reduction of agents. "That would be monopoly instead of competition," Deere lunged back, "and monopoly in its most offensive form. It would be an attempt to make a farmer buy one brand of plows in one county and another brand in another county."

The reporter next raised another contentious point. Could farmers "dispense with the services of the middleman?"

"They cannot succeed," Deere responded sharply. "They cannot improve upon the Natural Laws of Trade." In short, farmers had always enjoyed the privilege of selecting from a large stock of implements carried by dealers and salesman as well as the convenience of returning to the same salesman for repairs and new parts. "When the poor emigrant has secured a homestead, and, with the last vestige of his means, has put up a little shanty, he finds that he needs implements to till the soil," what can he do? "He goes to the middleman, tells him he has nothing left, and asks to be trusted for the things which are indispensable to his success. The middleman has confidence in his honesty, and gives him credit and, with it, a substantial start in life."

Deere's observations on the financial risks incurred by manufacturers and of the role of the middleman were a savvy dig at the Grange's lack of organization and inability to provide such service. He had outlined several important steps toward a mutually satisfying solution: the adoption of the cash system, the maintenance of equipment, the extension of credit only when necessary, and the continuation of fair, albeit limited, competition. Why, then, could the Grange not be included in manufacturing plans if Deere truly believe that if "rightly directed, much good will grow out of it"?

The Grange was still in its infancy and as yet unorganized, Deere suggested, and at present its inadequacies were merely a matter of the economics of scale. Grangers had no distribution system and could not arrange large quantities of orders to ship in bulk. With twenty-five principal companies already supplying the Western market with a limited amount of space on railroad cars, distribution would become a nightmare. A railroad car could hold 150 plows, or 100 cultivators, and organizing shipments from twenty-five suppliers for shipment to a particular agent would be impossible. Wait times would be extended, repair parts longer in coming, and extra costs would inevitably fall upon the farmer.

The reporter next interrogated Deere about price fixing, specifically the Deere & Company pricing system and the flexibility of its agents. Deere provided a forthright explanation. Dealers were allowed to charge customers up to a maximum amount set by the front office; their profit equaled the difference between the manufacturing price and the retail price. Their ability to sell would dictate their own income. Deere controlled overcharging to some degree by setting a maximum price on each implement but could not always control what his agents did at the point of sale. In essence, if anyone was to blame it was the middleman, however indispensable, for companies were the only checks upon exorbitant pricing in the field.

Deere & Company's catalogs listed three prices: a manufacturing price, a dealer price, and a retail price (the maximum dollar amount a dealer could charge for an implement). The overall markup between the figures depended on the item's popularity, the interchangeability of parts with other machines, and the overall manufacturing costs. The No. 1 clipper plow, for example, had a manufacturing cost of $10.25 and a retail list price of $26.00. The dealer paid around $16.00 for the plow, which gave him ten dollars of bargaining space with his customers. A heavier, twenty-four-inch breaker plow cost $19.70 to make, sold to dealers for about $31.00, and carried a retail list price of $51.00. That system had been in place at Deere since Grand Detour and the first days in Moline. In 1854, the wholesale price of a two-horse plow was $8.70, and the retail price was $11.00. In negotiating the final price, the salesman took into account the quantity of the order and his relationship with the customer. Charles also still followed his father's original business plan of flooding the market with more of his products at a lower price and thus driving out competition by mere numbers.[31]

Questioning became more adversarial. "You asserted, I believe," the reporter continued, "that you could place plows in the hands of farmers through your agents . . . at lower rates than small local Granges can supply them. Have you any evidence to offer on this point?"

The evidence was common sense, the entrepreneur argued. Deere & Company shipped plows across the country, and their business increased every year "while the small local shops, without the advantages of the accumulated capital, perfecting machinery, skilled workmen and experience can scarcely maintain an existence." Plow manufacturing on a small scale was not profitable, and, if not for the larger factories capable of mass production, plow prices would be 20 percent higher.[32]

The large factory was a reality of post–Civil War America. Centralization, acquisition, and incorporation became commonplace as businesses increased their market share through mass production and diversification in efforts to offer more complete lines of products. A prime example of this trend, Deere & Company was slowly moving from plow production toward a more complete line of cultivators and harrows. Deere's small experimental department continued to develop new products, and Deere also purchased the patents of outside inventors, a trend begun with the Hawkeye Riding Cultivator in 1862. The Kansas City branch house offered a complementary line for anything Deere & Company did not produce, thereby allowing for a single point of purchase for customers. The branch house was proving successful, and in 1875 Deere and Alvah Mansur again partnered for a new branch in St. Louis. More were soon to follow.

The *Tribune* was impressed by Deere's candid discussion. "This conversation shows that the plow makers have not assumed their present position without due reflection and thus, in their estimation, any other course would have been suicidal."[33]

The *Prairie Farmer,* on the other hand, accused Deere of surreptitiously manufacturing unmarked, generic plows to sell to Grangers. Deere was furious. "The allusion in the article . . . is so pointed that we cannot let it pass without this explicit denial," Deere told the reporter, noting that selling plows without the Deere trademark would make them no less recognizable as Deere plows. The quality of the plows and the shape of the beams were dead giveaways.[34]

Not only was Deere & Company not producing unmarked plows, but in 1874 it introduced a new way of distinguishing its products from competitors. The Illinois Supreme Court permitted the Moline Plow Company to continue labeling plow beams with markings similar to Deere's, and a new system for Deere was long overdue. It was John Deere, during his term as mayor, who prompted the move. The idea came from an engineering discussion between Deere and city engineer Melvin Gould. Gould lived not far from Deere in Moline, and the two had most recently worked together on the sewage and waterworks plans for the city. In the course of discussions, the two devised an idea of a new and unique trademark. Gould made the original drawings and cut his original brass stencil from a final design approved by Deere, a leaping deer. Little could Gould know that what he had drawn, a lone deer leaping over a log, would eventually become one of the most recognizable trademarks in American business.[35]

The trademark was another effort to distinguish Deere & Company from the overcrowded field of competitors, but it did nothing to help Charles wrestle with the press. The newspaper exchanges sparked a flurry of letters from customers, dealers, salesmen, and implement companies, each defending his own point of view. Yet there was no evidence of progress toward a resolution. Charles remained immovable, and the debate continued. His factory made Deere implements, his railway cars transported them, and his dealers sold them. How then, he wondered, could anyone tell him what products to sell and what prices to charge? The dictates of the market were the only legitimate authority. His company had earned its reputation over the course of two generations. More important, Deere & Company's success had not come at the expense of its customers, but for their material improvement. Still, his reasoning fell on deaf ears.

Grangers continue to organize, and loose confederations of farmers began attempts to manufacture implements on their own. The Grange and new farmer organizations were gaining a louder political voice, but by the late 1870s they were beginning to drown each other out. After 1870, Illinois began the transformation from an agricultural to a manufacturing state. Bigger and more productive machines—the Deere plow, the McCormick grain reaper, and new makes of harvesters and binders—allowed farmers to do more with fewer hands in the field. Low crop prices, high transportation costs, and outwardly self-interested manufacturers created a powder keg with a short fuse. Meanwhile, a more formal changing of the guard had occurred in Moline. John Deere appeared less frequently in the office and the workshops. Charles was now well documented as a strict advocate of competition and an opponent of credit. His growing wealth and influence propelled him toward future opportunities for himself and the business but now left him more open to criticism than ever before.

MOLINE, ILL.

"'Tis Purely Business"

Amid the pressures of the Grange and ongoing economic crisis through-out the country, Moline continued to thrive and Deere & Company's ex-ecutives had little to complain about, or so it seemed. They were build-ing elegant homes overlooking their factories, and the company's laborers had the luxury of steady work and wages comparable to, and most often higher than, wages in other American factories. Charles Deere retreated to Overlook and returned to his normal low-profile sta-tus after his *Chicago Tribune* interview, though his stance on the subject of the Grange, which would soon translate into a similar strong-fisted and immovable stand against organized labor, was now public record.

Boycotting manufacturers who refused demands for lower prices, Grangers continued their attempts to manufacture and distribute farm equipment on their own. Some machines were manufactured and sold at lower prices, but the intensity of production and the lack of much-needed capital for factory expansion and for product development, com-bined with the cost of litigation and a general economic recession, left Grangers with a manufacturing nightmare, just as Deere had predicted. But still they struggled along. Many of the loosely affiliated farmers' groups had united under the banner of the Illinois State Farmers' Associ-ation, an organization fighting the farmers' war through political ac-tivism. Despite signs of progress, success at the ballot box and in the leg-islature was slow in coming.

Charles Deere and his able advisors, meanwhile, strengthened the company's market position. Deere & Company and Alvah Mansur not only renewed their contract for the Kansas City branch in the fall of

1875 but also established another branch in St. Louis, the Mansur and Tebbetts Implement Company, which Mansur agreed to manage.

The Moline headquarters continued to supply Mansur with innovative, quality products at competitive prices. That year Gilpin Moore patented his Gilpin Sulky Plow, a riding, wheeled plow built as an improvement on the Hawkeye Riding Cultivator and similar machines. Moore had received other patents, but this was the first product to carry his own name. The Gilpin was a riding plow, designed for simplicity and ease of use: single lever controls replaced complicated systems of gears. Its patent was a breakthrough, and its sales would inaugurate a new era of prosperity for Deere & Company. Three thousand Gilpins were sold in the first year, Deere's 1876 catalog stated, "and the unbounded satisfaction they have given to every farmer using them—and this in view of the fact that many other makes of sulkies had been on the market three to six years previously—is ample proof of the authority of our claim to the best Sulky Plow in existence."[1]

Deere & Company executives, nonetheless, were ever wary of an economic crisis that might obliterate their good fortune. Veteran businessmen, they had witnessed cycles of boom and bust that seemed to recur every two decades. The nation's centennial year found it trembling at signs of an uneasy future. As the United States staggered into its fourth year of economic depression, it witnessed the first national work stoppage in its history. Even in the little town of Moline, not everyone was happy. In comparison to the violent strikes elsewhere across the nation, local labor disputes were minor and quickly resolved, yet, following close on the heels of the Grange movement, the labor movement was gaining momentum.

In May 1876, the St. Louis, Rock Island, and Chicago Railroad Company elected Charles Deere chairman of its executive committee, and thus he found himself officially aligned, in the eyes of the laborer, with the epitome of corporate greed. His dependence on the railroad had led him into consulting positions with several railroads that passed through Moline and the surrounding areas, and, as he joined their governing boards, opponents saw their conspiracy theories realized. Deere's relationship with the railroad industry was reactionary, because the ever-escalating cost of raw materials and transportation hobbled his company's growth. Ethically, he was of two minds about the political and economic power of railroad tycoons, although in public he remained silent. He disapproved of some of their more suspicious business tactics but considered the railroad's incentives offered to customers with the largest accounts a smart marketing strategy. Drawing an analogy from his own business, he compared such incentives to offering a free plow to a farmer who had just purchased fifty.[2]

Railroad monopolies could benefit customers, but they could also deeply wound Deere & Company and its nationwide network of dealers, who relied on the efficient transportation of goods, as the Panic of 1873 demonstrated. Between 1860 and 1868, almost 1,500 miles of track was laid, followed by another 25,000 miles over the next four years. For American investors, the railroads seemed a bottomless pot of gold—until the collapse of banking firm Jay Cooke and Company in New York. The bank's collapse had a domino effect, and over the next few years a quarter of the country's 364 railroads went bankrupt. Nationwide, unemployment hit 14 percent. Meanwhile, as small railroad companies were absorbed by a few major players, their proprietors and stockholders cashed out with enormous dividends. Outraged, the public accused the railroad tycoons of corruption, and there were a number who were indeed guilty.

Similar charges also fell on Charles Deere, as a result of his affiliation with three local railroads. First, he gave most of his local shipping orders to the Chicago, Rock Island & Pacific Railroad. Along with his father and John Gould, he had helped to bring the Chicago, Milwaukee & St. Paul Railroad Company (formerly the Rockford, Rock Island & St. Louis Railroad Company) to Moline. The strongest evidence that he was in league with the hated tycoons was his position as chairman of the executive committee of the St. Louis, Rock Island, and Chicago Railroad Company. Deere should not have been surprised that many of his fellow citizens considered him guilty by association.

The effects of high unemployment spilled into Moline in 1876. That spring, strikes erupted in West Virginia and along the seaboard. By the end of July, organized labor had burrowed its way through much of Illinois. Predictably, much of the focus fell again on Chicago, the country's great railroad hub. By 1872, Illinois had more miles of track than any other state in the Union, a crisscrossing network of more than 6,300 miles, with Chicago at the center. On July 24, mobs went for the jugular, forcibly closing railroad yards in Chicago, Bloomington, Peoria, Galesburg, Decatur, Carbondale, and other Illinois cities.

Suddenly, as if a lit fuse burned down Main Street, workers began to strike throughout Moline. In April 1876, laborers at a local sawmill walked out. Deere & Company was hard hit by the panic, but Deere refused to lay off his employees. Instead, he had opted to impose a 10 percent wage reduction. His well-intentioned move quickly backfired. In August the company's molders walked out.

Life in the blacksmith shop, the foundry, and the woodworking shops was not as comfortable as in the neighboring Main Street offices. Early mechanization efforts were making the work more efficient, but long days, polluted air, and a general primitiveness still reigned. Grinders often suffered from consumption caused by the minute particles of steel and the dust of the shop. Blacksmiths, woodworkers, and polishers suffered similar complaints. Days started with the ringing of a bell, and only certain sections of the shops were lighted. In addition to the torches that lit the plant at night, each man carried his own kerosene lamp. Men hauled iron and steel on their shoulders and in wheelbarrows from storage sheds over to the factory, where thirty-five or forty blacksmiths and their backhanders, or assistants, worked to mold and shape the material. The thick, heavy smell of coal emanated from every corner and crevice, where assistants kept the fire raging hot to form the moldboards and shares, weld the landsides and frogs, and plate the shares with a smooth sheeting of steel. One "Alligator Shearing Machine" made heavy cuts, a pair of planers were used to plane shares and moldboards, and two slow-operating bolt machines provided the final assembly. Then the assembled pieces went to the fitting or cultivator department, where final adjustments and welds were made. Handles were prepared in the fitting shop by cutting and boring each beam individually, then the plows were sent to the grind shop and the finishing shop to be primed, painted, and varnished.

The process of building a Deere Gang plow, a wheeled plow similar to but lighter than the Gilpin, was much slower and more labor intensive than building a walking plow, but then a wheeled plow was still a considerably new machine. In 1874 Deere workers could produce only four per day. Improvements in machinery and processes more than doubled production the following year, but work was still slow and tedious. Factory hands were thinking hard about their working conditions and their futures. They demanded to know why their bosses continued to grow wealthy while they themselves accepted pay cuts.[3]

Deere attempted to pacify his men by reassuring them that their wages were still comparable, if not higher than pay scales at similar establishments throughout the country. One of Deere's greatest struggles had always been taming the Mississippi River, which flooded regularly during Moline's damp spring and summer. Intermittent work stoppages due to flooding made establishing guaranteed pay for workers a

gamble. If the river overflowed, Deere would have found himself paying for work not completed. If the river stayed low, his employees
would have found themselves working more hours than they were
paid for. Nonetheless, Deere was willing to address the laborers' demands, and, as early as November 1872, his company was one of the
earliest to experiment with the eight-hour system. For the moment,
unfortunately, such progressive efforts did nothing to assuage the
workers protesting the wage cut.[4]

When a small group of molders walked out in August 1876, Gilpin
Moore, Deere's longtime superintendent of iron works, gave them until
noon the next day to change their minds. Only one man returned, so
Moore shipped in replacements from Indiana and nearly triggered a riot
among the strikers. "There is no trouble to find men who are glad to
work at these figures," a local paper reported. After a week without
wages, the molders returned to work. Deere had again held firm, and the
pay cut remained, although low-wage jobs for apprentices and assistants
saw no reduction. According to the *Moline Review,* the terms relied
"upon the Company's sense of fairness and justice."[5]

Berating the company as it usually did, the *Rock Island Argus* charged
Charles Deere and company secretary Stephen Velie with coercion. The
episode, the *Argus* asserted, justified the appearance of a new labor party
in the Tri-Cities. The Greenback Party, founded as the National Party,
was an organization of Southern and Western farmers pushing for the
elimination of farm debts through inflated currency and less dependence on the gold standard. In the same way that the Grange had organized farmers, the Greenback Party planned to organize labor.[6]

In Deere's defense, the *Moline Review,* the city's Republican newspaper,
insisted that his company's political stance represented the best interest
of its employees. "The *Argus* charges that the workmen of Deere & Co.
have always voted as Mr. Deere and Mr. Velie dictated at the polls. We
have a better opinion of the manly independence and intelligence of
their workmen than to believe this and believe that both Mr. Deere and
Mr. Velie are too true gentlemen to endeavor to dictate to their men
how they shall vote."[7]

Deere and Velie did have a tremendous influence on their employees,
and although they did not yet rely on strong-arm tactics, they did offer
certain incentives. Whereas more unscrupulous employers offered cash
bribes, Deere offered, for example, a corn planter to the employee who
came closest to guessing the total number of popular votes the winning
candidate received on election day. More persuasively, Deere made his

support for particular candidates very public, oftentimes directly telling his employees for whom to vote and outlining the dire consequences—layoffs, unemployment, wage reductions, and the like—of voting for the wrong candidate.

The tough talk had repercussions for Deere and did little to improve the reputation he had acquired over the past few years of labor negotiations and iron-fisted business maneuverings. In 1880, Deere & Company and a large group of other Moline businesses were again facing accusations of impropriety at the ballot box. That year Deere & Company promoted the Republican presidential ticket of James Garfield and Chester Arthur with banners draped across the street between the warehouse and the foundry. Maintaining control of local elections in Moline was important to Republicans both locally and nationally. Deere relied on a high tariff to prevent foreign products from flooding the American market. He blamed Democratic politicians for the high unemployment that followed the Panic of 1873, and he believed that the Democratic policies threatened American jobs. Republicans had put men back to work, he argued, and would continue to protect the interests of working men.[8]

Protesting a series of published letters claiming that Deere & Company and eleven other employers were forcing their employees to vote Republican, Deere printed a denial on the behalf of his fellow businessmen. Manufacturers were anxious to bolster Moline's prosperity and "would use all honorable means to convince everyone engaged in manufactories, either as an employer or employee, that our interests are mutual, and that the prosperity of one is the prosperity of the other." Deere further dismissed accusations that the businessmen would bully their employees by "questionable means."[9]

Deere's reaction to the molders' strike had not surprised anyone, nor had his denial of coercion at the polls. Both moves, sensible as they were from his perspective as a businessman, were triggered by personal feelings as much as by business considerations. That his workers would force his hand in spite of all he had done for them was difficult to accept, and he began to feel that the camaraderie he had always sought was perhaps more imagined than real. Deere continually strove to ease the strains of factory conditions, but social pressures and the growing influence of labor organizations inspired workers to demand improved conditions and greater pay, demands that were unattainable in the current unstable economic climate. For the time being, managers and employees worked amid the uneasy tensions. Yet, in view of his clear alliance with the railroads, together with his emergence on the political scene, Deere struggled to convince his employees—a force of 900 in Moline alone—that he was truly working for their best interests and not merely his own.

Back in Court

In his quest to offer a more complete line of farm implements, Deere entered several new agreements in the late 1870s. He owned such a large share of the plow market that there was little room for growth there. Only new product lines could provide additional business. In 1877 Deere formed a third partnership with Mansur. Like the branch houses, the new corn planter business that they founded was not fully owned by Deere & Company but was instead a partnership agreement between Deere and Mansur, providing for exclusive distribution agreements with Deere agents as well as access to all of the resources of the Deere businesses. The partners named their new enterprise the Deere & Mansur Company.

Deere and Mansur purchased an old quilt factory on the Moline riverfront, a short distance west of the plow works, and outfitted it for production of their new corn planter. The mechanical corn planter had evolved into one of the farmer's greatest friends, especially in the Midwest. As was the case with all mechanical equipment, the corn planter had evolved from a laborious process of walking the land and hand planting one seed at a time, to a riding planter that prepared the hole, planted the seed, and then covered it with soil. The premier manufacturer was located in Galesburg, a small railroad town fifty miles southeast of Moline. There George Brown was making and selling a two-row corn planter that required two people to operate—one to drive the heavy wooden sled and the second to hand feed the planter. Unlike Brown's fully patented slide-drop planter, the Deere & Mansur planter featured a rotary mechanism that Brown himself had invented but abandoned. Deere & Mansur also offered stalk cutters, spring tooth harrows, drills, and cutters.

The business immediately proved successful. Profits of $10,000 in the first year steadily rose to $48,000 by 1882, though the revenue did not come easily. Brown had all but abandoned his business to make his living suing competitors for patent infringements. In January 1881, he filed a claim against Deere and Mansur for making the rotary drop corn planter. Although the circuit court judge understood that Brown was not actively using his design and in fact "seemingly attached very little value to his patent until the defendants and their associates introduced and popularized it," he maintained that "the plaintiffs' rights exist and must be protected" and upheld Brown's suit.[10]

Deere quickly filed an appeal, because, at that time, the rotary drop planter was the Deere & Mansur Company's primary product. The appeal process bought time to develop another model, and the company set to work immediately. To assure customers of continued service for planters they already owned, Mansur began a media campaign through the St. Louis and Kansas City branch houses. Rivaling the battle between Deere & Company and the Moline Plow Company eight years before, in which John Deere's integrity was put on trial, *Brown vs. Deere & Company* centered on the question of character. Brown had filed against Deere for infringement of five patents, but dropped four of the charges, "thus admitting that *even in his opinion* we were not infringeing [sic] any other of his patents." Mansur promised customers a new and improved planter in the near future, "differing wholly from, and therefore not infringeing [sic] this old, abandoned and worthless device."[11]

A professional plaintiff in court proceedings against copyright infringers, Brown was using newspapers and company circulars to denounce Deere and Mansur and to intimidate dealers so that they would refuse to carry the company's product line. In response, Deere issued another circular announcing intentions to take the case to the higher courts, not in defense of the product, but in defense of principle, "as we believe the day of old and worthless re-issued patents, coming in to levy royalty upon practical and valuable inventions to the country, is at an end." He made sure to point out that Brown's reissued patent was due to expire on February 28, 1882.[12]

Brown hit back and filed an injunction on February 7. Tensions escalated three days later, when Mansur reviewed Brown's threat to "claim full damages and triple damages under the law." And, as for anyone giving Brown assistance, Mansur, the fiery Civil War veteran, printed defiantly, "We will take care of both you and him." Mansur's reputation for combativeness, already well known throughout the industry, continued to grow. By the time the case was resolved in mid-1881, with Deere paying a settlement of $3,052.68, the Deere & Mansur Company had abandoned any use of a mechanism resembling Brown's and instead put into production a new line of check-row planters: the "Deere" and, perhaps in defiance of the eight-year-old Moline Plow Company ruling, the "Moline" in late 1881. Brown protected his outdated patent, as he had been doing for years, and in the process managed to bankrupt his own business.[13]

In the fight against Brown in the courts, Deere and Mansur set aside their differences, although they began to disagree on other matters. Deere had always approached business conservatively, whereas Mansur was more aggressive and certainly more short-tempered. The branch houses were created to sell complementary agricultural products, that is, products not manufactured by Deere & Company (and now the Deere & Mansur Company), but Mansur had taken the initiative in selling competing plows as well. Disagreements over matters of prices and product warrantees further exacerbated tensions between the two men, and, just as their corn planter business began to see substantial gains, a contract renewal for the Kansas City house in 1879 led to open conflict. Always a proponent of executive profit sharing, Deere suggested giving Charles Wheeler, the branch's manager for the past four years, a small but well-deserved piece of ownership in the business. Mansur insisted instead on a salary and a share of annual profits. In the ensuing argument, Deere eventually won.

Deere and Velie did not want Mansur's independence to set a precedent for current and future branch house managers. Branch operations—product lines, prices, and warrantees—were still determined by the home office in Moline. Despite his faith in his abilities, Deere questioned Mansur's devotion to the Deere brand, especially in light of his recent decision to sell competitors' plows alongside Deere plows. Mansur was not related to Deere by blood or marriage, and the way in which Deere and Velie handled the situation made it clear that this lack of family ties was a severe disadvantage. Velie, who normally navigated between Deere and Mansur, took a hard-line approach, telling Mansur that it might be time for a complete split in their business relationship. "While we have no doubt that personal friendship and confidence will continue to have with us its due weight in all our business transactions, we cannot see it to our own interests to accept your proposition," Velie wrote, referring to Mansur's desire to sell competing brands. Whereas Mansur believed this move would increase revenue, Deere and Velie thought it would send a message that they could not sell enough of their own product. Velie went on, "I have inferred that nothing but an apprehension of the future in the plow trade would lead you to propose so radical a change in our business relations. Our faith—and your lack of it—is doubtless the principle [sic] cause of this difference in our propositions."

As could be expected, Mansur, a fifteen-year veteran of the company, was disappointed at what he took to be the "matured view of Deere & Co." and was "glad to be warned of your true position and feelings relative to our future connection. Stripped of its generalities, what you say is that if you can see a larger profit by discontinuing your connection with us, you will do so. I do not for a moment complain of this, for as you say, 'tis purely business.'" Mansur argued that he was not operating under the same principle. "But now," he warned, "I am forced by your action to take this same position and to stand henceforth squarely upon your own platform."[14]

Despite their differences, Deere and Mansur recognized that their relationship was too profitable to abandon, and they finally came to terms in July. As Velie pointed out, however, it was just business. Negotiations did little to sour Deere, Velie, or Mansur personally, though after a candid discussion of their differing opinions, Deere had established that final authority rested with him alone.

Deere moved forward with additional branch houses without Mansur. In 1880, he entered into a partnership for the company's third branch, this one in Minneapolis, Minnesota. W. J. Dean had been running Christian & Dean, an implement business that Deere had been dealing with for years. Unlike Deere's original partnership with Mansur, which included all of Deere & Company's stockholders on one side and Mansur on the other, the Minneapolis agreement gave Charles Deere and Dean an equal stake, with each investing $10,000. Mansur had hired his son-in-law to run the Kansas City house, and now Deere countered by hiring his own nephew, Charles C. Webber, to assist with running the Minneapolis house. The son of Ellen and Christopher Webber, C. C. had graduated from Lake Forest Academy in 1876. The following year, he cut his teeth as a mail boy and worked his way into a traveling salesman position before assuming his new position in Minneapolis.

The branch house system was an integral part of Deere & Company's success. Serving as regional product distribution centers for Deere products, branches usually replaced relationships with independent jobbing houses, as was the case with William Koenig in St. Louis and Christian & Dean in Minneapolis. Like the Moline Plow Works, branch houses were built at important geographic locations, along rivers and railroad lines. They also created a point of entry into new markets, operating as middlemen between the plow works headquarters in Moline and distant customers. Each regional branch was built on the expertise of its employees, most often former dealers and farmers who knew the territories well enough to advise Deere & Company's engineers on the specialized equipment needs of their particular territories. A Minneapolis catalog, for example, offered plow varieties suited to the soil in its own territory, but not a Texas Ranger plow designed especially for Southern soils. Branches also shortened delivery times. Instead of waiting for orders from Moline, a farmer in Minnesota need only visit Minneapolis to pick up an order.

Now with three branch houses and a corn planter factory to complement the plow works, Deere looked to less traditional sources of revenue. Concurrent with the opening of the Minneapolis branch in 1880, John and Charles Deere and Velie signed a contract with the Moline Wagon Company, manufacturer of farm, spring, and freight wagons, run by Deere & Company's head of collection and trade, Lucius Wells. The $45,000 agreement provided for three parties: the Deere team, the Moline Wagon Company, and Lucius Wells personally. The agreement also created a fourth branch house under the name of Deere, Wells & Company, located in Council Bluffs, Iowa, a key link west of the Mississippi with important transportation access via the Missouri River.

With a flurry of recent activity, by 1880 Charles Deere's direct agricultural interests included Deere & Company, the Deere & Mansur Company in Moline, the Moline Wagon Company, and four branch houses, strategically placed in Kansas City, St. Louis, Minneapolis, and Council Bluffs. In addition, he had major financial and executive interests in a plethora of railroads, banks, timber companies, and insurance companies. American business had now fully recovered from the Panic of 1873, and the future looked bright. Aggregate sales of 70,000 plows and cultivators, grossing more than $1.1 million, were reported for the 1879 fiscal year, and a new Corliss steam engine, which cost nearly $27,000, promised greater efficiency and productivity at the plow works. At a special board meeting in July, Deere & Company's stockholders rejoiced over a 20 percent dividend.[15]

The Good Life

In 1878, as his father vacationed at the rejuvenating baths in Hot Springs, Arkansas, Charles made the long voyage with a Gilpin Sulky Plow, a walking plow, and a Deere Gang Plow to participate in the Paris Universal Exhibition. The days when John Deere traveled in person to county and state fairs were gone. Charles had taken plows to Vienna in 1873, and he now made the overseas journey to display the latest Deere line in Paris.[16]

A skilled plowman since his youth, the middle-aged entrepreneur was a great hit. The Gilpin Sulky Plow made quite an impression, because many of the spectators had never seen a riding plow before. But it would prove more than a curiosity when it was put into competition with a French walking plow. The two teams of four horses were swapped when half of the field had been plowed. At the halfway point, the Gilpin's driver stepped off the plow and ran in front of his horses in an attempt to slow his horses down so as not to embarrass the French. He also managed to smuggle both of his whips to his opponent, while the driver "had only his umbrella to poke up the four horses on his plow." A winner of one of only seven awards given for performance excellence, the Gilpin received the Sevres vase, valued at 1,000 francs, and a gold medal.[17]

In the United States, the Paris exhibition provided Deere & Company with an opportunity for some marketing slight-of-hand. Advertisements announced that the Deere Gang Plow—not the Gilpin—had won the championship. The Gilpin already had strong sales, so evidence of the merits of the newer Gang Plow was more necessary. The Gang Plow was lighter and pulled two plows, but in construction and performance it was identical to the Gilpin, which Deere and Velie considered sufficient reason for interchanging the two products in advertising. In this particular case, they were right. In September 1874, both the Gilpin and the Gang Plow won first premiums at the Illinois State Board of Agriculture trials.[18]

Deere returned to Moline in good spirits after his trip to Paris. He was one of only a handful of the city's men, the *Moline Review Dispatch* reported, who, "since we used to meet them in everyday business, eight or ten years ago . . . have managed to glide into the ranks of mature life without material change in their physical appearance." He had put on a few pounds, his face had barely aged, and overall he remained slender and sleek. He was the master of his business, although now he struggled to hold the undying affection that his company's workers still felt for his father. Deere was still trying to earn the unconditional trust of his employees and build on well-established traditions of integrity, but the relationship remained tenuous. John Deere was one of the men, but Charles was an executive in a suit whose course of action often seemed at odds with the best interests of those in the shops. Moreover, his outwardly shy and passive demeanor contrasted with his father's charismatic ways. The times had changed around them, and the reality was that Charles could never have the intimate relationship with his employees that his father enjoyed.[19]

Nonetheless, the success of Deere & Company was globally recognized as the result of the work of both John and Charles, and due credit was given to both men and the individual qualities they had brought to the business. John was stubborn and hands-on. He had earned his success through amazing perseverance, yet he had never possessed the intellectual prowess that seemed to come so easily to his son. Charles, meanwhile, continued to prove his entrepreneurial brilliance by taking a large view of the business.

Shared ambition aside, John's role as a figurehead of the working class was ingrained. Despite the success of his business or the property and vacation homes he accumulated, he was and always would be middle class in his outlook on life. John spent his days on the farm or in the shop. In the evening, he returned to the home where he had spent almost three decades. For laborers, he exemplified what they themselves could become through hard work and perseverance. Charles, by contrast, seemed distant. He spent his days in the executive office next door to the plow shop, and when he was not traveling, attending parties, or vacationing, he passed his evenings at his stately home on the bluff. Yet both John and Charles shared a love for the business and a fatherly dedication to the men who worked for them.

To those who knew him well, Charles retained much of his middle-class outlook on life, although he possessed an ambition unmatched even by his father. Charles's most significant triumphs in court, in the boardroom, or at the negotiations table were less visible than a row of shining steel plows. He was still the first man in the office and the last to leave. He still personally read the company's mail every morning when he was in town; on Sunday the post was delivered to him at Overlook. He had built a 5,000-square-foot mansion on a sprawling hillside, but it was accessible and modest for a man of his wealth, in comparison to the great American castles erected by other entrepreneurs who moved far away from the factories that had made them rich. He also shared his father's thirst for invention. Whereas John delighted in the shape of a new moldboard, Charles reveled in the day's most modern marvels and luxuries. With an insatiable appetite, Charles had mastered patent law, developed a sharp mind for engineering, and even tried his hand at inventing new products in the company's experimental department.

At age forty-three, Charles retained a unique perspective on his family's heritage and the importance that his father's early struggles played in the family's daily life. In July 1879, he took Mary and the girls to Grand Detour to visit the place where John Deere had made his first plow. It was a visit to the only place, other than Moline, that Charles had ever called home and an opportunity to teach his children about humility, hard work, and perseverance. "One of my earliest recollections of my father's business dates back to the time when he used to take me to his blacksmith shop and set me on the forge while he was working at the anvil," he later wrote fondly.[20]

Demarius and Mary Deere were as different as their John and Charles. They shared the same love for home and family. Yet even here was a contrast: Demarius bore ten children, but Mary had only two daughters. Almost no records about Demarius exist; she did not even receive an obituary in the newspaper. The only insight into her life can be found in the silence of the records. She traveled with her husband, often returning home to Vermont to visit relatives, yet whether she was an energetic, hard-nosed woman or a soft-spoken, demure wife and mother is unknown. Lusena Deere, John's second wife, is just as elusive.

Mary, the daughter of wealthy parents, played the part of the socialite, hosting grand parties at her home. Donating her time and influence to charities, she became a well-respected philanthropist in Moline. She enjoyed painting, shared her husband's fondness for horses and dogs, and took great pleasure in travel. She shared her mother-in-law's tendency for illness, and often her itinerary took her to treatment spas for the well to do. She also traveled frequently with her daughters while her husband was on the road visiting branch houses and attending conventions, fairs, and meetings throughout the country. Mary hated the times spent apart from her husband, and her affectionate letters always spoke of her longing for his return.[21]

Railroads had shrunken the country. The long and uncomfortable wagon trips taken by John to county fairs had been replaced by shorter, more luxurious trips by train. Then again, Charles traveled more frequently and for longer periods of time. The first-class accommodations offered by his good friend George Pullman made riding the train feel like sitting in a front room parlor. Occasionally Mary and the girls accompanied him, although he usually checked into a separate hotel so that he could better conduct business.

John and Lusena Deere traveled extensively as well, most often to Vermont or California, places the transcontinental railroad had only recently made accessible. Their Moline home sat only a few blocks from the plow works, and the sulfur emissions from coal-burning factories and hundreds of passing trains added to the nagging physical ailments John seemed unable to shake, although, according to the newspapers, his health was slowly improving. In June 1875, he put a new roof on his two-story house, giving all indications he would continue to occupy the home. Then again, the home improvement may have only been the beginning of a clean-up effort.[22]

Not to be overshadowed by his son's towering "Swiss villa," John Deere was now finally inclined to display some of his wealth. In 1875 he purchased the newly built Italianate house of the grocer William Dawson at the top of Central Avenue, only a few blocks east of Overlook. Dawson had defaulted on his loan, and ownership of the three-story house and its three lots had reverted to the Moline Water Power Company, which had added real estate to its business portfolio. John bought the entire property for a mere $675. It helped that his son was on the power company's board. Over the next five years, Red Cliff, as his daughter Emma named the house, was transformed into one of the most spacious and beautifully adorned residences in the county. Deere hired the local contractor who had built Overlook, J. G. Salisbury, to remodel the house. Red Cliff's view of the river and the factories below were as spectacular as those commanded at Overlook. To strangers visiting Moline, the two majestic mansions on the bluff clearly announced who built the town and kept watch over it.

Before Red Cliff's completion, a local reporter toured "the spacious halls and elegantly furnished rooms of Hon. John Deere's modest but magnificent home on the bluff." Designed in the ostentatious Second Empire style, the three-story house was far from modest. Contradicting himself, the reporter confessed that it "reminds one of the luxurious residences seen in and about Boston and other New England cities." Yet it was difficult to describe, since there were "no sides, no back parts, no ends—in fact, the residence is all front. The approaches from four different directions are equally convenient and pleasant."[23]

The first floor included Deere's library, family room, sitting room, and parlors. Bathrooms with both hot and cold running water were on every floor. Black walnut trim finish gave the decor a warm tone in the glow of gas lighting. Parquet floors, Brussels carpets, expensive paintings and sculptures, and thick lace curtains adorned the home throughout. The parlors were decorated with ebony furniture from Chicago. The fireplace mantels were installed by E. W. Spencer of Rock Island. A grand staircase led to the second floor's five bedrooms, each with a private bath. The third floor held two more bedrooms, yet another bathroom, and a large recreation room. In all, the house displayed all that "comfort and good taste could command. As a residence, it is a model of architectural skill, and adds one more to the many which adorn the bluffs." A few weeks later Deere completed a new sidewalk that looked "as though it might outlast his grand children."[24]

Red Cliff was the product of a lifelong innovator, displaying some characteristic Deere touches. Besides gas lighting and fireplaces that doubled as steam heat vents, Deere anchored the bluff-top home with full-length iron rods sunk into the foundation and running through the top floor. His most ingenious creation was a large clay pipe that pulled cool air from the bluff and circulated it from the basement through the rest of the house on hot summer days.

As heart and respiratory problems started to take their toll, Deere spent more and more of his days at Red Cliff. It was magnificent, but ironically it only strengthened his bond with the workers who still toiled in the plow works. They felt as if Deere's home belonged to all of them and visited there frequently. The fairy-tale quality of Red Cliff, overlooking the sprawling city its owner had built, also added to the nostalgic Deere legend. By this time, John Deere was rarely absent from the news, and the most trivial day-to-day events began to take on a mythology rarely dedicated to the living. Stories of his great concentration and determination peppered local newspapers. Even the most mundane events were news. His vitality was considered a barometer of life in Moline. "By, Goli," Moline citizens read one morning, "there's nobody seems to enjoy this crisp, bracing, Winter weather any more than our pioneer plow share pounder, the Hon. John Deere. He makes that pair of black ponies 'git up and git' about as lively as any team on the street when there's anything urgent gnawing at the old gentleman's brain."[25]

Deere's nephew and personal secretary, William Ball, along with his wife and daughter, usually took Sunday dinner with the Deeres, first when they lived as neighbors on Main Street and later at Red Cliff. Young Nellie Ball remembered riding on her uncle's broad shoulders and the excitement of Christmas Eve at Red Cliff. The adults would decorate the tree behind massive folding doors, and, after what she thought an endless wait, the doors would be flung open to reveal the candlelit tree and piles of gifts.

Documented facts about John Deere's personal life are few, yet the anecdotes about his eccentricities are revealing. In January 1868, the *Union* reported that one of his horses broke from a hitching post in town and pulled his wagon wildly through the streets. On another occasion, he and Ball once stopped by Ball's house on Main Street, and Ball ran inside. When he came out again, Deere was gone. Later Deere explained that he had thought of something that needed to be done, and, forgetting all else, he simply drove off to handle the business. Another time, Ball's daughter later remembered, Deere had made arrangements to pick up his wife from the Ball house on his way home but forgot until he reached home and found her gone. His apparent absent-mindedness, she claimed in his defense, was "due to concentration."[26]

Economic crises, labor negotiations, and politics seemed unavoidable as Charles Deere continued to drive his business forward. The differing management styles of John and Charles were becoming more evident, as time-honored traditions were balanced with new challenges for financial growth, product development, and worker relations. A greater number of plow works employees had never worked for John Deere personally and knew him only through reputation or a chance meeting when he slipped into the shop. Charles faced risky times as multitudes of outside forces— farmers' groups, organizing labor, and numerous suppliers—attempted to dictate how he should run his operations. Yet he was eyeing the expanding market in the West and even beginning to break into markets overseas. Meanwhile, at home, his father's waning health was beginning to evoke comparisons between father and son, as townspeople reflected on all that John Deere had done for Moline.

MOLINE, ILL.

Father Deere

John Deere had become a legend in his own time, especially to the men who toiled in the plow work's blacksmith, molding, painting, and wood shops. In the late nineteenth century, men would retire from Deere & Company with thirty or forty years of service. Despite a number of strikes, employees retained almost unheard-of job security at that time. Many were German, Belgium, or Swedish immigrants who arrived speaking only two words of English—John Deere.

While John Deere was entering his twilight years, Charles was making a debut on the national scene. Because he had built a diverse, multimillion-dollar agricultural implement business, political opponents counted Charles among the most scandalous and corrupt tycoons of big business. Those who knew him personally, however, considered him a champion of the middle class, driven only by his dedication to his family, its business, and the tradition it represented. While he spent more time away from Moline to promote his hometown's interests in Washington, outside forces began to attack the moral and cultural fabric of the business through his employees, a battle that became harder and harder to win. Charles would face the most devastating setback of his life as he worked to balance his family commitments, business responsibilities, and political aspirations and, above all, maintain the integrity of the Deere name. After his father's death in 1886, he would have to face these challenges alone.

Moline had grown with the prosperity of John Deere, its most famous and colorful citizen. It had been sixty-two years since the first steamboat passed the city along the Mississippi River, thirty-eight years since Deere made his first plow along its banks, thirty-one years since the railroad first blew its whistle in the City of Mills. By the early 1880s, Moline and its southern suburb Stewartville claimed more than 10,000 citizens. Three railroads intersected the city, and riverfront manufacturers included Deere & Company, the Deere & Mansur Company, the Moline Plow Company, the Union Malleable Iron Company, the Moline Furniture Company, the Victor Scale Company, the Moline Boiler Works, and the Wheelock Paper Manufactory. Educational facilities included three brick school buildings and several wooden ones, as well as a 6,200-volume library funded by Stillman Wheelock. Ten churches offered worship. Both a police force and fire department kept watch over the city whose downtown was now illuminated by gaslights.[1]

For many, John Deere was an American icon, a folk hero of a bygone era who had made his way from humble beginnings into the country's business pantheon. Biographical directories focused on Deere's strength, declaring him "capable of almost unlimited endurance" and pointing out his "strong" features. Known for his "open" and "frank" manner, he was a "hearty, genial" man of "tender, social nature, and noble character." Biographers euphemistically described his explosive, often inflexible single-mindedness as "feelings near the surface."[2]

He stood as a shining role model in a world of robber barons who thrived on oppressing the working class. Despite the fact that he had long since retired from the business, Deere & Company's employees still felt an overwhelming affection for him. For the immigrants in the shops, John Deere was the man who had given them opportunity and freedom. So too, Charles Deere and his fellow executives still honored the company's founder. In February 1882, on his seventy-eighth birthday, the entire executive force sneaked from their riverfront offices, south across the railroad tracks, through downtown "in line of battle," and up the Central Avenue hill to Red Cliff to his doorstep. "Completely taken by surprise, the old gentleman surrendered at discretion," a local reporter wrote of the jovial event.[3]

Few in Moline could imagine a world without John Deere, and it seemed that he cultivated eccentricity intentionally to keep Moline's citizens amused. On one occasion, for example, he traveled to Grand Detour for a meeting of the Ogle County Old Settlers Association. He and John Gale, another early settler, sat down to reminisce in a local tavern and became rather boisterous. When the landlord attempted to intervene, he was forced to take refuge behind a barrel of salt fish. Deere's nephew and future company executive, Burton Peek, recounted the scene: "The two Johns, each with a salt fish, stood over him, and every time he raised his head they smacked him."[4]

Deere enjoyed revisiting the familiar sights, sounds, and smells of days past. In the summer of 1885, he traveled to Minneapolis to attend the Minnesota State Fair with his grandson C. C. Webber. A photograph taken that same year at the Lethin Brothers shop at 1514 Sixth Avenue in Moline, however, shows that his legendary strength was clearly failing. At eighty-one years old, his features had lost their definition, and his hair had grown white and crept up his forehead and down around his long ears into short sideburns. Yet his eyes and pursed lips still testified to his deep concentration and resolve. As was his custom, he wore a dark suit, a dark vest, and a white, high-collared shirt with a distinguished black bowtie.[5]

During the warm months, Deere divided his time between his spacious mansion on the bluff and his Moline farms, but he spent the winters with his wife Lusena on the West Coast. In October 1885 they rode the train to Santa Barbara with two of his daughters, Jeannette and Ellen. They also visited San Francisco, Los Angeles, and Riverside, where his nephew George Deere was a pastor at the All Souls' Universalist Church. George corresponded regularly with his cousin Charles and reported on John's vigor and faculty, which seemed to wax and wane. "Uncle is evidently in a state of senile imbecility," George wrote; he was suffering from the "weakness of age."[6]

California's warmth and dryness did little to improve John's health. Jeannette and Ellen were frustrated, as was their father, who refused their constant attention. He wanted to return to Moline, although the thought of January cold made him hesitate; his company was on his mind. Writing to his son in a shaky, almost illegible hand, he hinted at the prospects for the farm implement business in California. "Farmers are plowing—sowing wheat and barley, garden vegetables, fresh from the garden. They raise 2 and 3 crops in one year; alphalfa [sic] hay 4 and 5 crops a year; hay 4 and 5 tons to an acre."[7]

On February 14, his hand too shaky to write, John dictated a letter from Santa Barbara. He expressed disappointment that Charles had not yet embarked for California with his family. "If you come as I hope you will do," he urged, "come right here." Charles soon made the trip, but he could stay only a short while.[8] April at last arrived in Moline, and John returned home. When he reached Moline, the *Daily Republican* reported, he "looked many years older than when he left" and was "apparently badly used up."[9]

Deere was indeed "used up." By mid-May, his fragile hold on life slipped as he struggled in and out of consciousness. Charles, who was in Colorado on business, boarded a train as soon as news of his father's failing reached him. As family members gathered around their patriarch in the early evening of May 17, 1886, John Deere finally fell into an unrecoverable sleep. Weary and travel beaten, Charles arrived the next morning, too late to say good-bye. His father, the *Daily Republican* informed Moline citizens, had "passed peacefully away full of years and honors."[10]

"MR. JOHN DEERE IS DEAD," announced the *Chicago Tribune* the following day. His death in many ways marked the end of the humble, self-made entrepreneur and left American business to the age of the oppressive, self-centered, robber baron. Deere was mourned from coast to coast, but nowhere more so than in Moline. Deere & Company sent out a simple, bifold announcement of his death, trimmed in black and printed on heavy stock. The only accolade was his title: "Founder and President of Deere & Company's Moline Plow Works."[11]

Deere & Company's shops and offices were draped in black, as were most of Moline's factories and businesses. Flags hung at half-mast, and the windows of private homes were filled with photographs and sketches of Deere framed with mourning drapes. Private services began at Red Cliff at eight o'clock on the morning of May 20, followed by a long procession from the bluffs of Red Cliff to the First Congregational Church at Fifth Avenue and Seventeenth Street. In spite of heightened national labor troubles, during the next hour more than 2,000 men, women, and children paid their respects. Before noon more than 4,000 said their final good-byes. From the church and then down Sixth Avenue, the police department led a procession of Deere & Company workmen, pallbearers, hearses, mourners on foot and in carriages, and finally Moline's mayor and city council. Plow works employees served as pallbearers, and among the ten honorary pallbearers were John's old partner John Gould and the Moline Plow Company's Stillman Wheelock. The entourage arrived on the bluffs of Riverside Cemetery, several miles directly east of Red Cliff, before one o'clock; and after a short service, John Deere was laid to rest.[12]

For Charles there were great lessons in reflection, as obituaries recalled his father's simplicity and ability to withstand the great temptations of wealth. "He was not a theorizer, or one who dealt in impracticable things, but in solid facts," Reverend C. L. Morgan of the First Congregational Church eulogized at his funeral. "To him it was a victory in death, having lived to a good old age, fought the battle, kept faith and gone to his reward."[13]

John Deere had bequeathed his property, stock, and other assets to his wife and daughters. Charles and Mary received only a silver tea set, because "assistance was given him while living, including an advantageous position in business," placing him "above want" and providing him with "a good share of this world's goods." The tea set carried an engraving: "Presented to Charles H and Mary L Deere, by their Father, John Deere."[14]

Upon John's death, Lusena, his wife of twenty years, began a steady decline. That fall she asked her niece, Grace Ball, who was enrolled in a teacher training program in Moline, to move to Red Cliff for a few days. Lusena was having a difficult time sleeping and wanted someone to be with her at night. When Lusena soon took to bed ill, Grace left school and moved to Red Cliff permanently to care for her aunt, whose condition worsened until her death, on August 14, 1888. Eight years earlier, when John and Lusena had built Red Cliff, his daughter Alice and her husband Merton Yale Cady had moved from Chicago to take up residence at his Alderney Hill Farm. Now the couple moved into Red Cliff. John Deere's majestic home was once again occupied, but no one could replace him.

Life without John Deere

On May 18, 1886, John Deere's death brought the entire city of Moline together. Laborers walked side by side with bankers, temperance crusaders beside saloonkeepers, and lively children beside stooped old-timers. Together they mourned the man who had been a father to thousands of immigrants, a friend to thousands of farmers, and a benefactor to all Moline citizens. But the country had finally closed in, and, despite the temporary display of camaraderie and affection in tribute to John Deere, the city was fast falling victim to the nation's erupting labor crisis. Despite nearly three decades of experience at the helm of Deere & Company, Charles may have felt unprepared to face the future alone. The times were changing, and in the coming years he would be forced to reconsider not only the company's long-standing approach to labor, but also question the desirability of the keeping the business within the family.

On July 13, 1886, Deere & Company's stockholders met to elect new officers, and four days later the board of directors—Charles Deere, Stephen Velie, Gilpin Moore, C. O. Nason—gathered in Moline. At last, Charles Deere acquired the official title of president, but in fact the title merely acknowledged the role he had played for thirty years. Moore assumed the position of vice-president, Nason was named treasurer, and Velie remained secretary.[15]

Fortunately, Charles faced the future with assets his father never possessed. Despite branch house conflicts and struggles to maintain centralization, he was surrounded by a loyal clan of able businessmen. Even business disagreements with Alvah Mansur had no effect on their personal relationship, because Charles had learned from his father how to separate business and friendship. Charles needed all of his partners now. The age of organized labor and corporate monopoly was upon them.

Of this large group of family and colleagues, Deere had grown most intimate with Velie, his brother-in-law of twenty years. Velie was a hard-line businessman, meticulous and thorough in his work, always forthright in giving his opinion. His motives were transparently genuine, and his heart was always in the right spot. Although Deere had an affectionate, yet authoritarian, relationship with his daughters Anna and Katherine, he may have harbored a jealousy for Velie's three sons, who were being cultivated for leading roles in the family business.

Velie would often write to his sons about the moral virtues and business values of successful men. In 1884, he took the occasion of Deere's eightieth birthday to teach his oldest son, Charles Deere Velie, the lessons of a good life, with examples the young man had probably heard many times. John Deere had "started in life with no advantages of education," but he had achieved success through "hard work, integrity of purpose, and a natural faculty of concentrating all his powers on 'one thing at a time.'" After weighing the options and determining the right thing to do, he set his course and let nothing cloud his vision. His "faculty of concentration combined with a strong charity, a lively sympathy with struggling humanity and a sterling integrity has given him the character and made him the reputation he now enjoys—Concentration of effort has been the ruling practice of his life."[16]

A twenty-five-year veteran of the company, Velie enjoyed his freedom when Charles was out of town. Velie frankly told his old friend that he sometimes took "advantage of your absence to give my views more in detail than I can at any other time, and consider it good to you and to me that you have them." Velie's conservatism sometimes restrained Deere from taking great risks on untested products and markets. "Sometimes a great deal of money is made by taking great risks but it seldom happens that any honor or profit comes," he wrote in a personal note.

"My living depends upon the success of this company—yours does not and this is why I evince the most timidity." Velie's leadership would be needed now more than ever.[17]

Confident in his Moline force, Deere had become a regular in Chicago, Springfield, and Washington, D.C. With railroad manipulators, mining speculators, and oil barons determined to prove that in business bigger was better, domination had become the name of the game. The formula for success seemed to be a mix of uncompromising labor practices and under-the-table politics, both of which Deere understood but refused to practice or endorse, despite tempting opportunities.

The power base Deere had built among implement manufacturers was secure, and his ties to one of the country's largest constituencies—the farmers—made him a prized political ally. Close friends were pushing him to take a more visible role in political circles. Viewing a political career as a potential detriment to his business pursuits, Deere repeatedly declined.

On January 19, 1886, George Vinton, who had left Deere & Company to take a position as president of the Burlington Wheel Company, sent a letter to his cousin containing an introduction to a Mr. Southwell, owner of a Burlington, Iowa, newspaper. Southwell wielded "great influence in your district," Vinton pointed out bluntly. "He says you are the *preferance* [sic] *for congress* in your district"; the only competition was a judge in Aledo, a tiny village thirty miles south of Moline. "If you have any aspiration of the nomination," Vinton urged, "you will do well to cultivate Mr. S. My private advice is for you to *go for it*. You can attend to your business by proxy and it will not occupy your whole time and you are at the write [sic] time of *life* for this office." Instead of trying to influence change, "You may see several changes that you can *make yourself useful*."[18]

Deere's only previous experience with running for political office was not of his own doing. In 1881, Moline Republicans had entered his name on the mayoral ticket. The Republican Stillman Wheelock had already served two consecutive terms as mayor, and a local contingent of the party wanted him replaced, not because of his political agenda, but because it seemed time for a changing of the guard. To his relief, Deere lost the nomination by one vote; and in 1881 Wheelock won a third consecutive term.[19]

Deere was spending a great deal of time in Washington, which seemed, the *Daily Davenport Democrat* observed, "to have some peculiar fascination for him." As with all his pursuits, the fascination lay in the challenge. He envisioned the United States as a huge corporation with the president as its chief executive. Consequently, like other business tycoons of the era, Deere made little distinction between the president's status and his own at Deere & Company. Mark Twain and Charles Dudley Warner best described the Washington that Deere knew, where there was "a feverish, unhealthy atmosphere in which lunacy would be easily developed," where "everybody attached to himself an exaggerated importance, from the fact of being at the national capital, the center of political influence, the fountain of patronage, preferment, jobs and opportunities."[20]

Deere had himself been monitoring the climate in Washington for several years. Upon his return to Moline after a trip to the nation's capital in 1884, he told the *Moline Review* that "everybody is making presidents in Washington." Only a well-known name stood a chance for election, however, and a "statesman and soldier" had the best chance of winning the vote. That combination was getting harder to come by, as most of the great Civil War leaders were beyond their active years. The scandalous presidency of Ulysses S. Grant had also proven that not all war heroes made great politicians.

In the early 1880s, Deere spent most of his time in Washington lobbying for support for the next great transportation route through Illinois, the Hennepin Canal (formerly named the Illinois and Mississippi Canal), a proposed waterway to connect the Illinois and Mississippi rivers. In 1884 the discussion was already ten years old, though the idea for the project could be traced back fifty years. The first and second conventions to discuss plans had been held in Rock Island in 1874 and 1875. Now at last, the movement had friends in higher places. Deere's greatest ally was Illinois senator Shelby Cullom, who, upon his arrival in the capital in 1884, made the canal one of his three primary objectives, together with the control of interstate commerce and the elimination of polygamy. Cullom was a junior senator but not an inexperienced politician. He had studied law under Abraham Lincoln, had served as Illinois Speaker of the House, and had taken his first seat in Congress a month before Lincoln's assassination. He spent six years in Washington, only to return to Illinois and win the governorship in 1877. Even then a promoter of internal improvement, as governor he called for the improvement of roads.[21] Upon his election to the United States Senate in 1882, Cullom resigned as governor and returned to Washington. Deere had known him for more than thirty years, since Cullom had attended the Mt. Morris Academy with Albert Deere, Charles's deceased older brother. When Albert first became sick in 1848, Cullom was the one who had brought him home to Grand Detour. Over the years, Charles Deere and Shelby Cullom had become formidable political allies as well.

Critically important to Deere & Company's growth, the proposed Hennepin Canal would run from Rock Island to Chicago, connecting the Mississippi River with the Great Lakes, via the Illinois and Michigan Canal, which was completed in 1848. Midwestern manufacturers hoped that the canal would dramatically reduce shipping costs, and they pointed to the 85 percent drop in freight charges when the Erie Canal opened between Buffalo and New York. Cheap alternative transportation to compete with the railroad was of tremendous interest to all Midwestern manufacturers and their customers. Indeed, the Chicago Board of Trade endorsed the Hennepin Canal's potential for reducing transportation costs and retaining higher profits for goods sold in foreign markets. The Hennepin Canal Central Committee, a citizen group lobbying for the canal, estimated that Midwestern farmers would save $31.5 million in shipping costs in 1879 alone.

The Hennepin Canal was a hard sell in Washington. On the one hand, the River and Harbors Bill, passed by a Republican Congress in 1884 over President Arthur's veto, provided $18 million for the improvement of rivers and harbors throughout the country. On the other hand, the bill had been criticized as an example of pork barrel politics. The U.S. House Committee on Railways and Canals requested a presentation on the Hennepin Canal proposal and a few days later agreed to support a $1 million appropriation. The sum was not sufficient. According to a study conducted by the War Department fourteen years earlier, construction then would cost $3,899,723. The Hennepin Canal Central Committee, based in Iowa, insisted that the actual cost would be 25 percent less than the original estimate, though opponents now placed the estimate as high as $6.7 million. But insufficient appropriations soon became a mute issue. Unconvinced of the need for the canal, daunted by the cost, and fearful of opposing railroad interests, Congress struck down the proposal. In August 1886, the Appropriations Committee for Rivers and Harbors allocated only $15,000 of the original $225,000 marked for initial work on the canal. Defeated but not discouraged, canal supporters continued the uphill fight.[22]

Meanwhile, back in Illinois, Rock Island, Moline, and Meredosia were squabbling over plans for the canal's route. It was estimated that the canal would provide for the transportation of 20,000 to 30,000 tons of freight annually, and the profits would be a boom to whatever community commanded the canal's port on the Mississippi River. In the debate, Moline was "acting the dog," according to the press, and the "perpetual and utterly selfish" Moline Water Power Company "has made more trouble in congress than any other interest in Illinois."[23]

Charles Deere pasted the articles that assaulted Moline's selfishness into a scrapbook, a system of record keeping he preferred to a diary. So far, labor organizations had come out in favor of the canal because they thought lower transportation costs would allow manufacturers to pay higher wages, but the quarrelling of entrepreneurs threatened labor's continued support. Next to his articles on the canal, Deere glued the report on an Illinois convention held by the country's largest labor organization, the Knights of Labor.

The Knights of Labor Come to Moline

Charles Deere was not among the most flamboyant corporate giants of the Gilded Age, but he gladly enjoyed the era's greatest luxuries. In contrast to his father's insistence on simple living, he had acquired a taste for fine cigars and finer wines, extravagant hotels, and resort vacations—all of the things that set him apart from the common workingman. He had nothing to be ashamed of, because he remained modest, approachable, and equally personable in conversation with the foreman of the grinding shop and the next president of the United States alike. His company's workers were well taken care of, and, were it not for the mounting strength of labor organizations, Deere & Company's workers would have seen no reason to strike. But by the end of 1885, as Moline's population continued to grow and its elites became more distant from ordinary citizens, its business-as-usual way of life began to crumble.

While his father spent the last winter before his death in California, Charles was in Salt Lake City receiving telegrams from Stephen Velie with the latest updates on Moline's labor unrest. The Knights of Labor had advanced on Moline with the intention of organizing workers into one union camp. The Knights found locals mostly unreceptive, but, after a great deal of persuasion, Deere & Company's grinders agreed to participate in a national walkout on May 1, 1886. Allegedly, they were protesting a wage decrease enacted two years earlier.

As always, Deere stood his ground, believing that he treated his men justly. In progressive efforts to increase production and provide safer working conditions, he had recently installed an extensive air-filtering system for his workers. His was also the first factory in the Tri-Cities to introduce electricity. Deere & Company spent more than $3,000 on electric lights for the blacksmith, grinding, and wood shops. Thanks to the lights, which replaced some of the torches and kerosene lamps, workers could see better on overcast days and work more safely on nights when fulfilling extra orders that required overtime. As a public relations spectacle, Deere also placed a rotating light on the roof of the Plow Works; residents on both sides of the river watched as he threw the switch.[24]

Comparatively, Deere employees were as well paid and well cared for as any in the nation. Both skilled and unskilled workers received upwards of a dollar and a half for a ten-hour workday. Genuinely convinced that he treated his employees well, Deere took every one of the strikes, which now seemed a monthly recurrence, as a personal insult. In this particular case, the grinders were demanding wages as skilled laborers, which the company maintained they were not, because "a laboring man with no knowledge of the work can become proficient at it in three or four weeks."[25]

"The status of the grinders strike remains about the same," Velie reported to Deere in late April 1886. The Knights of Labor had convinced the polishers to strike in support of the grinders; unable to fill the positions quickly, the company had closed the polishing shop for the week. Velie defended the men, telling Deere that they showed a "disposition to come back" and blaming the Knights of Labor for prolonging the strike. He also relayed rumors about a violent climax to the situation on May first—the day designated for the national walkout. The rumors soon proved only too accurate in other cities around the nation, but there was no serious incident in Moline. When several more days passed with no move from the other side, Velie predicted, "I think the labor troubles culminated on Saturday, and from now boycotts and other demands of labor organizations will simmer down. They have been 'sent on the ground' by the anarchists and communists, who control them. . . . When the laborers find they are being led to their extinction, they will desert the organization."[26]

But it was not the end of labor agitation, and Moline was not the unions' key target. Chicago was the center of the most radicalized forces of labor, with more than a quarter of the city's 240,000-person workforce committed to some type of labor organization. A third of Chicago's workers were German, the same ethnic group John Deere had defended while he was mayor of Moline during the temperance movement of the early 1870s. Charles Deere had a unique and vested interest in events in both Moline and Chicago. As president of the Illinois Bureau of Labor Statistics, which at that time was studying convict labor, the eight-hour workday, and wage issues, he may have felt that both sides were looking to him to provide a resolution. In truth, the escalating tensions were far from his control, spiraling into conflict across the nation.

At the front of Chicago's anarchist movement was Albert Parsons, a former Confederate cavalryman orphaned as a child and raised by a former slave. Upon reuniting with his surrogate mother sometime after the war, Parsons dedicated himself to the rights of freedmen and eventually moved to Chicago to take up the cause of the workingman. Parsons joined the International Working People's Association and published its Chicago-based newspaper, the *Alarm*. He soon was working with editor August Spies, who on May 1 led 80,000 thousand workers up Michigan Avenue, with the endorsement of Chicago's mayor Carter Harrison, in support of a national strike for the eight-hour workday.

Many of those workers came from the factories of the McCormick reaper works. As Deere had done once before, Cyrus McCormick II responded by replacing his employees with more-willing workers. Since taking over the factory in 1884, the younger McCormick had been replacing workers with machines, thus fueling the fires of discontent. The walkout at the reaper works went peaceably at first, but on May 3, a small contingent of police got too close to the protesters. Spies was addressing another large crowd nearby when a bell signaling the end of a factory shift at the reaper works prompted striking employees into action against the strikebreakers who had replaced them. A riot ensued. When the smoke cleared, one rioter was dead. Spies and other anarchists organized, and the next morning Parsons and Spies led a protest meeting in nearby Haymarket Square. By ten o'clock, the meeting had ended peaceably, but police arrived anyway to disperse the 200 men still lingering about. Both police and strikers were on edge when a bomb exploded within the police ranks. Officer Mathias Degan was killed instantly, and seven other policemen were fatally wounded. At least sixty more persons were injured as well.

Velie updated Deere on May 6, solemnly retracting his earlier predictions of a peaceful settlement. Parsons had fled, all of the other "anarchists" had been arrested, and Velie considered "the career of those Anarchists, Schwab, Spies, Fielding [sic], Parsons, is at an end. They have had full sway there, and for the last two or three years in their incendiary harangues on the lake front Sunday have been educating the rabble up to disregard of law and deeds of violence."[27]

The *Farm Implement News,* a leading farm implement journal staunchly protective of the workingman and the farmer, was more naïve about the workers, or perhaps just more optimistic. Men who save their money and find their way home after work were not tempted to join the unions, the paper claimed. "It is the shiftless men, who spend their earnings at the saloon, away from their families, who fall an easy prey to long-haired, wild-eyed and load-mouth agitators." Home and family, the paper argued, should replace the "gin shop and the street corners" where most "anarchists" are manufactured.[28]

Deere & Company executives did not have the luxury of such optimism. In an effort to forestall violence in Moline, Gilpin Moore settled the grinders strike the next day. Chicago's tensions were not as amicably settled, and a witch-hunt ensued to gather the leaders of the labor movement. Parsons had fled, but the rest were shortly in custody. Parsons then reemerged and was one of eight men who were tried and convicted within three hours. Seven were sentenced to the gallows—four of whom were actually hanged—and one was sentenced to fifteen years in jail. Before the execution, Governor Richard Oglesby stepped in to commute the death sentences of Samuel Fielden and Michael Schwab to life in prison following their requests for clemency. The others had not sought clemency and met their deaths by hanging more than a year later, in November 1887. Moore's settlement with workers, Deere & Company's executives hoped, would prevent such a tragedy in Moline.[29]

The 1880s were a tumultuous decade of personal and professional setbacks for Charles Deere. His father was gone. The generation of self-made pioneers who had populated the riverbank with homes, families, and sprawling factories was quickly disappearing. It seemed, at least to some Americans, that their legacy of dedication to the community was also disappearing. In fact, charities and social organizations were never better funded. If the wealthiest citizens no longer took an active role, they still gave millions of dollars. Yet, in an age where personal involvement was still treasured, a few fat checks could not assuage the public's resentment of the wealthy. The employees both Deere and his father had loved and watched over were growing discontent, thanks to the prodding of labor organizers. As tensions between the shops and the front office mounted, Deere took it upon himself to uproot the outsiders who threatened to topple his plow dynasty.

MOLINE, ILL.

NINE

The Plow Trust

Three issues—politics, labor relations, and corporate consolidations—dominated the final fifteen years of Charles Deere's career. Advances in communication and transportation facilitated the growth of monopolies throughout the United States, and in the 1888 presidential election both the Democratic and the Republican candidates called loudly for antitrust laws. At the same time, Deere began to reexamine his open praise for the benefits of competition as the overpopulation of rival firms led him to consider what had once been unthinkable: the creation of a trust with Deere & Company at the center. Negotiations for a syndicate takeover seemed to fly in the face of the business principles he had always stood for, especially when the Republican Party, of which he was a lifetime member, was questioning the merits of trusts. Yet he had a vested interest in banking, real estate, and insurance companies as well as in the railroad and other transportation facilities. Consequently, politics demanded more and more of his time, and old friends in Moline began to feel neglected.[1]

Deere's most important negotiations concerning the family fortune in the next few years would actually be the marriage of his daughters, Anna and Katherine. The girls had received much of their education at Miss Anne Brown's School for Young Ladies, on Fifth Avenue in New York. Brown had at one time taught school for the children of soldiers stationed at the Rock Island Arsenal, the site of the former Civil War prison camp that had since become a government military installation. Charles was so impressed with Brown that he helped to finance her first private school in New York and then sent his girls there to study with her. To complement their formal education, Anna and Katherine had traveled extensively and had seen much of the world before their twenty-first birthdays. At home in Moline, they attended extravagant social gatherings, for which Overlook was quite famous, and helped their mother manage the dozen or so maids, cooks, gardeners, and miscellaneous servants employed at their fashionable estate.

Anna and Katherine were in many ways polar opposites. Anna was a "tall brunette who closely resembles the southern beauties, of which she might be mistaken as a type," according to the *Davenport Sunday Democrat*. From her father, she had inherited her thin frame and features, but she had her mother's hooked nose. Anna seemed to overshadow her younger sister Katherine, who had acquired her father's reserved manners. Yet Katherine's energy contrasted with Anna's almost constant struggles with the flu and other maladies. Men of prominence were courting both girls, and their choice of husbands would have an immediate impact on Deere & Company.

In 1890 Anna married William Wiman, one of the most handsome and eligible bachelors in New York. His father, Erastus Wiman, was a wealthy industrialist and president of both the Great Northern Telegraph Company of Canada and the Staten Island Railroad Company. The press had dubbed him the "king of Staten Island." Wiman and Charles Deere also shared a common interest in baseball. Deere had played on a traveling team in his youth, and in 1885 Wiman, an avid supporter of the sport, purchased the New York Metropolitan Club (the "Mets"), a professional baseball team that belonged to the American Association.[2]

Wiman's oldest son, William Dwight Wiman, was a well-liked graduate in the electrical course at Lehigh University. He had been a practicing electrician for several years, and the *Chicago Tribune* was most impressed that "for two years he put in 10 hours a day, in a pair of overalls, as a common workingman in the Edison establishment" before becoming a manager at General Electric. Thomas Edison had such high regard for Wiman's work that he claimed "his knowledge of electricity is much more profound and far-reaching than that of any other young man who has gone out from that shop." Wiman resigned from Edison's company in 1890 to serve as the superintendent of the Richmond Light, Heat and Power Company.[3]

Anna and Will had grown so close over the years that marriage seemed inevitable, although Anna's overly protective father was not yet convinced. "I fully appreciated your reticence the evening I left Moline," Wiman wrote Deere in October 1890 after a visit, "for I was in to[o] dazed a condition to have answered many questions." It seemed that Wiman was expecting more of a personal than a professional interview, since Deere's obvious and warm regard had "raised my hopes to the highest pitch." In the meantime, Deere planned to discuss the match with his daughter as well as with Will's father, who was on business in Chicago.[4]

Will waited anxiously. "I will follow your injunctions not to write or go back to Moline until I hear from her, but to do so costs me a hard struggle," he promised. "I place myself in your hands, and will be guided only by what you think it best you to do. Next to finding that Anna is not lost to me, I am grateful for your interest and regard, and I hope to prove myself worthy of it."[5]

Deere had in mind not only the personal interests of his daughter but also the future of a family fortune. More pressingly, he wanted a son-in-law in the plow business, for which Wiman showed little interest or ability. Erastus Wiman took responsibility for his son's current financial standing. He had become such an asset as his father's personal assistant, Erastus assured Deere in a letter, that he had been unable to "break away and try his own ways" with other ventures that would surely be more profitable. Will was paid much less than his worth, yet his father believed that, as a result, he had learned moderation. Besides, the wedding gifts alone would allow the couple to maintain the living standard Anna was accustomed to. Will "has good capacity, is perfectly reliable, and in his own account in any sensible field will I believe achieve success," Erastus concluded.[6]

But money, Will soon realized, was not the primary issue. Deere feared losing his daughter if she moved East. "I know it would be hard for her to leave you all and hard for you to lose her but it is bound to come some time," Will wrote Deere, "and the knowledge that she will be happy & comfortable in her new life, will lessen the blow." Soon after this admonishment, Deere agreed to the marriage, and it quickly became the talk of social circles in New York and in the Tri-Cities.[7]

On October 9, 1890, Anna and Will were married in a lavish ceremony held at Moline's First Congregational Church, the likes of which the Tri-Cities had never before seen. More than a hundred carriages filled the streets surrounding the church. Anna wore a white satin gown with embroidered marguerites and orange blossoms and finished in a rare Venice lace. After the ceremony, the couple left for a honeymoon in Europe. In addition to giving the couple stock in the Staten Island Rapid Transit Co., the Wiman in-laws had constructed a new home near their own on Staten Island for Will and Anna. Not to be outdone, Charles and Mary Deere gave the newlyweds "gilt-edged securities" valued at $1 million.[8]

At age sixty-five, remembering how well he and his father had worked together in the formative years of the company, Deere must have longed for a son of his own, especially when Anna gave birth to his first grandson and namesake, Charles Deere Wiman, in early 1892. Perhaps he had resigned himself to the likely possibility that a Velie or a Webber, not a Deere, would carry the company into the future. Stephen Velie had three sons—Charles, Willard, and Stephen, Jr.—all working in various minor positions at the company. Meanwhile, Deere's nephew C. C. Webber had developed into an able businessman with a sharp eye for detail and quality. He had been controlling the on-site interest as general manager in the Minneapolis branch house since the mid-1880s. Thanks to him, the establishment netted more than $770,000 in the 1891 season alone. His experience with the branch house system made him an expert on the subject, and his intelligent and insightful observations in the field were of the greatest benefit to the Moline force.

If Deere had given up the hope that his daughters' husbands would act as the sons he never had when it became clear that Will Wiman would not join the business, the man who asked for Katherine's hand revived that hope. Twenty-four-year-old Katherine Deere married William Butterworth, the handsome, well-spoken son of Ohio congressman Benjamin Butterworth, in June 1892. A middle linebacker on the football team and a pitcher on the baseball team at Lehigh University, Butterworth was also intellectual and theatrical, a member of both the Glee Club and the Dramatic Club. At Lehigh, he and Will Wiman became fast friends. Butterworth stood with the groom during Wiman's wedding to Anna Deere, and it was on that occasion that he first met Katherine. Deere was already acquainted with Butterworth's father, a well-known congressman and solicitor general to Chicago's Columbian Exposition, of which Deere himself was a commissioner.[9]

In September 1891, William Butterworth wrote to Charles from Washington, D.C., to ask for Katherine's hand. Butterworth had obviously consulted with Wiman, and he displayed his prowess as a negotiator. He had already received consent from his future sister-in-law, Anna. In his first proposal to Deere, he provided the details of his financial situation. "My ancestors," he continued, "all of them, had to work for their bread and I am no exception to the rule." The couple would live in Washington, where Butterworth worked as secretary to the commissioner of patents, or at his home in Cincinnati, where he would soon pass the bar exam and "would have to begin on $2500 a year." Katherine claimed that she would be "satisfied" with either arrangement. The young man was sure that her support would better ensure his success, because Katherine would "encourage me through any adversity." With Katherine by his side, he insisted, "I can win against anything."[10]

Whereas Will Wiman pursued his bride as a man overwhelmed by love, Butterworth approached Deere like a businessman and followed all the rules. And whereas Wiman had difficulty winning the approval of a doting father, Butterworth had apparently made a better first impression. Following her sister's wedding by two years, Katherine's wedding at Moline's First Congregational Church was equally an occasion for opulent celebration. The weather, however, refused to cooperate. A ferocious storm pounded the ground and washed out the railroad tracks, delaying the couple's trip east. Two days after the wedding the couple took the train to Chicago, they headed to New York and embarked on their European honeymoon. Having lost Anna to her new home in New York, Charles and Mary made sure that Katherine stayed close. As a wedding gift, they built a mansion for Katherine and William across the street from Overlook.

The newlyweds spent the summer in England. William frequently reported long walks through Hyde Park, past the Parliament house and Kensington Palace. "Katherine was too energetic to be of any use," wrote her husband one morning. "I think she would be walking yet if we had not seen everything."[11] After the honeymoon, William Butterworth resigned his position in Washington to join Deere & Company's Moline force. His father-in-law was delighted. Over the next few years, the company would need his legal expertise and negotiation skills.

Consolidation Schemes

In early 1872 John D. Rockefeller tamed threatening fears of oil overproduction. In a move that he thought was inspired by the best of social Darwinism, he bought twenty-two of the twenty-six oil refineries in Cleveland, Ohio, and created the Standard Oil Company. Almost overnight, Standard Oil's capital grew from $1 million to $3.5 million. A decade later, in 1882, Rockefeller created an even bigger trust with a capital base of $70 million. He now held the country's greatest commodity with American cash while other industrialists, eager to catch up, looked overseas for investors. British capitalists had become enraptured with America's trust builders, and a new wave of English money was flooding American markets, catalyzing the survival-of-the-fittest mentality that had encouraged the creation of monopolies over oil, steel, cotton, sugar, and other markets. In a country of farmers, a plow trust seemed imminent. There were plenty of men wanting to make it happen.

Charles Deere would entertain four consolidation offers between 1889 1892 and spearhead negotiations for a trust that, in the field of agricultural implements, would have rivaled the capital and structure of Standard Oil. Always a proponent of competition, Deere would begin to question his own stance on the issue when he found that a greater number of inferior products and a general decline in the business culture had become a threatening trend. More than 200 implement manufacturers had disappeared as a result of competition and attrition between 1860 to 1880. Yet almost 2,000 remained in production. On the surface, competition increased the farmers' options and held down prices. Deere himself had encouraged his fellow members of the N.P.M.A. to keep prices as low as possible, but he had grown increasingly dissatisfied with the large number of inferior products on the market. The farmer might pay less at the time of purchase, but the high cost of repairs and the need to replace implements sooner than expected would surely put him on hard times.

Deere considered himself personally responsible not only for Deere & Company, but also for the reputation of the entire implement industry. As the industry seemed to slip further away from the principles on which his father had built his business—integrity and quality—Deere found himself in the minority. In his own mind, the industry had reached a stage of uncontrolled competition, which drove prices down and forced him to impose lower wages on his employees, an option he was determined to avoid. The labor tensions of the 1880s made it all the more obvious that the only way to guarantee a continuation of business in Moline was to eliminate wasteful competition in other places. To succeed, Deere would have to find a way to balance his own integrity and the Deere & Company tradition with the often unscrupulous and self-interested capitalists he would need to build his plow trust.[12]

The summer of 1884 was a hard one in Moline, and prospects for the next year looked dim. While the price of wheat dropped, floods along the Chippewa, Black, and Wisconsin rivers portended a rise in the Mississippi that would interrupt waterpower at the plow works and interfere with production schedules. "The volume of business still remains small, and we may look for rather quiet general trade during October and possibly November," Velie reported to Deere, who was vacationing with his family in Europe, in September 1884.

Other implement companies, feeling the effects of prices driven down by competition, shared Velie's gloomy outlook for the future. During Deere's absence, Velie represented Deere & Company at a meeting of thirty-five manufacturers whose cooperative activities could be traced back to the earliest Civil War era meetings of the N.P.M.A. The group discussed the merits and pitfalls of what they called a "combination," which the smaller firms now considered advantageous and the larger ones "impracticable." With a depressed metals market and substantial losses by many plow manufacturers the previous year, Velie came away from the meeting with little expectation for any reduction in the previous year's implement prices to help the farmer regain his feet.[13]

Initially, Velie's worries seemed unfounded. In a single year, from 1885 to 1886, Deere & Company's profits almost quadrupled, reaching a high of $239,000. Then, suddenly, profits plummeted until by 1889 they had fallen to $156,000. Like many other Republican businessmen, Deere hoped that the presidential election of 1888 would turn the economy to his favor. He served as an elector for the party's nominee, Benjamin Harrison, and when Harrison won, Deere escorted his daughters to Washington for the inauguration.

In his inaugural address, Harrison spoke of a mutual covenant between the government and the people, where "neither wealth, station, nor the power of combinations shall be able to evade their just penalties or to wrest them from a beneficent public purpose to serve the ends of cruelty or selfishness." Deere took note as Harrison touched on several points critical to his company's future, including a promise to fight against the creation of monopolies and trusts. "I look hopefully to the continuance of our protective system and to the consequent development of manufacturing and mining enterprises in the States hitherto wholly given to agriculture as a potent influence in the perfect unification of our people," Harrison confided. "The men who have invested their capital in these enterprises, the farmers who have felt the benefit of their neighborhood, and the men who work in shop or field will not fail to find and to defend a community of interest."[14]

Deere had always denied the charge that he held a monopoly over the implement trade, so his investigations into a formal consolidation had everyone wondering what he would do next. The press, seeming to sense Deere's own inner conflict, wondered openly if his business aspirations might force him to abandon the Republican Party. By supporting Harrison, Deere had allied himself with efforts to end corporate corruption and greed. At the same time, however, he was making efforts to create the very animal Harrison openly denounced. Deere quickly answered those who questioned his party loyalty by taking on more responsibilities as treasurer of the Republican League of the State of Illinois and becoming more active with the Republican State Central Committee. Under Harrison, Congress unanimously passed the Sherman Anti-Trust Act in 1890 in an attempt to regulate the American trust builders and the British investors who assisted them. But by the time Harrison had signed the act into law in July, Deere had already spent a year putting together a proposal that Harrison and the Republican Party stood against.[15]

Deere & Company was not operating in a vacuum: all around trusts were seizing control of specific markets. The National Harrow Company had consolidated all twenty harrow makers in the United States, for example, and the American Wheel Company had accomplished the same for the makers of wagon and carriage wheels. Meanwhile, the steel makers, who were reaping enormous profits as a boom in railroad and bridge construction put the need for quality steel at an all-time premium, had also consolidated. They held implement manufacturers at their mercy and refused to negotiate prices with the N.P.M.A.[16]

The plow makers were an independent lot. Velie's position was typical. He continued to stress the need for N.P.M.A. members to stand together and fight, yet he remained suspicious of monopolies in any form. Deere, on the other hand, believed that the N.P.M.A. had outlived its usefulness. "Presume we are not now in position to act on a combination," he admitted to Stephen Velie in June 1888, "and must say that we have very little faith in effecting anything with the Steel syndicate."[17] The members of the N.P.M.A. were not bound to one another by formal legal or fiscal obligations, and their lack of cooperation put them at a disadvantage in the confrontation with the steel makers. Ready to fight fire with fire, Deere decided that the time for a plow trust had come.

Ignoring Velie's objections, Deere inaugurated discussions with outside investors. In 1889, F. L. Underwood, an investment broker from Kansas City, contacted Deere on behalf of a group of British capitalists. The proposed deal would combine Deere & Company, the Deere & Mansur Company, and the Moline Plow Company (formerly Candee, Swan & Company). At the time, Deere & Company, including its branch houses, held $2.8 million in assets. John Deere had distributed his stock to several of his daughters upon his death, and, although Charles voted on their behalf, he now purchased just enough to give himself a controlling interest of 51 percent. To create a more accurate assessment of the company's value, the board declared a $375,000 cash dividend and issued another half a million dollars in stock. Alvah Mansur, who was again in the midst of negotiations with Deere for branch house renewals in St. Louis and Kansas City, put aside his own pride, as well as the advice of others close to him. He would stand by Deere. "I told Underwood I would agree to anything you would on the Planter Shop," Mansur assured Deere, "and he said the price you fixed was $250,[000]." The only wild card was the Moline Plow Company, which had repeatedly suffered financial losses in recent years. In fact, it was already on the market with a $650,000 price tag.[18]

As negotiations with Underwood continued, an investment bonds broker from Boston named Thomas S. Nickerson attempted to undercut the deal by buying the Moline Plow Company. Underwood cautioned Deere that Nickerson's success could destroy their deal. Deere was well ahead of both of them. He had, in fact, begun secret negotiations with Underwood, who by November 1889 had arranged three different buyers for Deere, although the conservative entrepreneur had yet to disclose his company's financial details to either broker. "I trust you will soon decide to give me figures on your plant that I may present them to the same parties in London who have asked to get an option from you," Nickerson urged. Deere would continue to play a cat-and-mouse game with the two brokers until he got what he wanted. And it appeared that what he most wanted was a personal settlement of his longtime feud with the Moline Plow Company.[19]

Dispatched to Europe to investigate the financial soundness of the English investors, Velie warned Deere to watch his step. "They seem to be rushing things and of course it can't be kept up at present rate of speed—Underwood has nothing on foot but our scheme when I called on him," he wrote from Paris. Velie confessed that he was "prepared to see a black eye given to these ponderous financial schemes at most anytime." Unless it came at the hands of outsiders, consolidation per se was not a bad move. A trust capitalized by the company's own investors, Velie predicted, "will add more to our name and fame and perhaps to our purses . . . than it will to turn it over to alien hands."[20]

At 9:30 a.m. on Wednesday, July 16, 1890, the board of directors of Deere & Company met in Moline to vote on the sale of the company. Still in Europe, Velie did not attend, but he sent a letter in which he halfheartedly agreed to the sale, but only with strict terms that he privately hoped could not be met. After a "full discussion" of the proposal, the board passed a resolution to recommend to the stockholders that the three companies—Deere & Company, the Deere & Mansur Company, and the

Moline Plow Company—be sold for $3 million. Two million dollars of the payment had to be in cash. The Moline Plow Company immediately hiked its price to $800,000; the Deere & Mansur Co. too raised its value to $300,000. Combined with Deere & Company, the newly consolidated business would start with capital of approximately $4.85 million.[21]

But now that Deere & Company had agreed to sell, would there be a buyer? The valuation stunned both Underwood and Nickerson. The asking price was much higher than they had anticipated. C. C. Webber ("C. C. Webber the best," as he once called himself in a letter to his mother) shared Velie's pessimism and agreed that, if a consolidation were to be made, Deere & Company should launch the business itself with American financing. "It does not seem to me that it is necessary to go so far away from home to market so good a property," he wrote to his uncle Charles.[22]

Continuing to oppose the deal with an outside syndicate, Velie made the most compelling argument against the merger to date by invoking the integrity of his colleagues instead of the weight of their pockets: "Although a purely industrial institution, it has its moral and politico-economic aspects and an influence commensurate with its varied and wide spread connections and associations, and I cannot help but regard its managers whoever they are for the time being as trustees charged with the duty and under obligations to so mange its affairs as to transmit its standing and character unimpaired to posterity."[23]

By November 1890, Nickerson was getting anxious. As he waited for an answer from Illinois, London spiraled into an economic depression. Velie's instincts were also proving correct: Underwood and Nickerson gave conflicting reports on the financial climate. Underwood told Deere, "Nothing can be done with the business before the 1st of December because of the terrible depression," and "no one could float a company of any kind at the present time." Meanwhile, Nickerson wanted to proceed immediately and was still trying to get Deere to disclose the company's financial records.[24]

Just how the scheme would play out remained to be seen. Deere had successfully driven up the price of both Deere & Company and the Deere & Mansur Company at minimal expense to himself. To the brokers' dismay, Deere & Company's deep fraternalism seemed impenetrable, but it should have come as no surprise. Fifty-three years after the company's founding, ten of the eleven shareholders were members of the Deere family. The board voted unanimously on all decisions or did not vote at all. The only consolidation in effect so far remained within the family circle, and that grip seemed only to be getting tighter.

The End of Consolidation?

Europe was experiencing rough economic times. Apparently the crisis in London was not entirely debilitating, however, because T. S. Nickerson continued to write to Deere about the sale of the company. In October 1890, Deere received him as an agent of the American Exploration & Development Corporation in London, a third party interested in a combination of Deere & Company, the Deere & Mansur Company, and the Moline Plow Company. This time, Nickerson claimed to have a contract for the Moline Plow Company already in hand, although in time it turned out to be another futile ploy to prompt Deere to open his books to outside accountants.[25]

Deere made efforts to include Will Wiman in the family business and asked him to take time from his honeymoon to investigate the new offer and the men behind it. Finding the request beyond his means, Will approached his father, the king of Staten Island real estate. Erastus Wiman was in the midst of a great scandal resulting from his welcoming embrace of British capital. In an article in the *North American Review,* Wiman argued that absentee ownership was of great benefit to business, because the "impersonal character of a corporation rids it of the pride of possession inherent in personal proprietorship, and the impediments toward a union of interests, in rivalry, jealousy, and false or unjust estimates of value, are all removed." Wiman's argument discredited Deere & Company's long-standing heritage and the benefits of family leadership. Nonetheless, he provided Deere with an objective, if mixed, assessment of the American Exploration and Development Company. On the one hand, the individuals who formed the company were solid businessmen. On the other, Wiman found it impossible to determine what resources they held as a company.[26]

Deere continued to meet with Nickerson, but their negotiations were fruitless. In December 1890, Velie effectively slammed the door on British offers. Deere & Company executives agreed that their concern for the welfare of their employees and their hometown outweighed the temptations of personal profit from the proposed sale. "Our pride in the name and interest in the prosperity of Moline and its manufacturing establishments should, and doubtless will, preclude the possibility of our becoming a party to loading down the three under consideration with conditions calculated to prove their ultimate ruin," Velie declared in a letter to Nickerson.[27]

Nickerson quickly disappeared from discussions, just in time for Underwood to reappear with yet a fourth offer in the summer of 1891. The proposed deal would retain the Deere name and keep Deere, Velie, and Webber at the head of the company. Best of all, it would eliminate the influence of foreign investors. Underwood had managed to pull together a consortium of Boston men who would pay Deere's asking price—$5 million for the three companies—and more if necessary. With an American firm, Lee Higginson & Co. in New York, as the underwriter, Deere's executives were of one mind to move forward. Deere thought the "plan much better than the old one that was under consideration. Such an arrangement would do a concern good rather than harm." Both Webber and Velie concurred.

Not surprisingly, the pressures of the impending deal were weighing heavily on Deere's health. Since his father's death in 1886, he sometimes suffered from extreme stomach cramps, which doctors had been unable to diagnose, and in April he went to Hot Springs to rest and regain his strength. His trip was shortened by a new development that compromised the deal. On May 1 the *Moline Review Dispatch* broke details of the merger, forcing him to respond the next day. Addressing the entire agricultural community, Deere outlined the benefits of consolidation in the *Farm Implement News*. The "waste of competition" would be minimized, bringing the rampaging credit system under control. The newly created company would answer the farmers' complaints by centralizing manufacturing and thereby reducing retail prices. In addition, farmers would be able to share in the profits because Deere would sell company stock to the public.[28]

Investors came from New York, and Deere finally opened the books of both Deere & Company and the Deere & Mansur Company; all accounts were found to be sound. But in the meantime, the Moline Plow Company had dismissed Nickerson and backed away from the deal. Velie thought Stillman Wheelock had instigated an attempt to drive up the company's selling price once again, but his death in January 1892 proved Velie's suspicions unfounded. Deere began to buy Wheelock's shares of Moline Plow Company stock, but, as he did, other stockholders, led by Deere's longtime antagonist Andrew Friberg, ended the deal once and for all by voting against consolidation. The summer of 1892 found the proposed consolidation dead.[29]

What would John Deere have thought about consolidation? Would he have even considered the proposition? Probably not, but the abortive negotiations were a not waste of time. They gave Charles Deere an accurate assessment of the company's finances and a greater understanding of his company's core values and responsibilities. Velie again proved his dedication to Moline and to the Deere family. C. C. Webber showed himself to be a trustworthy, though somewhat conservative, voice of reason. The sixty-two-year-old company would remain in Moline and, more important, would remain a Deere enterprise. Charles Deere had weathered the storm, but attempts to balance conflicting political and business agendas while maintaining his family's good name had become tiresome. The overwhelming commitment to integrity he had inherited from his father may have felt like an ever-tightening noose at times, but so far, it had not failed him, his employees, or the city of Moline.[30]

Political Force

Since 1890, Deere had given weddings for both of his daughters and had entertained four serious offers to sell and consolidate his companies. His political aspirations continued to be teased, though he was well contented to work behind the scenes. Despite consolidation attempts, which appeared to conflict with the Republican Party's attempts to eliminate the formation of trusts, Deere renewed his dedication to the party. He made a careful distinction between his own consolidation efforts, which would compensate all parties and would continue to promote—not destroy—competition, and a trust, which would destroy everything in its path and award the spoils to a few. Politically, Deere had made considerable strides, and associates frequently tapped his influence in Washington. In 1890, for example, Deere's letter to President Harrison prompted the appointment of J. M. McCormick to the U.S. district judgeship of the Eastern District of Texas. Again, in September 1891, a young attorney (and future Illinois governor) from Jacksonville, Richard Yates, wrote to Deere. In accordance with the Republican state convention's tradition of placing a young politician on the state ticket, Yates asked Deere to help him obtain the nomination for congressman-at-large. Deere scribbled at the bottom of the letter, where he normally made short responses to such matters: "I am indisposed to be for the young fellows (boys) If they were made of the right stuff. . . . I wish you will sweep in the convention and at the polls."[31]

During consolidation negotiations of the early 1890s, Deere remained deeply involved in national discussions on a number of issues—currency, tariffs, and his pet project, the Hennepin Canal. With both a Republican House and Senate behind him, President Benjamin Harrison had moved swiftly on several critical issues, until the backlash against the McKinley Tariff, which established a high protective tariff (48 percent of the price of goods) in 1890, helped Democrats win control of the House of Representatives. The Sherman Anti-Trust Act had also backfired, as had the Coinage Act of 1890, which mandated the purchase of 4.5 million ounces of silver every month and sparked a heated debate on currency that carried into the 1892 presidential campaign.

For more than a hundred years the country had debated the merits of gold versus silver currency. Silver coins had been issued in very small quantities since 1789, and the government's practice of minting both gold and silver (bimetallism) was common; however, prices for each metal fluctuated independently, encouraging consumers to hoard the most valuable coins, depending on the market. Through the 1830s, silver was the metal of choice, but then gold strikes in the 1840s and 1850s reduced the price of gold. Predictably, Americans began to hoard silver. As it became harder to obtain, its value rose once again. Since silver had essentially been out of the market for twenty years, the Coinage Act of 1873 eliminated the silver dollar from future coinage.

European affairs added an unpredictable dynamic. First Germany, then France, Belgium, and other countries began to phase silver minting out of their own currency in deference to a gold standard. The result, coupled with silver strikes in the United States in the 1880s, again devalued silver. The "Crime of 1873" as it came to be called, had effectively taken silver out of the country's reserve. Consequently, inflation ran rampant.

Farmers suffering from depressed agricultural prices supported silver producers in hopes that the coinage of silver would catalyze the economy. The amended Bland-Allison Act, which had passed over the veto of Republican President Rutherford Hayes in 1878, aimed to do just that by authorizing the purchase of as much as $4 million in silver bullion per month for silver coins. In the meantime, increased demand for agricultural products overseas flooded the American market with gold, and the debate over currency continued to rage.[32]

Amid the political tumult of the 1892 election, the Republicans lost the presidency to Grover Cleveland. Unable to pull together the sale of his business to British capitalists, Deere prepared for lean times. The normally unbendable Mansur, himself a full-blooded Republican, could not help but tease Deere about the election results. "How do you like living in a Democratic state?" he wrote a few weeks after the election. "You have my sympathies."[33]

By 1893, the seemingly unstoppable twenty-year economic cycle hit the country with a depression just as President Cleveland was opening the Columbian Exposition in Chicago, the grandest and most expensive celebration the world had ever seen. As the orchestra belted out "America the Beautiful," the model city lit up with sparkling lights and never-before-imagined electrical marvels. But the Exposition was bittersweet. In the course of its six-month, 27.5 million-visitor run, 600 banks closed, stocks crashed, railroads went bankrupt, and unemployment exploded. Deere & Company's profits dropped more than 34 percent, down to $138,000 during the worst of the panic. Even though Deere's longtime friend, Illinois senator Shelby Cullom, had helped persuade Congress to hold the Exposition in his home state instead of in New York, he criticized the event as "a great injury . . . to the city of Chicago," an exercise in excess while the country was collapsing.[34]

The Columbian Exposition marked something more than a celebration of the country: it also marked a visible beginning of the decline of rural America and the beginning of urbanization, a trend the lives of John and Charles Deere exemplified. Also apparent was the growing social and economic divide, spurred by unemployment and labor unrest. The social and ideological division was best illustrated at night, as millions of electric lights lined the streets and buildings to illuminate the Chicago shoreline. Electric appliances, telephones, and motion pictures spoke of an exciting future, while in Pennsylvania miners continued to strike over poor working conditions and low wages. In other cities across America, workers with little hope for such luxuries as electricity fought for living wages. The scientific wonders were nothing new to Deere. His wealth had provided him the benefit of many of them already. The clear social divide, which Deere well recognized, was a revelation to many. Rarely could a business leader be found who still lived within walking distance of his factories, who entertained employees if they called on him at home, and who lived in opulence not in spite of them but among them, as Deere did. But despite the accessibility of Overlook, to the workingmen the mansion's spiraling turrets towering over the trees on the bluff were a daunting reminder of the separation between them and their company's owner. The next few years would prove Deere's greatest test yet and would show both him and his employees whether there was indeed a common ground.

MOLINE, ILL.

TEN

Sick Forever

The press often portrayed Charles Deere as a ruthless tycoon, responsible for the repression of the working class, but throughout his entire career he never made a business decision without first considering what was best for his employees. He predicted that the election of Democrat Grover Cleveland would hinder the country's economic growth. The Panic of 1893, which Cleveland conveniently blamed on outgoing Republican president Benjamin Harrison, substantiated his predictions. Meanwhile, organized labor caused upheaval throughout the nation as striking workers resorted to violence and government officials retaliated in equal measure.

Deere's foresight doubtless saved his company from the worst of the panic and labor agitation. As president of the Illinois Bureau of Labor Statistics, he had ready access to vital information about industries throughout the state, and in the early 1890s, he had begun preparing Deere & Company for the anticipated depression. Despite the failure of the first consolidation effort, he would once again enter negotiations, which, if successful, would create one of the most lucrative trusts in American history. Convinced that his employees enjoyed superior working conditions and above-average wages, he took labor protests as a personal affront. As he discovered, however, the paternalism that Deere & Company had exercised since John Deere had worked in the shop shoulder to shoulder with his men was no longer suitable in the modern business world, where executives sat in the front office and employees sweated in the factory. Charles Deere and his company painfully adapted to changing times.

As a compromise for a high protective tariff, President Harrison signed the Sherman Silver Purchase Act in 1890, nullifying the Bland-Allison Act, which had been passed by Congress to provide for more liberal coinage of silver, and requiring the U.S. Treasury to release legal tender notes redeemable in either gold or silver. In addition, the new act required the treasury to purchase a significantly larger quantity of silver and to increase the coinage in circulation. Not surprisingly, this policy undermined the country's gold reserves and drove down the price of silver, resulting in a decline in the value of the legal notes issued by the Department of Treasury. Faced with the fact that most European nations held to the gold standard and the likelihood that, on the silver standard, the U.S. dollar would lose value, investors across the country panicked. "If Cleveland would call Congress together and they would repeal the Sherman law and [the] Govt. insure 100 million bonds the thing could be stopped, but if he puts it off to Sept. there will be greater trouble than we have seen yet," Alvah Mansur predicted. After a hard-fought battle in Congress, the Sherman Act was finally repealed in October 1893. The fiasco was only a precursor to the currency debate to come.[1]

As Deere had predicted at Cleveland's election, the plow business was stunted and the workers became restless. Deere & Company always strove to provide its employees with the best working conditions and the most equitable wages. At a time when the average wage for American factory worker was nine dollars per week, the average employee in Deere & Company's iron shop, wood shop, or grinding room was earning between ten and twelve dollars for a fifty-four-hour workweek.[2] Nonetheless, still smarting from the previous strike and ever watchful for an infiltration of labor organizers, in 1892 Deere hired the Pinkerton National Detective Agency to investigate employees in the grinding shop, traditionally the source of discontent within the company. The Pinkerton operative, who went only by the initials "W. H. B.," played dice and billiards in the local saloons by night but had difficulty getting close to the men because they spoke Swedish. After a few days, he decided he would better blend in with workers by joining them in the shop, where he quickly detected a strong, underground opinion that "if the Swedes stick together they can run this shop, but they have no union." A bartender on Third Avenue suggested that the grinders and polishers, who had already staged two strikes, should walk out again. Unable to gather more concrete evidence of a labor conspiracy, the Pinkerton agent reported to Deere that workers were more inclined to talk big than to take action. His duty done, W. H. B. went on to his next case.[3]

The big talk turned into outright threats the following year. In October 1893, Deere's son-in-law William Butterworth, who had recently joined the company as an assistant buyer and soon after became treasurer, received a threat from an unemployed laborer. Butterworth passed the warning along to Deere: "Some bloody anarchist has threatened in an anonomous [sic] letter that unless we started up soon he will blow up the place with dynamite."[4]

Preparing to answer protesters with the voice of reason, in 1894 Deere & Company conducted an extensive labor survey of manufacturing companies to make wage comparisons. The Studebaker Bros., maker of carriages and wagons, offered a typical response. The firm had been unable to establish a rate of pay, because the factories were not running at full capacity. In fact, Studebaker was dividing the work among as many men as possible so that each could earn enough money to survive. Deere also found an unlikely ally in the Moline Plow Company. The two companies conversed about labor rates and shop regulations. "I think it advisable that we should act in harmony so far as is possible," the Moline Plow Company's new president, G. A. Stephens, proposed behind closed doors, "although it will, perhaps, be unwise if the labor presumed there was a concerted action indulged in by us."[5]

Moreover, in an effort to demonstrate solidarity with their workforce, Deere & Company's directors declared only a small 3 percent dividend at the July 1894 board meeting. Pointing to the lean economy, the board further resolved that future dividends would be declared only "from time to time when the finances of the company are in condition to pay them." Company executives too accepted salary cuts. For example, Gilpin Moore, superintendent of the iron works, saw his annual pay drop from $3,700 to $3,000. It is not likely, however, that the workers heard of these decisions or, if they did, that they took comfort in the sacrifices of stockholders and executives. After all, some could remember when, at the conclusion of the Civil War, from January 1865 through July 1866, unskilled laborers were earning as much as $1.67 for working a ten-hour day, or about ten dollars per week, though that wage was a temporary spike lasting only six months. The average rate for common, unskilled labor from 1867 through 1875 was $1.50 per day. From 1875 through early 1894, it was $1.35.

In October 1894, Deere & Company uniformly reduced wages by 10 percent for both skilled and unskilled workers. The company had spent more than $486,000 on labor in 1893, and the pay cuts, as well as cuts in production to compensate for the depressed market, reduced labor expenditures by more than 25 percent. The current cutback reduced a skilled worker's daily pay to between $1.40 and $1.60. Unskilled laborers earned only $1.25, or about $7.50 per week.[6]

In the midst of the crisis, Deere suddenly found himself alone. On the evening of February 14, 1895, Stephen Velie, recently recovered from a bout with the flu, bid Deere goodnight with the promise to visit him the next morning before the Velie family left for a short vacation in California. Later that night, Velie died in his home in Moline. For Deere, who found his brother-in-law a man of the "strictest integrity" in whom he "built an absolute trust," Velie was irreplaceable, both as a business partner and a personal confidant.[7] He had always played the role of intermediary between Deere and his employees. His sensitive and good-hearted handling of explosive situations would be greatly missed.

Deere closed the factory until after the funeral, but, as always, he immersed himself in activity. At the moment, he was considering whether he might best serve Deere & Company and Moline from Washington. He was getting a steady dose of Washington politics and seemed more inclined to toss his hat into the ring. As labor unrest continued, however, popular support diminished. Moline's *Republican Journal,* a paper allied with the Populist Party, asserted that Deere's only claim to recognition was the "supposed fact that he is Moline's richest citizen." He had caused eighteen months of "sufferings of our laboring people" through "selfish and coercive methods" that were "little short of cruel." Furthermore, the paper insisted that Deere was personally responsible for unnecessarily reducing work and wages. While he and his family traveled through Europe, his dedicated workforce starved. Therefore, the article concluded, "the less he is talked of as a congressional candidate, at present, the better."[8]

In September 1895, Deere & Company's grinders again went on strike. At last convinced that their pay was well above the average for workers in other American factories, they now protested the introduction of new equipment. The plant had installed safer grindstones that did not chip with wear. Workers preferred the old grindstones, which could be operated by one man instead of the two necessary for the new machines. In Velie's absence, Deere turned to Moore, who was to restore some of the old machines "where practicable." The grinders refused to compromise.

Now, according to the *Dispatch,* the grinders were using the new equipment as an excuse to organize a union, and when Moore called their bluff by offering to return all of the old equipment per their request, they demanded a reinstatement of 1894 wages. The cycle continued. Moore told strikers that if they could provide evidence that another manufacturer was paying grinders a higher rate Deere & Company would reinstate the wage. In the meantime, Moore brought in nine replacement workers from Indiana, six of whom were beaten by strikers after their first day on the job. The next morning, one of the strikers was arrested when he entered the shop carrying an iron spike. At the height of the tensions, Deere's fox terrier, Toby, was poisoned. Hoping to plead their case, the grinders approached the Illinois Board of Labor Arbitration. They soon recalled their protest, however, admitting that matters "are too largely in our favor." At last they agreed to return to work under the condition that the company would restore some of their old equipment, as Moore had proposed, and reinvestigate the contentious issue of wages.[9]

The New McKinley Era

As in previous elections, Deere's position on a number of political issues was the source of debate preceding the 1896 presidential campaign. On the one hand, as a businessman, he was a known advocate of the Republican Party. He served on the Republican Money Raising Committee for the state of Illinois, and, as was usually the case, when Deere offered his influence and personal services, other entrepreneurs offered their money. Standard Oil alone contributed $250,000 to the cause.[10] Deere supported high tariffs, the gold standard, and the protection of American manufacturing. Again, currency was a key issue in the election. William McKinley was the Republican Party's foremost authority on tariff questions, and he favored closing the American economy to foreign trade long enough to get it back on its feet. Republicans blamed Democrats and their low tariff for the Panic of 1893. In this election, though, McKinley's opponent, William Jennings Bryan, viewed the tariff as secondary and instead focused on the silver question. McKinley had the vote of most of the manufacturers and the laboring class in the East and Midwest.

On the other hand, Deere's industry was tied to agriculture, and he sympathized with the Populist Party on issues regarding the special interest of farmers. Consequently, despite vocal opposition to the manufacturers, the Populists found it difficult to snub Deere. For Deere it was not a matter of politics, but a matter of protecting his customers—and thus his own interests—regardless of party lines.

Amid swirling speculation about Deere's political alliances, he gave several newspaper interviews in which he placed himself clearly in the McKinley camp. He openly denounced both William Jennings Bryan and Arthur Sewall of the Democratic Party as representatives of the "anarchist element of the country." Deere defended American manufacturing interests through support of a high tariff and a dedication to the prevention of exporting jobs. Yet he also declared that he was "for the dollar of the highest value of purchase power the world over, and believe that all dollars whether gold, sliver or paper, should be of equal value."[11]

On the currency question, Deere cited the repercussions of the silver craze as the cause of unemployment. In a vicious statement far from the diplomatic tone he usually adopted, Deere accused the "mouthy classes," namely, the silver barons, of pushing their propaganda on the less-educated and mixing a "good deal of vitriol and venom into it and make what success follows, working on the passions and prejudices of the people."[12]

In a final interview in the *Chicago Tribune*, in September 1896, Deere made it clear that laborers must vote for McKinley or suffer the consequences. Most of Moline's factories were idle, and work would resume at his own immediately after McKinley's election. If McKinley lost, the plants would remain closed. Currency was worth a mere fifty-three cents on the dollar, and "no business firm of any ability whatsoever would be so foolish as to throw away 47 cents just for the sake of keeping in operation," Deere stated. McKinley's election would restore confidence in American business.[13]

It was a logical argument, but not one the unemployed grinder or blacksmith could understand. It was also undisguised encouragement for the plow works employees to vote for McKinley. Deere predicted a Republican landslide in Chicago and was "making all my calculations accordingly. I can hardly take into account the chances of a Bryan victory since the consequences from my standpoint would be disastrous." Further predicting that no factory in Moline could operate more than ninety days in the next year should Bryan win, Deere emphasized that factory employees "should not put the business interests of the country at this time to the task of remodeling their operations to a silver basis." Voters should not be "led off by clap-trap stories gotten up to influence their votes," he warned.[14]

McKinley was elected in November, but the election brought no immediate relief for Deere. The following July the molders, who had yet to see any benefit from McKinley's election, went on strike to protest another potential wage cut. A few days later the drillers went on strike, followed by the Deere & Mansur paint department. The Moline Plow Company's core makers followed suit, as did molders and core makers at the Union Malleable Iron Works down the street.

The Deere & Mansur painters strike was catalyzed by false reports that their pay was low in comparison with employee wages at other plants. The Illinois Board of Labor Arbitration heard their case in December and threw it out on account of bad information. Deere's position was again upheld, as the painters were in fact among the highest paid workers in the nation.[15]

With local elections upcoming in 1897, Deere and Butterworth, who, besides his duties at Deere & Company, was serving as second ward alderman for the city of Moline, were again being butchered by the press. The opposition party painted the two as greedy entrepreneurs who wallowed in luxury while the workingman suffered. The *Daily Dispatch* still defended the businessmen, although Moline's Populist paper, the *Republican Journal,* which claimed that Deere held interest in eighteen Moline factories, cast them as "public enemies of Moline." The *Dispatch* editor said he did not know or care about the number of factories Deere controlled but only wanted to see them all prosperous and filled with "busy men." If it were not for Charles Deere, the editor argued, Moline would still be an insignificant town with no jobs available for anyone. It was an easy argument to justify.[16]

By early 1897, Deere's hopeful predictions were finally fulfilled. For the first time in almost a decade, his employees were at work and seemingly content in the Deere factories. Deere, now sixty-two, spent the spring of 1899 in Bermuda investigating new business opportunities. His labor problems appeared to be behind him, at least temporarily, allowing him time to begin proceedings on what, to date, had been his greatest business disappointment. In a diary he had begun to keep, amid the mundane entries, an old subject resurfaced: "plow company combine is now the topic."[17]

The Plow Trust

In May 1899, Deere began to look anew at the failed consolidation efforts of the previous decade. Labor unrest was again consuming much of his time, and the guidance of longtime partners was disappearing. Stephen Velie's death in 1895 was followed by that of Alvah Mansur, Deere's partner in the St. Louis and Kansas City branch houses and corn planter business, in 1898. Gilpin Moore, the almost forty-year superintendent of the iron works and board member, died in 1900. With his most trusted advisors gone, Deere assumed an even greater workload. Still unable to diagnose nagging stomach problems, doctors were telling him to retire, advice he refused. Despite frequent illness and chronic fatigue, Deere remained mentally sharp and continued to tackle new projects. He inspected his factories with an acute awareness of processes and techniques and still drew upon his thorough mechanical knowledge to offer design improvements. In many ways, it was as if the Charles Deere of forty years earlier had returned, if only for a short while.

In the decade since his last attempts at consolidating Deere & Company, the Deere & Mansur Company, and the Moline Plow Company, the country had witnessed the height of the trust-building era. Auditors were busy nationwide, as more than 300 companies were disappearing annually, most absorbed by mergers. In 1899 more than a thousand companies disappeared. The following year saw the consolidation of companies such as Du Pont, International Harvester, American Tobacco, and U.S. Steel, a conglomerate valued at $136.5 million.[18]

Deere, meanwhile, revisited C. C. Webber's advice to organize under Deere & Company's own plan and with local capital. A half-million dollars in new equipment and facilities had been installed in the plow manufactory, which now boasted floor space equivalent to a forty-acre farm. By 1900, Deere & Company and the Deere & Mansur Company collectively employed 1,400 workers in Moline. In preparation for future periods of depression, and in an effort to prevent future unemployment, Charles Deere would even agree to operate the company under a name other than Deere.

For thirty years the cost of labor had risen as plow profits declined. Farmers were buying less expensive but more efficient machinery, and, although competition had been reduced by almost two-thirds since 1890, it continued to cut into profits. Illinois produced one-third of the more than one million plows sold nationally in 1900, yet with 700 American implement manufacturers pushing their products, profits were slim, and finding capital for new branch houses, research and development, and raw materials and transportation was becoming more difficult by the year.[19]

Putting his thoughts about consolidation on paper, Deere wrote a note to himself: "To retain trade, manufacturers have been forced to become merchants, building branches, and covering the country with jobbing depots, until now they have the most perfect system of selling machinery in existence." It was a "situation that has necessitated large investments outside of legitimate manufacturing capital." Predicting that the trend would only continue, with manufacturers earning less and less, Deere concluded, "there [is] but one remedy for the situation . . . but the adoption of this remedy cannot be avoided,—it can only be postponed."[20]

The *New York Times* first broke the story of a possible plow trust in March 1899 but did not provide further details for two months. The trust would consist of a $65 million partnership between New York capitalists and implement manufacturers, most of which were based in Illinois. At the same time the *Times* released this information, members of the N.P.M.A. discussed the trust and by all accounts seemed to be working against its formation. In September, in fact, Deere attended an antitrust conference held by Governor John Tanner in Chicago.

Over the next year, accountants secretly poured over the financial statements of nineteen companies while occasional updates in New York and Chicago papers kept the spotlight on the potential consolidation. In April 1901, the *Farm Implement News* reported that the plow combination was "practically assured," though other details were sketchy. At its head stood the president of one company that was yet to be publicly linked to the impending trust: Charles Deere. Quoting an unnamed "leading manufacturer prominently connected with the organization of the proposed plow combination," the *Farm Implement News* provided a list of nineteen companies firmly committed to the venture. The list included Deere & Company, the Deere & Mansur Company, the Grand Detour Plow Company, and the Rock Island Plow Company. The action of at least these firms was assured. The Grand Detour Plow Company was on hard times, and Deere owned almost a majority stock in the Rock Island Plow Company, which he had purchased from Gilpin Moore, who had helped save it from bankruptcy a few years earlier. With several of the leading organizations located in Moline and Rock Island, Deere saw the opportunity to establish Moline as the official and indisputable farm implement capital of the United States—a status that, in reality, it already held.[21]

On April 29, 1901, Deere issued a statement confirming plans for a $75 million consolidation under one of three names: the United States Plow Company, the American Plow Company, or the American Plow & Implement Company. Until this point, Moline had been recognized as the obvious location of the consolidated company's headquarters, with Deere as its president, but speculation began to swirl about his health and declining competency. The *Farm Implement News* doubted that

Deere would live long enough to see the combination through and reported that it "was only Mr. Deere's ill health and desire to retire from active business that made him consent to the Trust proposition at all."[22]

Deere kept his nose in the details from home while representatives met in New York to draw up the company's articles of incorporation. Deere assured the papers, "If the deal has not already been complete, it will be in short time."[23]

Meanwhile, in private, Deere confided to his Kansas City branch manager that the deal was far from done, thus provoking internal dissention. Branch manager George Fuller asked for permission to buy Deere and Company's interest in the Kansas City house if the trust did go through. Only 30 percent of Fuller's goods were Deere & Company or Deere & Mansur products, and, seeing no personal advantage in the trust, Fuller wished to go his separate way. Uncharacteristically, Deere seemed caught off guard by Fuller's fleeting loyalty, and as opposition continued to mount from within, he might have been reconsidering consolidation.[24]

For Deere, the creation of the trust—he always referred to it as a "consolidation"—would merely formalize the confederation of factories and branch houses now under his direction: Deere & Company and the Deere & Mansur Company in Moline as well as twelve branch houses, including St. Louis, Kansas City, Minneapolis, Council Bluffs, and, more recently added, Dallas and California. If the deal went through, the branch houses of all of the other participating companies would join the conglomerate, although many of them would be phased out so as not to compete with one another.

Therein, however, lay a problem. Deere did not have a full interest, and in many cases not even a controlling interest, in the semiindependent branches. Alliance with the trust, therefore, required independent approval from each branch. If successful, Deere would consolidate at least nineteen manufacturers and their affiliates, which collectively accounted for more than 90 percent of the country's farm implement production.

In May 1901, the *Moline Dispatch* had called the trust a certainty, but by the end of the summer it seemed to be slipping away. The New York capitalists bankrolling the deal now wanted the headquarters to be established in Chicago, not in Moline. The press also began to speculate that many of the larger agricultural manufacturers had lost interest in the trust and that the investors were soliciting smaller businesses with more diverse manufacturing lines in an attempt to pull the deal together.[25]

In the midst of the negotiations, Deere's reasons for pursuing the consolidation were confirmed by further labor dissension. For all practical purposes, the Orders of the Patrons of Husbandry, the official name for the Grange, were gone, as was the Greenback Party, which had made only a minor impact on politics in Moline, but other organizations had replaced them. One of the strongest labor unions in the United States, the National Association of Machinists, organized a nationwide strike in May 1901. Deere went to New York to consult with the National Metal Trades Association, an organization created at the height of machinist strikes in 1899. Manufacturers in Moline, Rock Island, and Davenport responded by founding their own group, the Tri-City Manufacturers Association. Quickly disgusted with collective negotiations, the manufacturers simply canceled their recently created union contracts and, on June 29, 1901, adopted their own "declaration of principles," authorizing each employer to negotiate with individual workers. The manufacturers' declaration denounced strikes and lockouts, promised not to discriminate against men on account of membership in organizations of any kind, and gave employees the right to quit their jobs without consequence. Most important, it established the rights and responsibilities of individual employers. First on the list was the recognition that "employers are responsible for the work turned out by our workmen, we must, therefore, have full discretion to designate the men we consider competent to perform the work and to determine the conditions under which that work shall be prosecuted."[26]

Privately, Deere thought that the labor unions were taking advantage of his employees. After one walkout, he met a committee of blacksmiths, noting in his diary that they were "gentlemen, all of them . . . good men who have made a mistake. [T]hey honestly want to get to work and appreciate the firm and their jobs."[27]

A year later, the plow consolidation was still not a done deal and Deere was fighting old ghosts. C. C. Webber was livid because Deere had not consulted the branch house managers, who as of yet had no idea where their fate lay if the trust was completed. Webber did not approve of consolidation. "Don't let it go that way," he wrote his uncle, "it will be a great mistake."[28]

Bad press for a proposed combination of harvesting manufacturers also affected the companies involved in the plow consolidation. Previous attempts to consolidate in 1890–1891, under the guise of the American Harvester Company, were ultimately unsuccessful, and it was dissolved soon after its organization. Critics considered the American

Harvester Company only a front for the alliance that would be reconstituted in August 1902 as the International Harvester Company, a trust of grain binders and other harvesting equipment manufacturers that included the McCormick Harvesting Machine Co., the Deering Harvester Co., and the Milwaukee Harvester Co. At the time of consolidation, IHC controlled 90 percent of the country's grain binder production and 80 percent of mower production. By 1904, it had managed to buy out most of the remaining competition and began branching out into other pursuits, threatening the plow makers who were still attempting to form a trust of their own.

Webber's investigations of IHC revealed the wrongful use of confidential information collected during negotiations and other questionable business tactics. To a man, Deere's executives watched closely to assure that, if the plow consolidation did succeed, Deere & Company's corporate culture, with its emphasis on integrity, would endure even if the newly formed company did not survive under the Deere name.[29]

As plow trust negotiations reached the deadline, it was again Deere's old nemesis, the Moline Plow Company, that stood in the way. President George P. Stephens told the press that his executives wanted to be left alone to run their business and announced publicly that the Moline Plow Company wanted nothing to do with the trust, although stockholders would sell out if the price were right. When no buyers appeared, the company remained in the trust negotiations but with no intentions of following through. On July 1, 1902, while Deere met with bankers in New York, the investors who had purchased the options to the Moline Plow Company failed to make a $500,000 deposit toward the consolidation fund. Deere returned to Moline the next day and refused to talk to reporters. Two days later, with mixed emotions, he confirmed the collapse of the deal and pointed to labor unrest as the cause.[30]

The collapse of the proposed trust had repercussions for Deere, as in the final few years of his life he attempted to hold on to familiar ways of doing business. The nature of American business had changed dramatically in his fifty years at Deere & Company. Deere was still acting president, but he had recently turned much of the day-to-day operations over to his son-in-law William Butterworth. Along with Butterworth, Webber and Velie's three sons, Willard, Charles, and Stephen, Jr., who together had more than five decades of experience in the implement business, eagerly exchanged Deere & Company's outdated, paternalistic management style for a more democratic one.

During the trust negotiations, a small movement had been forming against Deere, as his waning health and extended absences offered some of the younger executives a glimpse of a company without him. His business sense had always been acute, but his willingness to take necessary risks was waning. At times he seemed overly protective and uncharacteristically cautious.

The failed plow trust had left Webber, a member of Deere & Company's board of directors and general manager of the Minneapolis branch house, somewhat cynical about Deere & Company's future. He was not looking for a hostile takeover but for recognition for past service and greater authority. He had been discussing the effects of the proposed trust with his cousin Willard Velie, who remained on the company's board of directors despite his decision to leave the Deere offices a few years earlier and pursue his carriage-making business. Neither of them had been enamored with the idea of consolidation in the first place, and they were now working to protect themselves against such a consolidation in the future. They felt that a decentralized advisory board would best promote the interests of Deere & Company. Most important for Webber, it would guard the interests of the branch houses.

Deere expressed some apprehension, but the company directors agreed to create an advisory board, which would hold no formal power but would serve as an instrument of inclusion. Directors, stockholders, and even outside experts were eligible to join. Nobody wanted to go to Moline monthly merely to visit, Webber told Deere, and the distance was prohibitive for branch house managers. "We want to go there for business, and while we are there on this Advisory Board business our business would be at Deere & Company's office and shop."[31]

Neither Deere nor Butterworth attended the board's first meeting in October 1903. Furious at the implication that they were shunning the board, Webber protested loudly, "I do not believe that it is proper to handle the matter in this way." Over the next year, the advisory board began to hold monthly meetings as Webber wished. It seemed superfluous, however, because the company's executives decided important or potentially controversial questions in their offices, without ever consulting the board. By 1905, it was disbanded.

If Webber and Deere had their differences of opinion, both men nonetheless held to the creed upon which John Deere had founded the business. As Charles Deere put it, "Good plows and good material in plows counts." Webber agreed, "You hit it right. . . . If that was not so, Deere & Co. would not hold the place in the trade that they hold to-day."[32]

The End of an Era

Charles Deere was aging rapidly. In 1904 he saw doctors in Chicago, New York, and Boston and was diagnosed with pernicious anemia, a blood deficiency that had troubled him for years. In November 1904, his fading health was further taxed with the care of his bedridden wife, Mary.[33] Despite having lost the use of her legs, she still attended meetings of the Daughters of the American Revolution and continued activities with the First Congregational Church, City Hospital, and other civic and charitable organizations. Charles and Mary spent the summer of 1905 on their houseboat, docked at nearby Campbell's Island, with an occasional excursion to St. Paul or elsewhere.[34]

Charles's oldest daughter, Anna, and her husband, Will, too suffered frequent illness. Hoping that the dry western air would provide a cure, the couple moved to Santa Barbara, California, in 1902, to a home on the northwest corner of Garden and Mission streets. Apparently, the change of climate made little difference. On June 1, 1906, Anna died at age forty-two. "The death of our daughter our great sorrow," Deere mournfully wrote in his diary. Her passing left Will to care for their two children, fourteen-year-old Charles and ten-year-old Dwight. Her body was taken by rail to Moline, and funeral services were held at Overlook. A fifteen-foot-high white granite crucifix was erected over her grave on the family plot on the bluffs of Riverside Cemetery.[35]

Charles and Mary were devastated, and the health of both took a decided turn for the worse. After spending the winter of 1905–1906 in North Carolina and Florida, Mary returned home in February while her husband took a separate car to Washington. He returned to Moline in May looking thin and tired. He and Mary again spent the summer living on their houseboat.[36]

Deere was now traveling to Chicago for weekly medical treatments. Mary could not travel, so he often made the trip alone or with an assistant. Dr. W. E. Taylor, an authority on nervous diseases, as well as a longtime family friend and physician at the nearby Watertown hospital in East Moline, had been conducting laboratory tests for months. Like other specialists, however, he had been unable to ease Deere's pain.

Late in the afternoon of August 22, George Vinton, Deere's cousin and business associate of sixty years, visited Deere's houseboat to try once again to convince him to "unload of the responsibility of his business" or "his health would be impaired by constantly thinking and anxiety." Deere was "very weak and nervous," but the two talked of business and old times. They walked to the back of the boat. "Charlie, you're pretty sick," Vinton said plainly.[37]

"George," he replied, "I'm sick forever. I ought to have quit business twelve years ago."

Vinton tried to persuade him to return to Overlook and phoned his driver to bring the car and meet them at the train station. Initially, Deere refused, not wanting to bother his wife who continued her own battle. Perhaps lacking the energy to argue, he at last yielded and set out for town with Vinton. "Be sure and come down to my office tomorrow at 9 o'clock," Deere told his cousin. The next morning when Vinton appeared, Deere was nowhere to be found. During the night he had been put on a train bound for Chicago.[38]

The news soon reached the streets of Moline. "Moline people have been given much alarm during the last two days by rumors rife on the streets that Charles H. Deere is dead in Chicago," the *Dispatch* reported. But he had not yet succumbed, and until his last breath he would remain a leading figure. Even while he lay ill, Governor Deneen appointed him as the delegate to the "deep waterways convention" to be held in Memphis in October with President Theodore Roosevelt in attendance.

For months Deere's condition had been "so grave, so discouragingly hopeless that many another man would have bade fate take its course," the papers reported with solemn optimism. He was unable to digest or keep down food, and journalists credited his survival to a "magnificent will and remarkable vitality." He was put under the care of Dr. Charles Kahike, whose family was prominent in Rock Island circles, at the John Streeter sanitarium on Calumet Avenue. A team of specialists continued to monitor him. "Mr. Deere is overworked," Dr. Kahike told news reporters, after he discovered that, despite repeated medical advice that he retire, Deere had only given up work three months before. "At present he is improving and I hope to build him up steadily."[39]

At his own request Deere was moved to the Hotel Lakota at Thirtieth Street and Michigan Boulevard. Katherine and William Butterworth, who had been traveling in Mexico, arrived shortly afterward. Mary had made the trip with her husband, and she stayed by his side day and night, reading and talking to him the day through. On October 6, 1907, Charles slipped into a coma, and doctors gave him no more than a few days to live. Mary stayed by her husband for twenty-three more days.

Charles Deere died on Tuesday, October 29 at 1 a.m. at the Hotel Lakota. That night in Moline, the train was met by more than a hundred people who silently stood in a light rain to watch the casket as it was taken from the train and driven to Overlook. The family paid their respects the next morning at Overlook, then held a public service at the First Congregational Church, the scene of many Deere weddings, baptisms, and funerals. At noon, by proclamation of the mayor, the City of Moline closed down just as it had twenty-one years earlier to mourn the death of John Deere. Early in afternoon, workmen gather at the Deere factories then marched together to the church to pay their final respects. "The city joins as one large family in a tribute of sorrow at the passing of him who for years was conspicuously a leader," the *Review Dispatch* observed.[40]

On November 26, the board of directors of the John Deere Plow Company of Omaha, a branch house in Nebraska, sent a fitting resolution to Mary Deere. "Resolved, That in the death of Charles H. Deere, this Company has lost its great head and advisor, a man of pronounced views and policies but ever ready to consider the counsel of his associates; a man of large affairs, often looking far beyond the activities of the present time and always enjoying the personal success of those interested with him in the operations of the allied branches of Deere & Company."[41]

The tribute was highly appropriate. Deere could have easily propelled himself into the American business pantheon that included the richest and most ruthless capitalists of the era, but a devout responsibility to his family, his employees, his customers, and his town would not allow him to dishonor his father's vision. Together, the lives of John and Charles Deere had spanned more than a century of change and progress. Their company's product line had expanded from John Deere's plows to Charles Deere's riding sulky plows, planters, wagons, and buggies. He had even entered the automobile business. The family had risen from poverty and debt in small-town Vermont to rank among the country's financial and social elite. But through all that time, John, the self-made man, and Charles, the architect of a vast business empire, had remained true to the family ideals that had always motivated them. In the end, Charles was the one who venerated his father the most and who made the name John Deere an enduring legacy known the world over.

Yet his own name, in large part by his own doing, was to be lost. Charles Deere's greatest failure, his failure to create what would have been one of the nation's largest trusts, was actually the greatest testament to the vision he and his father shared. It was his adherence to a belief in cooperative partnership—not a ruthless destruction of competitors—that prevented the consolidation of the trust. Future Deere & Company president Burton Peek, recalling his early days working for his uncle Charles, gave all due credit for the company's survival to its second president, recognizing that "all great institutions are but the lengthened shadow of some one man." Peek understood, as did those who had seen the company grow from its earliest days, that Charles was the man who had ultimately put his father's vision into practice. Yet it was only through the combined efforts of father and son that the family name—the name Deere—could endure.

MOLINE, ILL.

Epilogue

Deere & Company's great Moline rival, the Moline Plow Company, struggled through financial problems at the end of the nineteenth and early twentieth centuries. In 1919, George Peek (who was related by marriage to the Deeres through John Deere's nephew Samuel Charters Peek), became the Moline Plow Company's chief executive officer, resigning after selling the company to the International Harvester Company in 1923. International Harvester merged into the Minneapolis-Moline Power Implement Company in 1929. It has since been bought and sold several more times.

Although Mary Deere was an invalid when her husband died, she lived another six years before passing away at the age of seventy-two. She was recognized nationally for her philanthropy, especially her efforts on behalf of the Daughters of the American Revolution, in which she held national office. Upon her death, she bequeathed Moline the property that is now Velie Park, located on the bluff between Overlook and Red Cliff, once the site of Stephen and Emma Deere Velie's home. Her home for thirty-three years, Overlook is one of three Deere-related properties now open to the public. The John Deere Historic Site in Grand Detour, the Butterworth Center, and the Deere-Wiman House (Overlook) remain visual reminders of how far the family came in just two generations.

The death of Charles Deere did not end his family's dominance over the plow industry. It was not until 1982, a full 146 years after John Deere built his first plow in Grand Detour, that a nonfamily member was named president of Deere & Company. The most visible reminder of

John Deere's legacy today is the leaping deer logo that was conceived by John Deere and Melvin Gould in the 1870s. Today it represents a global, multibillion-dollar business.

Upon Charles Deere's death in 1907, his son-in-law William Butterworth was elected the third president of Deere & Company, a position he retained for twenty-one years. From 1910 to 1912, Deere & Company completed a series of mergers and acquisitions, realizing Charles Deere's earlier efforts by consolidating eleven factories and twenty-five sales organizations under a central accounting and financial office. This created what is considered the "modern" Deere & Company. It was a realization of Charles Deere, Stephen Velie, and C. C. Webber's attempts at consolidation under family ownership.

An early twentieth-century engineer at Deere & Company noted, "Charlie Deere pumped information into him [Butterworth] as to how the business of Deere & Company should be managed. William Butterworth took all that in, and as a result of the high esteem for the judgment of Mr. Deere, he aimed to carry out the ideas and wishes of Charlie Deere." Butterworth bridged the gap between John and Charles Deere and the future of agricultural manufacturing. Despite the great reluctance of Butterworth, who held firm that Deere & Company was a plow company, engineers undertook experimentation with the tractor. In 1918, only eleven years after Charles Deere's death, Deere & Company purchased the Waterloo Gasoline Engine Company. It marked the company's entry into the tractor business and ensured John Deere's second century of doing business.

Deere & Company Organizational Time Line, 1836–1907

1836   John Deere moves from Vermont to Grand Detour, Illinois

1837   Charles Deere is born, March 28

1843   L. Andrus & Company is established, March 20

1846   Andrus, Deere & Lathrop is established, October 20

1848   Deere, Atkinson & Co. is established in Moline, Illinois, in May and is dissolved the same month

1848   Deere, Tate & Gould is established, June 19, and a new factory is erected

1852–
1857   Company is called "John Deere" for miscellaneous periods

1854   Deere & Chapman is established, November

1857   John Deere & Company is established, July 1

1858   John Deere & Company is dissolved, March 13

1858   Deere & Co. is established, October 5

1860   Deere & Co. is dissolved, November 5

1860   Moline Plow Manufactory is established, November

1864   Deere & Co. is formed with partners John Deere and Charles Deere, July 1

1868   Deere & Company is incorporated, August 15

1869   Deere, Mansur & Company branch house is established in Kansas City, Missouri, July 15

1873   Leaping deer trademark is introduced; in 1876 it is patented

1875   Revenues exceed $1 million for first time

1875   Deere, Mansur & Company branch house is established in St. Louis, Missouri, September 1

1877   Deere & Mansur Company, manufacturers of corn planters, is established in Moline, Illinois

1880   Deere & Company branch house is established in Minneapolis, Minnesota, December 1

1881   Deere, Wells & Company branch house is established in Council Bluffs, Iowa

1886   John Deere dies, May 17

1889   Mansur & Tebbetts Implement Company branch house is established in Dallas, Texas, August 3

1889   Deere Implement Company branch house is established in San Francisco, California, August 5

1901   John Deere Plow Company branch house is established in Indianapolis, Indiana, October 8

1902   John Deere Plow Company branch house is established in Portland, Oregon, January 1

1906   John Deere Plow Company branch house is established in Baltimore, Maryland, October 1

1907   Charles Deere dies, October 29

Notes

Abbreviations Used

CCW Papers   Charles C. Webber Papers, Deere & Company Archives

CHD Papers   Charles Henry Deere Papers, Deere & Company Archives

DA   Deere & Company Archives

IRAD   Illinois Regional Archives Depository, Western Illinois University

ISHL   Illinois State Historical Library

RGD   R. G. Dun & Co. Collection, Baker Library, Harvard Business School

RICHS   Rock Island County Historical Society

SHV Papers   Stephen Velie, Sr., Papers, Deere & Archives

1—Young and Enterprising

1. *Middlebury Mercury,* April 14, 1806; William Rinold Deere to William Deere, Jr., June 26, 1808, copy in DA.

2. *National Standard,* May 15, 1816; ibid., May 22, 1816.

3. Neil M. Clark, *John Deere: He Gave to the World the Steel Plow* (Moline, Ill.: privately printed, 1937), 21; H. P. Smith, ed., *History of Addison County* (Syracuse, N.Y.: D. Mason & Co., 1886), 290, 304; Theo Brown, "The Early Life of John Deere In Vermont," August 1902, DA.

4. S. Augustus Mitchell, *Illinois in 1837* (Philadelphia: S. Augustus Mitchell, Grigg & Elliot, 1837), ISHL.

5. *John Perry vs. John Deere,* Book B, Ogle County Circuit Court, Case Number 918, September 1843 Term, copy in DA.

6. John Gould, "Recollections of John Deere," DA; Harriet Martineau, *Society in America* (New York: Saunders and Otley, 1837), 265.

7. *Bicentennial History of Ogle County* (Ogle County, Illinois: Ogle County American Revolution Bicentennial Commission, 1976), 272–73.

8. James T. Allen, *Allen's Digest of Plows, with Attachments, Patented in the United States from A.D. 1789 to January 1883* (Washington, D.C.: Joseph Bart, Printer, 511 Ninth Street, 1883). A fire in 1835 destroyed many U.S. patent claims, for which no new patent numbers were filed. Charles Newbold received two patents on June 26, 1879, and Richard Chenoweth on November 25, 1808.

9. Ibid.

10. Joseph C. G. Kennedy, *Agriculture of the United States in 1860: Compiled from the Original Returns of the Eight Census under the Direction of the Secretary of the Interior* (Washington, D.C.: Government Printing Office, 1864), xix.

11. *Vermont Aurora,* January 4, 1826.

12. Testimony of John Gould, *Candee, Swan, et al. vs. Deere et al.,* 54 Ill.; Gould, "Recollections of John Deere," DA.

13. Edward C. Kendall, "John Deere's Steel Plow." *Contributions from the Museum of the History and Technology: United States National Museum Bulletin 218* (Washington, D.C.: Smithsonian Institution, 1959).

14. John Deer [*sic*], 1840 U.S. Census, Ogle County, Illinois, Grand Detour Precinct page 16, line 11.

15. *Rock River Register,* April 7, 1843.

16. *John Deere vs. Levi Dort,* February 22, 1841, Book A, Ogle County Circuit Court, Case Number 424, copy in DA; *John Deere vs. Peter Wertz,* April 9, 1842, Book A, Ogle County Circuit Court, Case Number 178, copy in DA.

17. *John Perry vs. John Deere,* Book B, Ogle County Circuit Court, Case Number 918, September 1843 Term, copy in DA.

18. Articles of Agreement between Leonard Andrus and John Deere, March 20, 1843, ISHL.

19. Testimony of Luke Hemenway and John Gould, *Candee et al. vs. Deere et al.,* 54 Ill. 439.

20. H. C. Peek, "Reminiscence of John Deere," DA; John Gould, "Recollections of John Deere," DA; Articles of Agreement between Leonard Andrus, John Deere, and Oramil Lathrop, October 20, 1846, amended June 22, 1847, ISHL.

2—John Deere, The Plow King

1. Frederick Anderson, ed., *Quad Cities: Joined by a River* (Davenport, Iowa: Lee Enterprises, 1982); David B. Sears, "Pioneer in the Development of the Water Power of the Mississippi River," *Illinois State Historical Society Journal,* 8 (2) (July 1915).

2. Gould, "Recollections of John Deere," DA.

3. Robert Tate, "Life of Robert Tate," May 25, 1847, 75–77, DA; Gould, "Recollections of John Deere," DA.

4. Tate, "Life of Robert Tate, May 13, 1848–September 26, 1848, DA.

5. "Oration of J. M. Gould at the dedication of the Rock Island County Courthouse, October 1, 1896," *Historic Rock Island County: History of the Settlement of Rock Island County from the Earliest Known Period to the Present Time* (Rock Island, Illinois: Kramer & Company, 1908), 82; Gould, "Recollections of John Deere," DA; Tate, "Life of Robert Tate," August 25, 1849, DA.

6. According to Tate, Cyrus Kinsey was hired on August 7, 1848. Tate, "Life of Robert Tate," August 7, 1848, DA. Comments about Deere come from testimony of Cyrus Kinsey, *Candee et al. vs. Deere, et al.,* 54 Ill. The other plow maker in Moline at the time was Daniel Beery. Deere told Beery, "he was going to do a big business, and that he would crush out the small plow factories in the neighborhood." Beery's affidavit of March 21, 1867, is included in *Candee et al. vs. Deere et al.,* 54 Ill., DA.

7. Gould, "Recollections of John Deere," DA; "Mr. Deere's Own Story," *Moline Review Dispatch,* October 7, 1907.

8. *Davenport Gazette,* February 8, 1849.

9. James M. Swank, *History of the Manufacture of Iron in All Ages* (Philadelphia: James M. Swank, 1884), 297. Swank's reference to Deere is not disputed, although he states that the cast steel was delivered to Deere in Moline in 1846. It was likely ordered in Grand Detour and delivered to Moline.

10. *N.W. Advertiser,* reprinted in the *Davenport Gazette,* September 20, 1849.

11. Gould, "Recollections of John Deere," DA.

12. Robert N. Tate to his brother (probably John Tate), September 20, 1851 (inset in Tate, "Life of Robert Tate"), DA.

13. Gould, "Recollections of John Deere," DA.

14. Ibid.

15. Tate, "Life of Robert Tate," March 27, 1849, DA.

16. Tate, "Life of Robert Tate," October 30, 1851–February 11, 1852, DA; Gould, "Recollections of John Deere," DA.

17. *Moline Review Dispatch,* November 8, 1907; Tate, "Life of Robert Tate," July 19, 1848–November 11, 1848, January 26, 1849, May 29, 1850, February 17, 1849, April 5, 1849, DA; "Allin" probably refers to Ellen Deere; Gould, "Recollections of John Deere," DA; Tate, "Life of Robert Tate," August 25, 1849, DA.

18. Tate, "Life of Robert Tate," April 9, 1851, DA; John Deere Account and Receipt Book, 1848–1855, DA.

19. *Portrait and Biographical Album of Rock Island County, Illinois* (Chicago: Biographical Publishing, 1885), 215–16; George Vinton to Charles C. Webber, May 13, 1908, 26651 DA.

20. Tate, "Life of Robert Tate," December 13–17, 1851, DA.

21. *Moline Workman,* November 1, 1854. The partnership notice also appeared on December 20, 1854.

22. Ibid., November 29, 1854.

23. Mechanics and Laborers' Timebook for 1852–1855, DA; *Moline Dispatch,* April 12, 1937; Tate, "Life of Robert Tate," January 12, 1856, DA; RGD, Rock Island County, Illinois, March 17, 1858.

24. *Moline Workman,* May 16, 1855; *Rock Islander,* January 10, 1855.

25. Tate, "Life of Robert Tate," February 23, 1854, DA; *Rock Island Advertiser,* March 31, 1852; Wayne Broehl, Jr., *John Deere's Company: A History of Deere & Company and Its Times* (New York: Doubleday, 1984), 93.

26. *Rock Island Daily Islander & Argus,* March 25, 1859; *Moline Workman,* June 7, 1855.

27. *Rock Island Advertiser,* July 5, 1854. For an article on their ineffectiveness see *Moline Workman,* June 30, 1855. Tate, "Life of Robert Tate," entry for July 8–13, 1855, 122, DA.

28. Tate, "Life of Robert Tate," September 5, 1857, DA.

29. *Moline Workman,* May 16, 1855; *Rock Islander,* January 10, 1855.

3—C. H. Deere's "Celebrated Moline Plows"

1. Kennedy, *Agriculture of the United States in 1860.*

2. Ibid.; *Twelfth Census of the United States, Taken in the Year 1900* (Washington, D.C.: U.S. Census Office, 1902).

3. *Country Gentleman* 10 (1857): 129. On seed drills, see "Moline Centre Draft Steel Plows and Seed Drills," *Prairie Farmer,* May 1851, and "Seymour's Patent Grain Drill Manufactured by Deere, Tate & Gould," *Prairie Farmer,* July 1851.

4. *Rock Island Advertiser,* September 28, 1853, October 19, 1853, October 17, 1855.

5. *Chicago Press* and *Wisconsin Farmer* quotations from page 62 of Reynold M. Wik, *Steam Power on the American Farm* (Philadelphia: University of Pennsylvania Press, 1953); Kennedy, *Agriculture of the United States in 1860,* xix; *Prairie Farmer,* April 1, 1858.

6. *Prairie Farmer,* September 23, 1858, September 30, 1858, October 21, 1858, November 18, 1858, September 29, 1859; Broehl, *John Deere's Company,* 120–22.

7. Dissolution, John Deere & Co. Co-Partnership, March 13, 1858, DA.

8. Gould, "Recollections of John Deere," DA.

9. *Country Gentleman* 10 (1857): 129.

10. *Moline Review Dispatch,* November 8, 1907; Tate, "Life of Robert Tate," August 27, 1850, DA; *Rock Island Weekly Advertiser,* October 31, 1855.

11. "Reminiscence of Carroll Remley of Rock Island, from an interview with P. C. Simmon dated July 15, 1913," DA.

12. RGD, Rock Island County, Illinois, March 17, 1858, May 18, 1858, June 30, 1858; John Deere household, 1860 U.S. Census, Rock Island County, Illinois, 294, line 2; *Moline Review Dispatch,* November 8, 1907.

13. Dissolution, John Deere & Co Co-Partnership, March 13, 1858, DA; Vinton to Webber, May 13, 1908, 26651 DA; Memorandum of Trade between John Deere and C. H. Deere, July 1, 1857–December 23, 1859, 67876 DA.

14. RGD, Rock Island Count, Illinois, August 1860; Rolf Achilles, *Made in Illinois: A Story of Illinois Manufacturing* (Chicago: Illinois Manufacturers Association, 1993), 33–34; Broehl, *John Deere's Company,* 123–24

15. "Mr. Deere's Own Story," *Moline Review Dispatch,* October 7, 1907; *Moline Review Dispatch,* November 8, 1907.

16. Charles Deere Memorandum Book, 1858–1869, 49824 DA.

17. Ibid.

18. Dissolution Notice, Deere & Co., November 5, 1860, 67879 DA.

19. Catalog and Price List from C. H. Deere's Moline Plow Manufactory, 1862, DA.

20. U.S. Patent Office, "John Deere, of Moline, Illinois, Improvement in Molds for Casting Steel," patent number 41203, January 12, 1864. Deere & Company's first patent was purchased from Thomas McQuiston of Morning Sun, Ohio, patent number 25,843 on October 18, 1859 for "improvement in Cultivators." John Deere's other patents were 42,172 on April 5, 1864, "Improvement in Cast-Steel Molds," patent 46,454 on February 21, 1865, "Improvement in Plows," and patent 63,369 on April 2, 1867, "Improved Method of Making Plows."

21. Catalog and Price List from C. H. Deere's Moline Plow Manufactory, 1862, DA.

22. George Vinton to Charles C. Webber, May 13, 1908, 26651 DA.

23. Broehl, *John Deere's Company, 150.*

24. Catalog and Price List from C. H. Deere's Moline Plow Manufactory, 1862, DA; Plow Manufactory of Chas. H. Deere circular, January 1, 1862, 76450 DA.

25. RGD, Rock Island County, Illinois, January 1863, August 1863.

26. Indenture between John and Charles Deere, July 1, 1864, DA.

27. Vinton to Webber, May 13, 1908, 26651 DA.

4—Raging Abolitionist

1. *Moline Workman,* September 6, 1854.

2. Ibid., October 11, 1854. While an early Republican Convention gathered in nearby Mercer County, Deere was still serving as chairman of the Whig County Convention.

3. Ibid., February 6, 1856; H. C. Peek, "Reminiscence of John Deere," DA.

4. *Rock Island Daily Islander and Argus,* September 28, 1858.

5. *Rock Island Evening Argus,* reprinted in the *Moline Daily Workman,* January 4, 1856.

6. *Moline Workman,* July 9, 1856; ibid., July 13, 1856.

7. Ibid., July 16, 1856.

8. Ibid., July 30, 1856.

9. Ibid., July 16, 1856; ibid., November 25, 1855; ibid., July 23, 1856.

10. Ibid., July 30, 1856.

11. Thomas Slattery, *An Illustrated History of the Rock Island Arsenal and Arsenal Island,* Parts 1 and 2 (Rock Island, Illinois: Historical Office, U.S. Army Armament, Munitions, and Chemical Command, 1990), 64–65.

12. *Portrait and Biographical Album of Rock Island County, Illinois,* 706–7.

13. *Rock Island Argus,* April 12, 1861, April 15, 1861.

14. "Mr. Deere's own Story of his Early Days and the Beginning of the Deere Industry." *Moline Review Dispatch,* November 8, 1907.

15. *Moline Review Dispatch,* November 8, 1907.

16. A. D. Bricham, *Twin Cities Directory,* for 1861–1862, 10, RICHS; Tate, "Life of Robert Tate," August 31, 1862, DA.

17. Kennedy, *Agriculture of the United States in 1860.*

18. *Rock Island Argus,* January 2, 1863.

19. Tate, "Life of Robert Tate," September 9, 1862, DA.

20. *Rock Island Argus,* January 2, 1863.

21. Ibid., January 3, 1863; ibid., January 14, 1863.

22. Ibid., November 17, 1863.

23. *Rock Island Evening Argus,* July 2, 1863, July 3, 1863.

24. Ibid., March 7, 1864.

25. Ibid., July 31, 1863.

26. Kate Perry-Mosher, "History of Rock Island, Ill., 1863," *Confederate Veteran,* 14 (1906), 28.

27. Benton McAdams, *Rebels at Rock Island: The Story of a Civil War Prison* (DeKalb: Northern Illinois University Press, 2000), 21–27.

28. *Rock Island Evening Argus,* April 15, 1865.

29. Tate, "Life of Robert Tate," February 14, 1859, February 22, 1861, February 20, 1865.

30. *Daily Argus,* March 4, 1865.

31. Vinton to Webber, May 13, 1908, 26651 DA.

5—The Case of "The Moline Plow"

1. *Rock Island Evening Argus,* July 14, 1865, DA.

2. *Portrait and Biographical Album of Rock Island County, Illinois,* 274–75.

3. *Rock Island Evening Argus,* November 27, 1863.

4. Charles Deere Diary, February 22, 1867.

5. Ibid., February 23, 1867, February 26, 1867, February 27, 1867, 25336 DA.

6. *Rock Island Evening Argus,* March 26, 1867.

7. Circular by Wm. Koenig & Co., St. Louis, Missouri, March 12, 1867, DA.

8. Tate, "Life of Robert Tate," March 19, 1867, DA; reprinted in Norman L. Freeman, *Reports of Cases at Law and in Chancery Argued and Determined in the Supreme Court of Illinois,* vol. 54 (Springfield, Ill., 1872), 439–68.

9. *Rock Island Daily Union,* April 27, 1867.

10. *Chicago Republican,* May 28, 1868.

11. Deere & Co. General Catalogue, 1867, DA.

12. "Another Runaway," *Rock Island Union,* January 4, 1868; Deere & Co. General Catalogue, 1867, DA; Candee, Swan & Co. Price List, August 1, 1866, DA.

13. Tate, "Life of Robert Tate," March 23, 1868, DA; Patent of Samson Felton of Huntingdon, Pennsylvania, "Improvement in Plows," November 1, 1830 (Allen, *Allen's Digest of Plows, with Attachments*); Patent of Charles B. Taylor of Bainbridge, Ohio, "Improvement in Plows," August 23, 1833 (Allen, *Allen's Digest of Plows, with Attachments*); Testimony of Robert Tate, *Candee et al. vs. Deere et al.,* 54 Ill.

14. *Chicago Republican,* quoted in *Moline Review,* June 1, 1868 (emphasis added).

15. Candee, Swan & Co. Circular, July 1, 1868, DA.

16. *Portrait and Biographical Album of Rock Island County, Illinois,* 219–20.

17. Testimony of J. E. Winzer, *Candee et al. vs. Deere et al.,* 54 Ill.

18. *Moline Review Dispatch,* March 26, 1868; *Rock Island Union,* October 23, 1867.

19. Tate, "Life of Robert Tate," April 5, 1868, DA.

20. Deere & Company Certificate of Organization, August 16, 1868, DA.

21. Appraisal is reported in "Journal of the Proceedings of the Board of Directors of Deere & Company," filed April 26, 1869, DA. Yearly output is reported in "Journal of the Proceedings of the Board of Directors of Deere & Company," July 18, 1890, DA.

22. Circular announcing formation of Deere, Mansur & Co., September 20, 1869, DA; RGD, Jackson County, Missouri, 1869.

23. Ibid.

24. Testimony of J. M. Gould, *Candee et al. vs. Deere et al.,* 54 Ill.

25. Testimony of Joseph Jaeger, *Candee et al. vs. Deere et al.,* 54 Ill.

26. Ibid.

27. Arvid Axel Kohler and Kitty Lee Cosentine, *The House of Kohler: A Family History 1300–1989* (Decorah, Iowa: Annundsen, 1989), 89.

28. Testimony of Andrew Friberg, *Candee et al. vs. Deere et al.,* 54 Ill.

29. Ibid.

30. Ibid.

31. Ibid.

32. *Candee et al. vs. Deere et al.,* 54 Ill.

33. Deere & Company Illustrated Catalog, 1871, DA.

34. *Candee et al. vs. Deere et al.,* 54 Ill.

35. Ibid.

36. Freeman, *Reports of Cases at Law and in Chancery Argued and Determined in the Supreme Court of Illinois,* 439–68.

37. Tate, "Life of Robert Tate," March 13, 1871, June 5, 1871, DA; *Daily Davenport Democrat,* October 24, 1871.

6—Supply and Demand

1. *Daily Davenport Democrat,* July 1, 1869.

2. Reverend Percy C. Ladd, *The First Congregational Church of Moline: A One Hundred and Twenty-Five Year History 1844–1969* (The First Congregational Church of Moline: Moline, IL, 1969), 20.

3. John Deere Papers, 19301 DA.

4. *Daily Davenport Democrat,* April 12, 1872.

5. *Moline Daily Dispatch,* October 13, 1933; The "Maine Law," passed statewide on June 2, 1851, made liquor manufacture, trade, and use illegal in Maine, except for medicinal or mechanical purposes.

6. *Chicago Tribune,* October 23, 1872.

7. *Rock Island Daily Islander & Argus,* September 28, 1858.

8. *Moline Review,* May 14, 1875.

9. *Rock Island Argus* quoted in *Daily Davenport Democrat,* August 26, 1874.

10. *Daily Davenport Democrat,* December 13, 1872; ibid., May 25, 1874; ibid., June 5, 1874; ibid., July 25, 1874; *Moline Review,* December 11, 1874.

11. *Moline Review,* July 4, 1873; ibid., August 15, 1873; ibid., August 1, 1873.

12. *Moline Review Dispatch,* October 3, 1884.

13. Robert Cromie, *The Great Chicago Fire* (New York: McGraw-Hill, 1958), 3–5. *Chicago Tribune* is quoted on page 128; "Excerpts from Diaries of William T. Ball," October 10, 1871, DA.

14. Ibid., November 10, 1873, January 9, 1874.

15. *Moline Review,* December 12, 1873; *Rock Island Argus,* June 20, 1875, July 1, 1875; *Moline Review,* July 1, 1875, July 5, 1875.

16. *Moline Review,* October 3, 1880.

17. *Daily Davenport Democrat,* March 21, 1871.

18. Ann and Atkinson streets are now Sixth Avenue and Eighteenth Street, respectively; *Moline Review,* September 11, 1874.

19. Edward Winslow Martin, *History of the Grange Movement; or, the Farmer's War Against Monopolies* (Philadelphia: National Publishing, 1873), 7.

20. Ibid., 420.

21. Ibid., 415–30; *New York Tribune* quoted on pages 415–18.

22. The Northwestern Plow Makers Association later became the Northwestern Plow Manufacturers Association. Its members included S. D. Morrison &

Sons; Moline Plow Company; B. D. Buford & Company; T. & H. Smith & Company; St. Louis & Peoria Plow Company; Hapgood & Company; Naperville Agricultural Works; T. Cumins & Company; T. D. Brewster & Company; Jas. Mairerhoffer, Parlin & Orendorff; Davenport Plow Company; F. K. Orvis & Company; Furst & Bradley; Deere & Company; Kinsey Manufacturing Company; Battell & Collins; Skinner, Briggs & Enoch; and St. Joseph Manufacturing Company; William T. Hutchinson, *Cyrus Hall McCormick: Harvest, 1856–1884* (New York: D. Appleton-Century, 1935), 88–89.

23. *Prairie Farmer,* January 23, 1864.

24. Martin, *History of the Grange Movement,* 415–18; *New York Tribune* quoted on pages 415–18.

25. Charles Deere to A. F. Vinton, November 15, 1872, 25332 DA.

26. Deere to Vinton, November 15, 1872, 25332 DA; Deere to Vinton, December 7, 1872, 25332 DA.

27. Kennedy, *Agriculture of the United States in 1860,* xiv.

28. Hutchinson, *Cyrus Hall McCormick,* 580–96; quotation is W. J. Hanna to E. W. Brooks, Red Wing, Minnesota, March 24, 1870, 582.

29. "Proceedings of Northwestern Plow Maker's Association Held at Chicago on the 2d of December, 1873," 71113 DA. *Chicago Tribune,* January 17, 1874. Price List, Moline Plow Works, Deere & Co., 1 July 1873, DA; Wholesale Net Price List, Moline Plow Works, Deere & Co., 1874, DA; Reduced Price List for 1875 of the Jno. Deere Moline Plows Manufactured for Wm. Loenig & Co., November 2, 1874, DA; "Proceedings of Northwestern Plow Maker's Association Held at Chicago on the 2d of December, 1873," 86641 DA.

30. *Chicago Tribune,* January 17, 1874.

31. John Deere Memorandum Book 3, 113542 DA; prices summarized in appendix exhibit 2 of Broehl, *John Deere's Company,* 792.

32. *Moline Review Dispatch,* December 25, 1874.

33. *Chicago Tribune,* January 17, 1874, February 11, 1874, February 23, 1874.

34. *Moline Review Dispatch,* December 25, 1874.

35. Ibid.

7—"'Tis Purely Business"

1. U.S. Patent Office, "Improvement in Sulky-Plows," Patent Number 164929, 29 June 1875; Deere & Company General Catalog, 1876.

2. *Daily Davenport Democrat,* May 22, 1876.

3. "Memories of John Kiel," DA.

4. Deere to Vinton, November 20, 1872, 25332 DA.

5. *Daily Davenport Democrat,* August 18, 1876, August 22, 1876; *Moline Review,* August 31, 1876.

6. *Daily Davenport Democrat,* April 18, 1876, July 26, 1876, August 19, 1876, August 22, 1876.

7. *Moline Review,* August 31, 1876.

8. Ibid., July 16, 1880.

9. Ibid., October 28, 1880.

10. *Galesburg Republican and Register,* January 17, 1881.

11. Deere, Mansur & Co. circular, undated, 76514 DA.

12. Deere & Mansur Company circular, February 4, 1881, 76514 DA.

13. *George Brown v. Deere, Mansur & Company and others,* Circuit Court, Eastern District Missouri, January 1881, 6 Federal Reporter, 484–93; Deere, Mansur & Co. circulars, undated, February 4, 1881, February 10, 1881, 76514 DA; Deere & Mansur Company circular, February 4, 1881, DA; Deere & Mansur Company Receipts, 43649 DA.

14. Alvah Mansur to Deere & Co., May 10, 1879, May 19, 1879, May 21, 1879, DA; Stephen Velie to Alvah Mansur, May 23, 1879, 3391 DA; for contract of June 1, 1879, 3296 DA.

15. Deere & Company Board of Directors Minutes, July 3, 1880, September 7, 1880, DA.

16. For John Deere's trip to Hot Springs, Arkansas, see *Moline Review,* April 26, 1878.

17. *Scientific American,* September 21, 1878; compilation of Historical Information by P. C. Simmon, DA.

18. *William Starling vs. Deere & Co. and Charles H. Deere,* Circuit Court, Southern Division of the Northern District of Illinois, April Term, 1891, 78651 DA; the trials held by the Illinois State Board of Agriculture occurred on September 8, 1874, 76649 DA.

19. *Moline Review Dispatch,* March 28, 1879.

20. *Moline Review,* July 5, 1879; *Weekly Implement Trade Journal,* 1906, DA.

21. *Moline Review,* July 23, 1880.

22. Ibid., June 26, 1874 for new roof; ibid., December 11, 1874, for Deere's health.

23. *Moline Review,* September 3, 1880.

24. Ibid., September 3, 1880; ibid., September 16, 1880.

25. *Moline Review Dispatch,* December 2, 1880.

26. "Another Runaway," *Rock Island Union,* January 4, 1868. Nellie Ball Rosborough, "I Remember John Deere," DA.

8—Father Deere

1. *Holland's Moline City Directory for the Years, 1885–1888* (Chicago: Holland Publishing), RICHS.

2. *The Past and Present of Rock Island County, Ill.* (Chicago: H. F. Kett, 1877), 325–28.

3. *Moline Review Dispatch,* February 10, 1882.

4. P. C. Simmon, "History of Deere & Company," DA.

5. Rosborough, "I Remember John Deere."

6. *Sioux City Daily,* May 1886, in Charles Deere Scrapbook E, DA.

7. George Deere to Charles Deere, November 20, 1885, December 14, 1885, CHD Papers; John Deere to William Ball, January 20, 1886, John Deere Papers, DA.

8. Mansur to John Deere, March 3, 1886, 43380 DA.

9. *Moline Daily Republican,* May 18, 1886.

10. George Deere to John Deere, May 11, 1886, CHD Papers; *Moline Daily Republican,* May 18, 1886.

11. Death announcement of John Deere by Deere & Company, DA.

12. *Moline Daily Republican,* May 20, 1886.

13. Ibid.; *Chicago Tribune,* May 18, 1886, reported that Deere died of "old age and dyspepsia."

14. On John Deere's death and funeral, see *Chicago Tribune,* May 18, 1886; *Moline Daily Republican,* May 18, 1886, May 20, 1886; *Daily Gazette,* May 18, 1886; Deere & Company announcement, 23662 DA. On his will, see *Moline Review Dispatch,* June 6, 1886, June 11, 1886; John Deere Will and Probate Records, IRAD; "Record of property of John Deere Estate Transferred to the heirs by Executors," 1886–1892, DA; "Executors Book of John Deere Estate," 1889, DA.

15. "Journal of the Proceedings of the Board of Directors of Deere & Company," July 13, 1886, July 17, 1886, DA.

16. Stephen H. Velie to Charles Deere Velie, February 4, 1884, SHV Papers.

17. Stephen H. Velie to Charles Deere, March 17, 1892, CHD Papers.

18. George Vinton to Charles Deere, January 19, 1886, CHD Papers.

19. *Moline Review,* April 8, 1881.

20. *Daily Davenport Democrat,* April 23, 1883; Deere makes this statement in an interview published in the *Chicago Inter-Ocean,* October 20, 1888; Mark Twain and Charles Dudley Warner, *The Gilded Age: A Tale of Today* (1873; reprint, New York: Penguin, 2001).

21. A thorough overview of the Hennepin Canal can be found in Donald W. Griffin's "The Hennepin Canal: Freight Regulation by Competition," *Journal of Illinois History* 7 (Spring 2004), 37–60. Shelby M. Cullom, *Fifty Years of Public Service: Personal Recollections of Shelby M. Cullom* (Chicago: A. C. McClurg, 1911), 222.

22. Hennepin Canal Central Committee letter to Congress, December 15, 1881, DA; Charles Deere interview in *Moline Review,* May 23, 1884; Ernest Bogart and Charles Thompson, *Centennial History of Illinois,* vol. 4, *The Industrial State, 1870–1893* (Springfield: Illinois Centennial Publications, 1920), 348–52.

23. Unidentified articles are pasted in Charles Deere Scrapbook E, 28–29, DA.

24. Broehl, *John Deere's Company,* 237–39.

25. *Daily Davenport Democrat,* April 27, 1886.

26. Velie to Charles Deere, April 28, 1886, SHV Papers.

27. Velie to Charles Deere, April 27, 1886, May 4, 1886, May 6, 1886, SHV Papers.

28. *Farm Implement News,* January 1888.

29. Donald L. Miller, *City of the Century: The Epic of Chicago and the Making of America* (New York: Simon & Schuster, 1996), 468–82. Albert Parsons, August Spies, George Engel, and Adolph Fischer were hanged after the Haymarket Affair. Louis Lingg committed suicide.

9—The Plow Trust

1. Charles Deere was appointed on July 10, 1889; E. E. Morgan to Charles Deere, April 30, 1891, 43379 DA.

2. *Davenport Sunday Democrat,* September 14, 1890.

3. *Daily Davenport Democrat,* October 8, 1890.

4. William Dwight Wiman to Charles Deere, September 13, 1889, CHD Papers.

5. Ibid.

6. Erastus Wiman to Charles Deere, September 29, 1889, CHD Papers.

7. Wiman to Deere, September 13, 1889, CHD Papers.

8. *Daily Davenport Democrat,* September 14, 1890, October 8, 1890.

9. William Butterworth Biographical File, 4118 DA.

10. William Butterworth to Charles Deere, September 15, 1891, CHD Papers.

11. Butterworth to Deere, July 10, 1892, CHD Papers.

12. "Manufacturers," *Twelfth Census of the United States, Taken in the Year 1900* (Washington, D.C.: U.S. Census Office, 1902), 347.

13. Velie to Mansur, September 4, 1884, SHV Papers; Velie to Charles Deere, September 17, 1884, SHV Papers.

14. Inaugural Address of Benjamin Harrison, March 4, 1886, *Compilation of Historical Material by P. C. Simmon,* "Statement Covering Period from Incorporation to Close of Business, July 1, 1910," 68791 DA.

15. Cullom, *Fifty Years of Public Service,* 249–52; James Nielson, *Shelby M. Cullom: Prairie State Republican* (Urbana: University of Illinois Press, 1962); *Dispatch,* February 1, 1889; Harrison Inaugural Address.

16. *Farm Implement News* 11, 2 (February 1891); *Farm Implement News* 12, 3 (March 1891).

17. Deere to Velie, June 2, 1888, SHV Papers; Velie to Charles Hapgood, October 7, 1887, SHV Papers; Velie to Mansur, August 9, 1888, SHV Papers.

18. Mansur to Deere, September 12, 1889, CHD Papers.

19. F. L. Underwood to Charles Deere, November 2, 1889, CHD Papers; Reports are dated as received by Deere & Company on November 5, 1889, November 7, 1889, and November 12, 1889, CHD Papers; Thomas Nickerson to Charles Deere, November 19, 1889, December 2, 1889, CHD Papers.

20. Velie to Deere, June 23, 1890, July 15, 1890, CHD Papers.

21. "Journal of the Proceedings of the Board of Directors of Deere & Company," July 16, 1890, DA.

22. C. C. Webber to Charles Deere, July 29, 1890, CHD Papers; "C. C. Webber the best" is in C. C. Webber to Ellen Webber, September 25, 1876, CCW Papers.

23. Velie to C. C. Webber, August 30, 1890, SHV Papers.

24. Underwood to Deere, November 15, 1890; Nickerson to Charles Deere, November 26, 1890, CHD Papers.

25. Alex Parkes to Charles Deere, October 30, 1890, CHD Papers, in T. S. Nickerson files.

26. Erastus Wiman, "British Capital and American Industries," *North American Review* 150, 1890; Wiman to Deere, December 1, 1890, with letter of Thomas Richardson to Erastus Wiman attached, CHD Papers, DA.

27. Velie to Nickerson, December 11, 1890, CHD Papers.

28. *Farm Implement News,* May 2, 1891.

29. Velie, Sr., to Deere, May 20, 1891, CHD Papers; Underwood to Deere, January 23, 1982, CHD Papers.

30. Underwood to Deere, January 5, 1891, January 26, 1891, CHD Papers; C. C. Webber to Deere, January 24, 1891, CCW Papers; Underwood to Deere, February 20, 1891, CHD Papers; Velie, Sr., to Underwood, July 27, 1891, CHD Papers; Velie, Sr., to Deere, February 27, 1891, February 28, 1891, CHD Papers, Mp; Underwood to Deere, March 7, 1891, CHD Papers; Close of negotiations in Velie, Sr., to G. P. Stevens, March 23, 1891, CHD Papers; Velie, Sr., to C. C. Webber, March 14, 1891, CHD Papers; *Boston Globe,* March 3, 1891; Charles Deere Letterbooks, 1885–1907, 20132–30132 DA; Velie, Sr., to Deere, April 18, 1891, April 22, 1891, May 20, 1891, CHD Papers; Willard R. Green to Velie, Sr., June 3, 1891, CHD Papers; Underwood to Deere, August 12, 1891, CHD Papers; Green to Deere, June 29, 1892, CHD Papers; Underwood to Deere, January 15, 1892, CHD Papers; Martin Kingman to Deere, February 20, 1892, CHD Papers; A. L. Bryant to Green, March 16, 1892, CHD Papers; Velie, Jr., to Deere, March 24, 1892, CHD Papers; Underwood to Deere, March 6, 1892, CHD Papers; Green to Deere, April 9, 1892, CHD Papers; Velie, Sr., to Deere, April 12, 1892, April 13, 1892, May 5, 1892, CHD Papers.

31. A. B. Taber to Deere, April 8, 1890, CHD Papers; P. H. Donnelly to Deere, September 19, 1891, CHD Papers; Richard Yates to Deere, February 1, 1892, CHD Papers.

32. H. W. Brands, *The Reckless Decade: America in the 1890s* (New York: St. Martin's Press, 1995), 193–214.

33. Mansur to Deere, November 28, 1892, 43380 DA.

34. Cullom, *Fifty Years of Public Service,* 256; *Compilation of Historical Material by P. C. Simmon,* "Statement Covering Period from Incorporation to Close of Business, July 1, 1910," DA.

10—Sick Forever

1. Mansur to Deere, June 30, 1893, 43380 DA.

2. "Journal of the Proceedings of the Board of Directors of Deere & Company," September 25, 1894, DA.

3. Reports of Pinkerton's National Detective Agency to Charles Deere, January, 9–15, 1892, CHD Papers.

4. Journal of the Proceedings of the Board of Directors of Deere & Company," July 13, 1894, September 25, 1894, DA; William Butterworth to Deere, October 3, 1893, CHD Papers; *Compilation of Historical Material by P. C. Simmon,* "Statement Covering Period from Incorporation to Close of Business, July 1, 1910," DA.

5. Studebaker Bros. to Deere & Company, letter dates as received July 18, 1894 (in 1894 price survey with notes by Charles Deere, 19329 DA); G. A. Stephens to Deere, June 27, 1893, CHD Papers.

6. Journal of the Proceedings of the Board of Directors of Deere & Company," July 13, 1894, September 25, 1894, DA; Butterworth to Deere, October 3, 1893, CHD Papers; *Compilation of Historical Material by P. C. Simmon,* "Statement Covering Period from Incorporation to Close of Business, July 1, 1910," DA.

7. *Moline Review Dispatch,* February 15, 1895.

8. *Moline Republican Journal,* January 17, 1895.

9. *Moline Review Dispatch,* September 10, 1895, October 11, 1895, October 12, 1895; for article on the death of Toby, see *Moline Review Dispatch,* September 14, 1895.

10. Charles Dick to Deere, October 17, 1893, CHD Papers.

11. *Moline Review Dispatch,* July 20, 1896.

12. Ibid.

13. Ibid., September 10, 1896.

14. Ibid., October 19, 1896, October 20, 1896.

15. Broehl, *John Deere's Company,* 273–75.

16. *Moline Review Dispatch,* April 5, 1897.

17. Charles Deere Memorandum Book, May 1899, 45006, copy in DA.

18. Ralph L. Nelson, Merger Movements in American Industry, 1895–1956 (Princeton, N.J.: Princeton University Press, 1959), 35.

19. *Twelfth Census of the United States, Taken in the Year 1900.*

20. Notes on consolidation, 1901, 19344 DA.

21. The nineteen companies named in the consolidation were Deere & Co., Deere & Mansur Company, Moline Plow Company, Grand Detour Plow Company, Morrison Manufacturing Company, David Bradley Manufacturing Company, B. F. Avery & Sons, Butcher & Gibbs Plow Company, Syracuse Chilled Plow Company, South Bend Chilled Plow Company, Fuller & Johnson Manufacturing Company, Kingman Plow Company, Pekin Plow Company, Peru Plow & Wheel Company, Sattley Manufacturing Company, J. Thompson & Sons Manufacturing Company, Minneapolis Plow Works, Union Malleable Iron Company, and Bettendorf Metal Wheel Company.

22. *Farm Implement News* 22, 18 (May 2, 1901).

23. *Farm Implement News* 22, 23 (June 6, 1901).

24. Fuller to Deere, June 20, 1902, CHD Papers.

25. Consolidation developments can be traced in the *Farm Implement News* 22, 17 (April 25, 1901); 22, 18 (May 2, 1901); 22, 19 (May 9, 1901); 22, 20 (May 16, 1901); and 22, 23 (June 6, 1901).

26. Tri-City Manufacturers Declaration of Principles, June 29, 1901, 3759 DA.

27. Charles Deere Memorandum Book, August 6, 1901, 45006, copy in DA.

28. Webber to Deere, June 20, 1902, CHD Papers.

29. *Farm Implement News* 22, 1 (January 1891); ibid., 22, 4 (April 1891).

30. *Moline Daily Dispatch,* July 3, 1902, July 5, 1901.

31. Webber to Deere, March 23, 1906, CHD Papers.

32. Ibid.

33. *Moline Daily Dispatch,* October 29, 1907.

34. Charles Deere Memorandum Book, February 10, 1905, 45006, copy in DA.

35. Ibid., undated entry, 1906, 45006, copy in DA.

36. *Moline Review Dispatch,* November 8, 1907.

37. Vinton to Webber, May 13, 1908, George Vinton papers, DA.

38. Ibid.

39. *Moline Daily Dispatch,* September 5, 1907.

40. *Moline Review Dispatch,* November 8, 1907.

41. Corporate Record Book, John Deere Plow Company of Omaha, 1899–1917, DA.

Works Cited

Note on Sources

Tracing the life of John Deere is a difficult task. Primary sources are few, and the bulk of what exists in his hand is in the form of account books, receipts, and business ledgers, which include both business and personal accounts, from his first two decades in Moline. In addition, hundreds of canceled checks, starting from the early 1870s, offer glimpses into the organizations and the people Deere supported financially. The best primary source is "The Life of Robert Tate," a series of diaries maintained by Robert Tate for more than fifty years. This source records much of the development of Moline and Deere's daily activities, although there are some inaccuracies as the result of Tate's adding a narrative compilation later in life. In the early 1900s, Deere & Company engineer Theo Brown spent a great deal of time in Vermont talking to people who once knew John Deere, taking pictures of the extant buildings and sites of Deere's years in several Vermont towns, and making copies of deeds and other pertinent records. The greatest insight into Deere's character is found in testimony during the *Candee, Swan & Co. vs. Deere & Company* trademark suit, which began after the Civil War. From these transcripts comes much of what we know about John Deere's character. Much of what else that is known about John becomes rather complex, because of the name's use by his company and also because Charles Deere perpetuated his legend.

Neil Clark privately published the first biography of John Deere in celebration of the company's centennial in 1937. It blends history and fictional dialogue. Dozens of short articles and theses on John Deere's company appeared, although, other than Darrah Aldrich's *The Story of John Deere* (1942), nothing else has been written specifically on John Deere the man. Many of these sources were useful in their compilation of secondary sources and statistics, but they served primarily as general starting points in the early stages of research.

The most comprehensive source for Deere & Company history is Wayne Broehl, Jr.'s, 900-page *John Deere's Company: A History of Deere & Company and Its Times*. This exhaustive history of the company and its leaders covers the years 1804–1984. Broehl presents in detail much of John Deere's early life in Vermont and Grand Detour, as well as the findings of an archaeological survey of the Deere home and shops in Grand Detour. To Broehl we owe a tremendous amount of gratitude.

Charles Deere's life at first seemed easier to grasp than his father's because a large collection of letters, scrapbooks, and diaries are available; however, tracing his life proved difficult because of the extraordinary number of projects that consumed his time and the random nature of the primary sources, many of which are not dated. The style of this book reflects the contrasting lifestyles of father and son, starting with one man and one product and ending with one man surrounded by many people and projects that are all integral to the story. Hundreds of letters from Charles Deere and from his close business associates, as well as colorful newspaper articles, supplied key information about his business and personal activities.

Newspapers provided a chronology of events. In addition, nineteenth-century city papers offer unique glimpses into personalities and provide tedious details such as the arrival and departure of important citizens, railroad schedules, and local government decisions. Despite this wealth of information, newspapers must be reviewed critically for bias and gratuitous errors, whether intentional or accidental. Papers at this time were political organs, and Charles Deere controlled the Republican press in Moline for much of the last quarter of his life.

Thousands of documents from the Deere & Company Archives, the Baker Library at Harvard Business School, the Illinois State Historical Library, the Illinois Regional Archives Depository at Western Illinois University, and the Rock Island County Historical Society provide the basis of *The John Deere Story*. Contact with the Henry Sheldon Museum in Middlebury, Vermont, the Chicago Historical Society, and the Wisconsin Historical Society also proved valuable in compiling information about business competitors and life in Vermont and Illinois during the nineteenth century. In addition, site visits to the John Deere Historic Site in Grand Detour, Illinois, were invaluable in recreating the first ten years of John Deere's life in Illinois.

Archives, Libraries

Deere & Company Archives (DA)

Illinois Regional Archives Depository (IRAD), Western Illinois University

Illinois State Historical Library (ISHL)

R. G. Dun & Co. Collection (RGD), Baker Library, Harvard Business School

Rock Island County Historical Society (RICHS)

Newspapers

Boston Globe

(Chicago) Inter-Ocean

Chicago Press

Chicago Tribune

Daily Davenport (Iowa) Democrat

Davenport (Iowa) Gazette

Galesburg (Ill.) Republican and Register

Middlebury (Vt.) Mercury

Moline (Ill.) Daily Dispatch

Moline (Ill.) Daily Republican

Moline (Ill.) Daily Workman

Moline (Ill.) Dispatch

Moline (Ill.) Republican Journal

Moline (Ill.) Review

Moline (Ill.) Review Dispatch

Moline (Ill.) Workman

National (Middlebury) Standard

New York Times

Rock Island (Ill.) Advertiser

Rock Island (Ill.) Argus

Rock Island (Ill.) Daily Islander & Argus

Rock Island (Ill.) Daily Union

Rock Island (Ill.) Evening Argus

Rock Island (Ill.) Union

Rock Island (Ill.) Weekly Advertiser

Rock Islander

Rock River (Grand Detour, Ill.) Register

Vermont Aurora

Wisconsin Farmer

Magazines / Periodicals

Country Gentleman

Farm Implement News

Prairie Farmer

Scientific American

Weekly Implement Trade Journal

Books, Articles, and Legal Documents

Achilles, Rolf. *Made in Illinois: A Story of Illinois Manufacturing.* Chicago: Illinois Manufacturers Association, 1993.

Aldrich, Darragh. *The Story of John Deere: A Saga of American Industry.* Privately Printed and Copyrighted by C. C. Webber, 1942.

Allen, James T. *Allen's Digest of Plows, with Attachments, Patented in the United States from A.D. 1789 to January 1883.* Washington: Joseph Bart, Printer, 511 Ninth Street, 1883.

Anderson, Frederick, ed. *Quad Cities: Joined by a River.* Davenport, Iowa: Lee Enterprises, 1982.

Ardrey, Robert L. *American Agricultural Implements: A Review of Invention and Development in the Agricultural Implement Industry of the United States.* Published by author, 1894.

Bicentennial History of Ogle County. Ogle County, Ill.: Ogle County American Revolution Bicentennial Commission, 1976.

Bogart, Ernest Ludlow, and Charles Manfred Thompson. *The Centennial History of Illinois.* Vol. 4, *The Industrial State, 1870–1893.* Springfield: Illinois Centennial Commission, 1920.

Brands, H. W. *The Reckless Decade: America in the 1890s.* New York: St. Martin's Press, 1995.

Bridge, James H. *The Inside History of the Carnegie Steel Company.* New York: Aldine, 1903.

Broehl, Jr., Wayne. *John Deere's Company: A History of Deere & Company and Its Times.* New York: Doubleday, 1984.

Chapman, Charles Edward. "History of Deere and Company, 1837–1911." Master's thesis, Iowa State University, 1949.

Clark, Neil M. *John Deere: He Gave to the World the Steel Plow.* Moline, Ill.: privately printed, 1937.

Cromie, Robert. *The Great Chicago Fire.* New York: McGraw-Hill, 1958.

Cullom, Shelby M. *Fifty Years of Public Service: Personal Recollections of Shelby M. Cullom.* Chicago: A. C. McClurg, 1911.

Deere, George. *Autobiography by Rev. George H. Deere, D.D.* Riverside, Calif.: Press Printing, 1908.

Ellinger, George. United States Department of Commerce. *National Bureau of Standards Test Report on Metallographic Examination of John Deere Plow Submitted by United States National Museum.* Washington, D.C., March 1963.

Freeman, Norman L. *Reports of Cases as Law and in Chancery Argued and Determined in the Supreme Court of Illinois.* Vol. 54. Springfield, Ill., 1872.

Fuller, Sarah Margaret. *Summer on the Lakes, in 1843.* Edited by Arthur Fuller. Boston: Charles C. Little and James Brown, 1856.

George Brown v. Deere, Mansur & Company and others, Circuit Court, Eastern District Missouri, January 1881, 6 Federal Reporter, 282–94.

Griffin, Donald W. "The Hennepin Canal: Freight Regulation by Competition." *Journal of Illinois History* 7 (Spring 2004), 37–60.

Historic Rock Island County: History of the Settlement of Rock Island County from the Earliest Known Period to the Present Time. Rock Island, Ill.: Kramer & Company, 1908.

Hoffman, Margaret J. *Preliminary Report on Archaeological and Historical Research on the Location of the John Deere Blacksmith Shop and Forge at Grand Detour Illinois with A Report on a Magnetic Survey of the John Deere Property by Prof. W. A. Longacre, Head, Physics Department, Michigan College of Mining and Technology.* July 24, 1962.

Howard, Robert P. *Illinois: A History of the Prairie State.* Grand Rapids, Mich.: William B. Eerdmans, 1972.

Hutchinson, William T. *Cyrus Hall McCormick: Harvest, 1856–1884.* New York: D. Appleton-Century, 1935.

Irwin, W. B. *William and Sarah (Yates) Deere and Some of Their Descendents.* Riverside, Calif.: privately printed, 1964.

Kendall, Edward C. "John Deere's Steel Plow." *Contributions from the Museum of the History and Technology: United States National Museum Bulletin 218.* Washington, D.C.: Smithsonian Institution, 1959.

Kennedy, Joseph C. G. *Agriculture of the United States in 1860: Compiled from the Original Returns of the Eight Census under the Direction of the Secretary of the Interior.* Washington: Government Printing Office, 1864.

Kohler, Arvid Axel, and Kitty Lee Cosentine. *The House of Kohler: A Family History, 1300–1989.* Decorah, Iowa: Annundsen, 1989.

Ladd, Reverend Percy C. *The First Congregational Church of Moline: A One Hundred and Twenty-Five Year History, 1844–1969.* Moline, Ill.: First Congregational Church of Moline, 1969.

Line, Esther Charlotte. "The Development of Deere and Company: An Illustration of the Growth of the Middle West." Ph.D. dissertation, University of Chicago, 1931.

McAdams, Benton. *Rebels at Rock Island: The Story of a Civil Prison.* DeKalb: Northern Illinois University Press, 2000.

Magnuson, Yngve P. "John Deere, A Study of an Industrialist on the Illinois Frontier, 1837–1857." Thesis, State Teachers College, St. Cloud, Minn., 1956.

Martin, Edward Winslow. *History of the Grange Movement; or, the Farmer's War Against Monopolies.* Philadelphia: National Publishing, 1873.

Martineau, Harriet. *Society in America.* New York: Saunders and Otley, 1837.

Miller, Donald L. *City of the Century: The Epic of Chicago and the Making of America.* New York: Simon & Schuster, 1996.

Mitchell, S. A. *Illinois in 1837: A Sketch Descriptive of the Situation, Boundaries, Face of the Country, Prominent Districts, Prairies, Rivers, Minerals, Animals, Agricultural Productions, Public Lands, Plans of Internal Improvement, Manufacture . . .* Philadelphia: S. Augustus Mitchell, Grigg & Elliot, 1837.

Neilson, James W. *Shelby M. Cullom: Prairie State Republican.* Urbana: University of Illinois Press, 1962.

Nelson, Ralph L. *Merger Movements in American Industry, 1895–1956.* Princeton, N.J.: Princeton University Press, 1959.

Observations on the Law of Trademarks and the Decision of the Supreme Court of Illinois in *Candee et al. vs. Deere et al.,* 54 Ill. Rep., 439. (Moline, Ill., 1877).

Paine, A. E. *The Granger Movement in Illinois.* Urbana: University of Illinois Press, 1904.

The Past and Present of Rock Island County, Ill. Chicago: H. F. Kett, 1877.

Perry-Mosher, Kate. "History of Rock Island, Ill., 1863." *Confederate Veteran* 14 (1906).

Portrait and Biographical Album of Rock Island County, Illinois. Chicago: Biographical Publishing, 1885.

Scott, Roy. *The Agrarian Movement in Illinois: 1880–1896.* Urbana: University of Illinois Press, 1962.

Sears, David B. "Pioneer in the Development of the Water Power of the Mississippi River," *Illinois State Historical Society Journal* 8, 2 (July 1915).

Slattery, Thomas, J. *An Illustrated History of The Rock Island Arsenal and Arsenal Island,* parts 1 and 2. Rock Island: Historical Office, U.S. Army Armament, Munitions, and Chemical Command, 1990.

Smith, H. P., ed. *History of Addison County.* Syracuse, N.Y.: D. Mason & Co., 1886.

Stillwell, Lewis D. *Migration from Vermont.* Montpelier: Vermont Historical Society, 1948.

Swank, James M. *History of the Manufacture of Iron in All Ages.* Philadelphia: James M. Swank, 1884.

Taft, Philip. *Organized Labor in American History.* New York: Harper & Row, 1964.

Trachtenberg, Alan. *The Incorporation of America: Culture & Society in the Gilded Age.* New York: Hill and Wang, 1997.

Twain, Mark, and Charles Dudley Warner. *The Gilded Age: A Tale of Today.* 1873. Reprint, New York: Penguin, 2001.

U.S. Census Office. *Twelfth Census of the United States, Taken in the Year 1900.* Washington, D.C.: United States Census Office, 1902.

Wik, Reynold M. *Steam Power on the American Farm.* Philadelphia: University of Pennsylvania Press, 1953.

Wiman, Erastus. "British Capital and American Industries." *North American Review* 150 (1890).

Wolman, Leo. *The Growth of American Trade Unions, 1880–1923.* New York: National Bureau of Economic Research, 1924.

Index